Four Scenes for Posing the Question of Meaning and Other Essays in Critical Philosophy and Critical Methodology

Studies in the Postmodern Theory of Education

Joe L. Kincheloe and Shirley R. Steinberg
General Editors

Vol. 79

PETER LANG
New York • Washington, D.C./Baltimore • Boston • Bern
Frankfurt am Main • Berlin • Brussels • Vienna • Canterbury

Phil Francis Carspecken

Four Scenes for Posing the Question of Meaning and Other Essays in Critical Philosophy and Critical Methodology

PETER LANG
New York • Washington, D.C./Baltimore • Boston • Bern
Frankfurt am Main • Berlin • Brussels • Vienna • Canterbury

Library of Congress Cataloging-in-Publication Data

Carspecken, Phil Francis.
Four scenes for posing the question of meaning and other essays in critical philosophy and critical methodology / Phil Francis Carspecken.
p. cm. — (Counterpoints; v. 79)
Includes bibliographical references and index.
1. Critical theory. 2. Postmodernism. 3. Methodology. 4. Meaning (Philosophy). I. Title. II. Series: Counterpoints (New York, N.Y.); vol. 79.
B823.C35   142—dc21   98-25585
ISBN 0-8204-3967-3
ISSN 1058-1634

Die Deutsche Bibliothek-CIP-Einheitsaufnahme

Carspecken, Phil Francis:
Four scenes for posing the question of meaning and other essays in critical philosophy and critical methodology / Phil Francis Carspecken.
–New York; Washington, D.C./Baltimore; Boston; Bern; Frankfurt am Main; Berlin; Brussels; Vienna; Canterbury: Lang.
(Counterpoints; Vol. 79)
ISBN 0-8204-3967-3

Cover design by Nona Reuter

The paper in this book meets the guidelines for permanence and durability of the Committee on Production Guidelines for Book Longevity of the Council of Library Resources.

© 1999 Peter Lang Publishing, Inc., New York

All rights reserved.
Reprint or reproduction, even partially, in all forms such as microfilm, xerography, microfiche, microcard, and offset strictly prohibited.

Printed in the United States of America

This book is dedicated to my two shining sons:
Sunil and Roly Carspecken.

TABLE OF CONTENTS

Foreword by Peter McLaren   ix

Introduction   1

Essay One
Paradigmatics of the "Paradigm Dialogue"   7

Essay Two
Power, Truth, and Method: Outline for
a Critical Methodology   30

Essay Three
Four Scenes for Posing the Question of
Meaning: Phenomenology, Form,
Feeling-Body, and the Origins of
Intersubjectivity   118

Essay Four
Five Third Person Positions and Their
Relevance to Reflection, Validity,
and Systems Analysis   258

References   279

Index   289

FOREWORD

Critical ethnographers, social theorists, and educational philosophers, inside and outside of the field of educational research would do well to read this important new book by Phil Francis Carspecken. Although admittedly Carspecken is interested in wisdom more than philosophy, there are few educational ethnographers who can rival him in sheer philosophical breadth of knowledge, and few that can keep up with his relentless precision in constructing categories of and approaches to meaning-making. While some may argue that existential phenomenologists have made a career out of being giddyingly imprecise, few educational thinkers have explored the issue of the vulnerability of meaning with more care and attention to detail than Carspecken.

Four Scenes for Posing the Question of Meaning is a work that surely will disturb the complacency of ethnography pundits who have not done their theoretical homework. It will also shake those up who are quick to jump on the postmodernist bandwagon and indulge themselves in cocktail party aphorisms followed by self-satisfying assertions such as: "There is no truth, only interpretation." "Truth is a regime that masks relations of power." "The subject is dead." "We are always already preconstituted by the discursive regimes that constrain the way we think about thought itself." These are not the comments of pseudo intellectuals dressed in black turtlenecks and chinos smugly intoxicated by feelings of self-importance. They belong to the lexicon of utterances that we hear our colleagues exercising over their tuna salads at the faculty club and which our students use to club their dreaded "modernist" classmates and grind to a halt their cries for truth and justice. It is not that these statements in themselves are false. It is rather that they are thrown about with such facile abandon and with little understanding of what they mean in the context of making hard and tough decisions about meanings and their defensibility.

Carspecken's book is underwritten by a reconstructed philosophy of praxis. Praxis, as Carspecken views it, is an essential drive to unify all dimensions of action under the control of a self-actualizing, autonomous subject. He revives this concept from its ethnographic slumber by attempting to bring it into an enlivening conversation with the question: How does power work within and through human agency to reproduce social inequalities? Carspecken doesn't really pursue this engagement by addressing the structural side of power as much as he connects and reconnects the concept of power to some of the themes orginated by praxis theory. Contra Foucault, Carspecken associates power with acts oriented toward understanding. It is precisely the internal connection between power and truth that Carspecken attempts to capture through a reformulated concept of praxis. Foucault's work is limited in this endeavour in the sense that he reduces truth to power. For Carspecken, as for his mentors, Habermas, Hegel, Mead, Husserl, and Derrida, power is never subject-less or anonymous. Truth cannot be reduced to the workings of an anonymous power. Power is always internal to communicative action in addition to action oriented to consequences. Following Husserl, Carspecken stresses the importance of expectation and action in experience and meaning. From this position he arrives at four "layered categories" of expectation—of action consequences alone; of action consequences mediated by actions of another; tacit intersubjective expectation and communicative action; and explicit intersubjective expectation and communicative action. Carspecken concludes that experience is knowledge-imparting only when it is intersubjectively represented in the context of an index of expectation horizons, that is, when the object of experience is examined in relation to bounded sets of expectations or what may be considered a hierarchy of expectations. To transform *experience of* into *knowledge of* means expecting and anticipating how an entire group of people will engage such experience. It means taking the position of others in relation to the object of experience. We are challenged by Carspecken with, among other things, understanding the role of audience-dependent recollection and reflection, and how second or third person audiences are related to meaningful action through preanticipated sets of possible responses and preconceptual understanding.

Foreword

Carspecken is relentless in his assertion that knowledge is always bounded by expectations of how communicative actions that reference the object of experience would be experienced by others. In the final analysis the object of experience serves for Carspecken as the limit reference of certain communicative horizons. Always already rupturing the object and the subject is the subject's expectation of the response of others.

If all acts of meaning carry truth claims internally because meaning must be understood as structured by intersubjectivity or horizons of expectation, then the central task of the research becomes, for Carspecken, that of addressing the thorny issue of validity claims. Analyzing the procedures and processes leading to normative evaluative agreements and exploring issues over internal and external validity claims power Carspecken's sojourn into the murky waters that disturb our grasp of the form and pragmatic properties of truth in relation to actions oriented toward understanding where much is implied but never within direct reach. For those of us engaged in empirical research, Carspecken's ideas (arrived at often at the intersection of Derrida's deconstruction of presence and Habermas's formal architectonic of truth) stipulate that the researcher be open to different categories of validity claims.

What is so fascinating about Carspecken's work is the way that it manages so creatively to reveal how identity claims and evaluative claims work within a praxis of resistance and opposition. What Carspecken has achieved is an entirely new vocabulary for discussing oppositional acts and the politics of resistance. For instance, Carspecken is able to explain how social relations of inequality place the goal-oriented dimension of action under the control of others and thus alienate it from the praxis of subordinate populations. At the same time, Carspecken shows how, in spite of existing social relations of inequality, cultural formations are able to mobilize to help affirm identities through normative-evaluative regimes designed to maximize affirmation of the self as it struggles against goal-oriented action that is controlled by others.

Carspecken's originary "scenes" (meaning-imparting contexts) and phenomenological sketches for posing the question of meaning constitutes a critical and densely conceptual strategy for doing critical work. As a task-master, Carspecken is not for the theoretically faint of heart. His project of investigating meaning in four different ways is demanding on the reader but the rewards are exceedingly rich for those willing to stick with the program. A major payoff lies in Carspecken's model of meaningful action for social researchers. Here we are challenged by questions about the "I-feeling mode" and the compression of somatic states; by the rigor of testing moments of universality operating within every validity claim; by the politics of self-reference that lies waiting in every act of implicit understanding; by the implications that arise when confronted by the idea that body postures and gestures not only indicate subjective states but also normative and identity references; by the process of "monitoring" whereby an actor takes second and third person perspectives on her thought/actions; and by the risk that obtains when the validity of a claim about the world or what is right and what is wrong breaks down and leads the actor to a state of despairing ontological insecurity.

Because Carspecken is able to specify so clearly and vividly the different types and workings of subjective and normative-evaluative claims, researchers are presented with a vital and important new way to approach their data analysis—a way that will enable them to understand how ideology works to uphold some meanings and interests and not others. Carspecken's work lies at the cutting edge of critical ethnography. Serious attention to the "scenes" phenomenologically crafted throughout this volume will help to take critical ethnographers to a different level of research. This pathbreaking volume is a welcome addition to the field of ethnography and to the broader domain of the social sciences.

Peter McLaren
UCLA

An Introduction to

FOUR SCENES FOR POSING THE QUESTION OF MEANING
And Other Essays in Critical Philosophy and Critical Methodology

When I was an adolescent, I developed the habit of taking walks alone. I often talked aloud to myself as I walked. I talked to review my life and consider my future. I explored the origins of my self through a collage of shades, forms, and faces that could each be traced to significant others. I speculated on such things as the nature of creativity, romantic desire, and the mysteries of space and time. A favorite activity was to notice in which phase the moon happened to be, and then recall what I was doing when it was last in that phase, and when it was in that phase a year before. I would also stand near the Wisconsin River to stare at the top of Rib Mountain, simultaneously trying to recall as vividly as possible the view of my position by the river from Rib Mountain's observation tower. This was like trying to be in two places and two times at once.

Time and space and self; I could induce the most marvelous feelings within by contemplating these things. I enjoyed these activities enormously but never told anyone that I talked to myself. It was a common idea, when I was young, that while speculating about the mysteries of life was totally acceptable, even admirable, only crazy people talked to themselves.

I had a wonderful experience on one of these walks, when I was seventeen years old. Or at least I have, since my early twenties, told my various life stories to myself with this wonderful experience constructed centrally within their plots. On this occasion I was walking near the banks of the Wisconsin River at night, talking to myself as usual, using a fallen branch for a walking stick. At some moment during this walk I noticed how much I enjoyed talking to myself but I also noticed how my talk never completed whatever ends it was directed toward. I started to wonder about these things. First, I wondered why I talked to myself at all, since I believed that talking was merely a way to put thoughts into words as a sort of encoding process. Why should I feel clearer about my own thoughts after talking them out than before? Why weren't my thoughts simply lucid in themselves, transparent to me as soon as they appeared? Why did I need to act them out in talk? What was the basis of this enjoyment I felt when talking my thoughts out, and why did it yet fail to fully satisfy?

Thoughts seemed to simply come without any effort or act of will, but once they emerged I had the choice of either ignoring them or acting them out with talking or more explicit thinking. Each thought was infused with a desire to have itself explicated in talk. Each thought carried a sort of promise that its full explication would be pleasurable. Yet talking never really did satisfy these desires. In fact, a lot of talking left me feeling depleted in some way.

On this special occasion during my seventeenth year mental imagery emerged spontaneously to represent my own thinking process to myself. One image was that of a stream bubbling forth from a dark and unknowable source. The stream was thought. The stream was many thoughts, each of which pointed toward a destination that I desired to reach. The "I," the self, my self, just escaped the imagery, but was felt. I could feel my self in and through each thought, and had the choice of either keeping it merged within the course of the stream, as thought moved toward some desirable goal, or withdrawing the feeling from the stream and leaving the thought to dissipate. I could act, by talking or thinking explicitly, or I could give the thought up, let it go.

Other images arose to represent what occurs when a thought is acted out by either thinking it through or talking it out. There was an audience for my acts that could first be felt as part of the desire, within the stream of thought itself. When a thought was completed this audience took a distinctive representation, differentiated from the act. The act completed was a performance for its audience. The pleasure I experienced was generated by performing for audiences. But the audiences were rarely anthropomorphic. They were impersonal, represented in abstract imagery like clear fields or points of light. My audience had no human features other than the bare principle of being an understanding other. It was a conscious other that could grasp what I had to say and see who I was through my performances. It was my own creation, or at least the creation of thought that streamed within me. It was both mine and totally other than me. The greater clarity I felt after talking an idea out came from the experience of taking the position of this audience to which my thoughts were addressed, but it was simultaneously a *felt* clarity about who I was at the moment of performing. I needed that audience to feel myself, and that was often why I talked. I needed to be my own audience in order to further become myself.

Now came the moment that seemed so wonderful. Rather than allow new thoughts to rise forth into performances I simply held my attention on this image of the abstract other, deliberately ascribing to this other the ability to understand all my thoughts *before* I acted them out. I did this deliberately, because I had the idea that thoughts should not need to be expressed in order to be understood. If my audience was really my own creation, all I needed to do was to concentrate on it, and it would understand all the thoughts streaming up within me without my having them expressed in words or images. Rather than take the position of the audience I objectified it as a light that gazed at and through me. I kept my sense of self in distinction from this light, as a fully transparent object to its gaze.

I immediately felt good, even in my body, when keeping my attention on the image of this omniscient other, represented as a light. There was no need to think because this other could understand me to my depths. The good feeling resulted in new streams of thought; desires to talk or think about this very experience I was having. But I resisted the new desires in order to keep my attention on the image of the other. I let the new desires go by bringing my attention back to the light and by remembering, through this same act, that the light already understood the new thoughts. The good feeling became stronger! And the urge to think about all of this was now even harder to resist.

Then for a moment I had a most elated feeling. My mind seemed to stop and an ecstatic sensation began to arise within me, within my body. Something important seemed close. I vaguely felt that I understood what time is: Time is born between the urge to act again in thought and the moment when the mind is stopped through contemplation of this omniscient other—this other that already knows the content of each new thought. Time is the result of a choice. I vacillated between these two states for a little while, ecstatic feelings increasing until I could stand it no longer. I started thinking explicitly again, but did not talk aloud. I was very excited.

In the life stories I have told since, I often give this moment significance. I have been fascinated for decades with the nature of thought, with the structure of meaningful acts, with the constituents of self, with the mystery of time. My life stories frequently place this solitary experience of my seventeenth year at the origin of these fascinations. But life stories always have something false about them. This moment within my own life is best considered a symbol for my ongoing preoccupations. It is a personal myth that encapsulates many of my current interests and many of the identities I currently adopt when thinking about my self and my work.

My life since the age of seventeen has been a rambling and largely unplanned affair. Somewhere, sometime during my twenties, I began investing a lot of myself in the art of understanding other people. I have worked as a therapeutic counsellor, a schoolteacher, a community organizer, and a political activist. Understanding other people has involved, for me, much the same imagery I ascribe to this solitary experience during my teens. It involves intuiting the thought streams of others beneath the overt actions and words they produce. It involves intuiting the desires that inhabit these streams, the audiences to which these streams are directed, and the senses of self that all of us pattern into our lives.

For the past ten years my job has been to teach social theory and qualitative research methods at a university. I have used the formal features of my job to continue explorations of meaning, self, desire, time, and other related things. Early in the 1990s I wrote a book-length manuscript entitled "The Phenomenology of Meaningful Action." I never sent the manuscript out for publication, as I was not satisfied with it. Someday I might complete it to my satisfaction. Meanwhile I have condensed many of its arguments into an essay that I have named "Four Scenes for Posing the Question of Meaning." This is the longest of the essays in this volume.

I also include here three other essays that deal with many of the same issues as "Four Scenes," but with an emphasis on critical research methodology. "Paradigmatics of the Paradigm Dialogue" was first written as I was clarifying ideas for my book on critical ethnography (Carspecken 1996). I did not use the essay in that particular book but continue to find it helpful for distinguishing the critical ethnographic method that I practice and teach from other genres of qualitative research. I have chosen to place "Paradigmatics of the Paradigm Dialogue" as the first of my four essays because it is very much a stage-setting sort of piece. It emphasizes what critical ethnography is *not*, and prepares the way for many of the ideas presented in the subsequent essays.

The second essay in this book is entitled "Power, Truth, and Method; Outline for a Critical Methodology." It explores the origins of critical ethnography, warns against postmodern themes that violate basic principles central to the critical perspective, and argues in favor of a revised theory of praxis to occupy the central position in critical epistemology.

"Four Scenes" comes next. It is the most difficult essay to read and my advice to readers who find it difficult is to skim through it and focus only on those portions that most appeal to them. Though the various sections of "Four Scenes" are connected within the logic of the essay as a whole, they also read autonomously and employ different styles of writing.

The last essay in this book, "Five Third Person Positions and their Relevance to Reflection, Validity, and Systems Analysis," is really a set of notes that were deleted from an article I published with Laurie MacGillivray (Carspecken and MacGillivray, 1998). These notes were portions of my contribution to our jointly authored article that were considered too dense by our editors. I wanted to see them published since they address a question that my students have repeatedly raised with me: Is there only one third person position, or are there more? If there are more, how might we distinguish them?

The four essays of this book complement each other well. I regard all of them as preliminary and exploratory. This book is meant to be a collection of related essays that represents my efforts to date at becoming a more conscious human being, social researcher, criticalist, and teacher. I have made no effort to tidy up loose ends, nor to fit each essay into a tight logical sequence that would impart a sense of totality to the book as a whole.

ACKNOWLEDGMENTS

I would like to thank Joe Kincheloe for inviting me to submit these essays to Peter Lang Publishing, and for his patience when I exceeded my deadline. Shirley Steinberg also displayed patience and support during the time I reworked the original essays.

A special appreciation goes to Barbara Korth, who has read many of my unpublished manuscripts and essays, including these four, and who has brilliantly developed, expanded, and otherwise employed some of my ideas in her own work. Barbara Korth's work on care as a pragmatic concept is stunningly sharp, original, and, to my gratification, completely congruent with my own work.

Thanks also go to Kathleen Babbitt for her outstanding job as copy editor and to Jackie Pavlovic for her tremendous support as production supervisor.

A one-semester developmental leave granted me by the University of Houston was enormously helpful for completing this book. My thanks to Phyllis Gingiss and Alan Warner. Several grants awarded me by the University of Houston also supported my efforts.

Essay One

PARADIGMATICS OF THE "PARADIGM DIALOGUE"

NATURALISTIC INQUIRY AND ITS WAKE
The publication of Lincoln and Guba's book *Naturalistic Inquiry* in 1985 was an important event. This widely read book attacked the epistemological position of mainstream quantitative research that has dominated sociological inquiry for many decades. It used fairly recent developments in both natural science and in the philosophy of natural science to argue that a "new research paradigm" is called for. In many ways, the authors echoed arguments made by Herbert Blumer and other members of the Chicago School against quantitative methods: even the term "naturalistic" can be traced to Blumer (see Hammersley 1989). But the detail Lincoln and Guba gave to their arguments was something new, as was their appeal to a wide audience.

Qualitative research is growing in popularity, and *Naturalistic Inquiry* is one of the reasons why. Perhaps the most effective feature of *Naturalistic Inquiry*, in terms of providing sound arguments against the assumptions of traditional practitioners, was its transformation of mainstream methodological vocabulary, almost term by term, into a newly coined vocabulary congruent with the "paradigm shift" Lincoln and Guba called for. Advocates of qualitative research have been able to use Lincoln and Guba's work to explain which concepts within the naturalistic, qualitative, orientation roughly correspond to such quantitative terms as "internal validity," "external validity," and "reliability." Frequent references to natural science and the philosophy of natural science have no doubt also contributed to the book's visibility and argumentative force as well. Lincoln and Guba found the right vocabulary to use and the right references to make for gaining the respect of a very wide audience.

Following the publication of *Naturalistic Inquiry*, a number of methodological theorists began conversing with each other, at conferences and through publications, about issues raised in that text. This academic conversation came to be called the "paradigm dialogue." A book edited by Guba in 1990 adopted this phrase for its title. Many authors contributed papers for the book. The general agreement among most members of this group is that there currently exist four distinctive "paradigms" through which social research is conducted: the positivist, postpositivist, critical, and constructivist paradigms. This typology, too, has become influential. But it has begun to mislead students of social research through its incorrect portrayal of traditions such as critical ethnography, as well as through the simplistic structure of a four-member typology.

The framework employed initially by Lincoln and Guba to highlight methodological issues was somewhat expanded by contributors to Guba's book. One finds fairly recent work in the philosophy of science cited, some attention to Habermas, some attention to postmodern works and feminist theory.

However, the way in which this paradigm dialogue was framed—the particular vocabulary favored, the concepts through which alternative methodological positions were conceptualized—remains limited. One still finds arguments made from developments within physical science, when in fact the core issues involved in the physical sciences are not readily transferrable to the social sciences. A kind of rhetorical appeal is made in this way that was effective in winning an audience for *Naturalistic Inquiry*, but that in fact always obscured problems specific to the human sciences. The logic is often based on the inappropriate use of analogy. Little is said about methodological debates that have taken place in sociology, rather than in natural science and its philosophy, since the 19th century.[1]

Not fully addressed by participants in the paradigm dialogue is the important challenge to traditional Western concepts of truth brought about by the loosely bounded intellectual movement called "postmodernism." When postmodernism is mentioned, one feels disappointed at the particular postmodern themes chosen for

---

[1] See Hammersley 1989 for an excellent scholarly discussion of these debates and their relevance for methodological theory today.

emphasis and at the shortness of the discussion provided. Even highly relevant conceptual schemes developed by contemporary social theorists like Anthony Giddens are missing from the picture. Habermas is frequently referred to, but primarily Habermas as the secondary literature has rendered him, or Habermas prior to his magnum opus, *The Theory of Communicative Action* (1981, 1987b). As Marki LeCompte aptly put it, the paradigm dialogue, despite its clear importance to a growing group of scholars who are moving away from traditional methodological theory, suffers from "intellectual ethnocentrism" (LeCompte 1990:247). It appears to be trying to reinvent the wheel in some places, to be blind to highly relevant intellectual traditions in others.

The limitations of the paradigm dialogue may be related to limitations in Western intellectual history. I have picked, rather unfairly, on this group and their terms of discussion primarily because the limitations under which they work are indeed common, and the commonness of such limitations is best displayed through a critique of those who have tried to summarize the work of an entire field. I have also picked on them because they are so visible and their way of framing the issues is probably quite widespread. I do not wish to downplay the significance of the paradigm dialogue for modern methodological theory. Since this community of methodological theorists has made efforts to be open to all sorts of contributions (Marki LeCompte's critical comments, for example, were published in *The Paradigm Dialog*) one can expect that limitations within the discussion will be overcome in time.

FOUR PARADIGMS? OR ONE?

Meanwhile, the four-member typology of methodological orientations developed by participants in the paradigm dialogue reads, at least to me, as only four *orientations* that may be taken within a single, true, paradigm whose characteristics remain unarticulated and in the background. I do not believe that all participants in the paradigm dialogue work entirely through the assumptions of this backgrounded and unarticulated scene (or "true paradigm"), but I do see that many formulations composed by these authors suggest it. As discussed below, this single common background scene underlies much Western philosophy since at least the Enlightenment, and played an important role, through neo-Kantianism, in the formation of both positivistic methodology and the methodology of symbolic interactionism. Moreover, this paradigmatic scene is precisely what critical theory, particularly Habermasian critical theory, directly opposes. Since Guba and his colleagues describe critical social research as if it, too, embraced this paradigmatic background, their description is misleading.

"Paradigms"

In the first chapter of *The Paradigm Dialog*, Guba presented his belief that social research is currently practiced within four competing paradigms. His use of the term "paradigm" is objectionable, but Guba was aware of this. He admitted that the term paradigm is vague and contentious. He invited readers to conceive of it in their own way. In some of his writings Guba displays profound insights into the nature of meaning and understanding by calling a paradigm "what you have left when you can't explain any more" (quoted in Peshkin 1990:348). We could infer from this insightful statement that Guba has conceptualized the term paradigm as an implicit and holistic mode of knowledge that defies full articulation. The same idea is developed within my other essays in this book, as a feature of all meaningful action. It is a correct insight that is related to hermeneutic theory, and ought not be limited to the concept of paradigm.

A paradigm, in Kuhn's use of the term, refers to a holistic, totalizing, and tightly bounded interpretative framework from which it is difficult to escape (Kuhn 1970). True paradigms win very wide consensus during some historical period, such that portions of them recede into deep regions of common sense. Yet social researchers seem well aware of the variety of orientations within which research is practiced today, have little trouble moving intellectually from one orientation to another, and frequently borrow terms developed within one orientation for use within another. Social research employs principles that are much

Paradigmatics 11

more openly contested and fluid than the term "paradigm," in its Kuhnian sense, would allow. In addition, there are probably many more than four orientations that could be described as operative at this time.

A "MetaParadigm"?

If one looks closely at the manner in which Guba described his four research orientations, an underlying scene, image, or "root metaphor" (McLaren 1993), that *could* perhaps be called a paradigm in something like the Kuhnian sense does appear. If one thinks about the task of creating a typology of methodological theories, one will see that such underlying imagery would be unavoidable. How can one compare diverse methodological schools unless one employs a few core concepts addressed by each school, showing how each methodological framework varies from the others in its particular rendering of the core concepts? To compare methodological schools in as rigid a manner as Guba attempted necessitates a set of standards that transcends the boundaries of each, so that the person comparing schools places herself outside any one of them and uses a single ruler by which to measure their differences from each other. Of course this same problem occurs within Kuhn's famous book on scientific revolutions. Kuhn's argument that scientific paradigms are incommensurable has been widely attacked, at times precisely because of the fact that diverse paradigms can be described and compared by a single author and for a single audience.

Since Guba used the term "paradigm" to describe each methodological school, he would have to agree, in his own terms, that he employed a "metaparadigm" when he constructed his typology: a "paradigm by which to describe paradigms." This metaparadigm, moreover, would involve core concepts shared by each paradigm in the typology: it would effectively outline a single view, underlying each orientation described by Guba, such that surface variations can be contrasted. I will shortly describe certain features of this metaparadigm, this core imagery used by those participating in the paradigm dialogue to describe each orientation in their typology. I will describe it, however, with a phrase different from those of "paradigm" or "metaparadigm." This phrase is "originary scene."

THE CONCEPT OF ORIGINARY SCENE

The common yardstick Guba used to compare his four orientations to social research could perhaps be simply called a paradigm, a "true paradigm" rather than an orientation, because it is deeply entrenched and broadly consented to, not only among methodologists but among many philosophers as well. It is so basic and fundamental that one can discuss it rationally only with great difficulty and therefore it meets some of the criteria Kuhn applied to his concept of "scientific paradigm," minus the emphasis on science and research alone. Kuhn believed that paradigm shifts occur in nonrational ways, or at least involve a different kind of rational argumentation from that used within paradigms (see Bernstein 1976 and 1983 for good discussions of rationality and the paradigm concept).

However, partly because the term "paradigm" has been so badly abused, I will avoid it in favor of a phrase I coined myself: "originary scene." Fundamental interpretative frameworks are often most directly representable through imagery: "scenes." This seems to be due to the nature of much human understanding, which foregrounds explicit symbolic representations against backgrounded metaphors that often involve imagery. A backgrounded scene, additionally, need not be quite so tight in setting conceptual boundaries as the term "paradigm" would suggest. Originary scenes *are* difficult to escape from and are difficult to defend rationally, but they need not be so totalizing in their effects as to bar movement from one to another save through dramatic "shifts." Originary scenes are not incommensurable. In fact, articulating their backgrounding imagery greatly facilitates movement from one perspective to another.

In addition, the term "scene" has the advantage of directly conveying the importance of imagery without limiting the idea of an interpretative framework to visual perception alone. A "scene" is meant to convey a "scene of *use*," a "scene of *meaningful action*." As discussed in the "Four Scenes" essay, I have taken this concept of "scene" from Henry Staten's work on Wittgenstein (Staten 1984). Staten used the term to indicate a meaning-imparting context, grasped holistically and in the background whenever an explicit meaning is grasped. He took the term from Wittgenstein's later writings, in which Wittgenstein occasionally wrote that the meaning of a statement is given through the scenes of its use. A "scene" of this sort must be grasped simultaneously when one grasps any explicit meaning. The scene is what makes the explicit meaning intelligible. It is in a sense "presupposed" by the explicit meaning, or tacitly referenced by it.

But the term "scene" alone is not enough to convey the idea of very fundamental interpretative structures capable of winning the tacit consent of a very large group. All human understanding will involve scenes that range greatly in their generality and depth. We need another term to qualify that of "scene" and I have taken the term "originary" to this end. "Originary" connotes fundamental grounds from which an entire epistemological theory, or an entire philosophy, may be built. An "originary scene" accordingly refers to the barest, broadest, and deepest meaning-imparting scenes within a culture or underlying a specific intellectual tradition. It plays a part in all or most acts of meaning and understanding made within a culture or tradition. It will be revealed most explicitly through efforts to describe conceptual beginnings and state logical foundations: to philosophize.

By choosing the term "scene" to refer to a context of meaningful exchanges, a scene of *use*, Staten and Wittgenstein put their fingers on several things at once. First of all, contexts of meaningful interaction are grasped by actors in holistic ways. Despite the extreme complexity of any context in which meaning is conveyed, actors possess an understanding of meaning that is singular in nature. Secondly, though one's actual experience of a meaning-imparting context will not directly involve imagery, one's effort to step aside from such a context in order to represent it for memory, or in order to talk about it, will usually begin with analogies from visual perception. As the American pragmatists realized (see discussion below), human experience occurs initially in a holistic manner, in which body feelings, desires, and sense objects are experienced without differentiation. When representing such experience for memory, however, images are often, initially, employed. The concept of "scene" is accordingly meant to escape the metaphor of perception. A scene of use is more than a visual scene, even though it *becomes represented* most immediately through imagery. In fact, the difference between holistic forms of experience and their initial representation in images may account for both the preference given to visual perception in Western conceptions of knowledge and the limitations entailed by this preference.

GUBA'S PORTRAIT OF CRITICAL SOCIAL RESEARCH

An originary scene, then, is an underlying holistic view fundamental to a very broad range of cultural activities and expressions. When we start to push against the background structures of those formulations that have to do with the barest and broadest of concepts, concepts like "reality," "knowledge," and "truth," we find that the imagery of an originary scene begins to take explicit form. This is what I will now do with Guba's depiction of critical social research and, eventually, with his depiction of the other three orientations in his typology.

Guba began his portrayal of critical social research by calling it "ideologically oriented inquiry" (1990:23). By this he meant that critical social researchers pursue their craft with explicitly acknowledged allegiance to an ideology. They differ from other kinds of researchers because they explicitly acknowledge this allegiance. Here Guba echoed descriptions of critical social research that can be found in the works of authors who themselves claim to belong to the critical school. Patty Lather, for example, has called her critical orientation "openly ideological research" (1986). This characterization tends to come up in reviews of critical social research as well (Anderson, G. 1989). When this expression is used, of course, its full meaning lies in an epistemological theory that takes *all* processes of inquiry to be "ideological." Critical social research, from this perspective, is distinguished by its open acknowledgment of the role played by ideology in inquiry. Other approaches, according to this view, are ideological but are unaware of it.

One must ask, however, what is meant by the term "ideology." Guba's clarification of this begins to reveal the underlying imagery I have mentioned. He says:

> Nature can not be seen as it "really is" or "really works" except through a value window. If values do enter into every inquiry, then the question immediately arises as to what values and whose values shall govern. If the findings of studies can vary depending on the values chosen, then the choice of a particular value system tends to empower and enfranchise certain persons while disempowering and disenfranchising others. Inquiry thereby becomes a political act. (1990:24).

Many critical social researchers would agree that research is a political act whether the researcher acknowledges this or not. But not all of us would affirm Guba's explanation of the intrinsically political nature of research. The political quality of social inquiry is not reducible to the effects of values on inquiry. The epistemological implication carried by Guba's quotation, that inquiry is akin to "seeing," is also objectionable. Let us break down the implications of this passage into four related assertions:

1) Values "enter into inquiry at choice points such as the problem selected for study, the paradigm within which to study it, the instruments and the analytic modes used, and the interpretations, conclusions, and recommendations made" (Guba 1990:23).

2) Thus, values exist *outside* the process of inquiry, while in some way determining its analytic procedures and its conclusions: primarily by determining preinquiry "choices" made by the researcher. That is, inquiry cannot *inquire* into the rightness or wrongness of particular values, only into objective features of the world. Yet all studies of the objective world are shaped by a value orientation because all had to begin with a choice of questions, instruments, and interpretative frameworks.

3) Values, while excluded from the legitimate objects of inquiry, are either "right" or "wrong" in the eyes of critical theorists. Yet values can somehow be known as, or believed to be, right or wrong prior to any act of inquiry. Guba seems to have it that critical theorists believe, given this prior conviction in one set of values over other possible sets, that research should begin with the choice of "right values." However, according to this logic no inquiry can ever be made to determine which values are the right ones.

4) Values influence the inquiry process analogously to the way in which a window both facilitates and limits what can be seen outside. Therefore, inquiry is akin to "seeing," to visual perception.

This is not a correct description of critical theory, at least critical theory in the form I adopt. The key underlying and unexplored terms in Guba's portrait of critical social research are *values*, and *seeing*. These terms are most closely associated with an originary scene implicit not only in Guba's writings but in a great deal of methodological and philosophical writing in the West.

The Scene of Passive, Solitary Perception

The most primordial imagery one can draw forth from Guba's manner of characterizing critical social research hovers about the core scene of an observer who gains knowledge of an external world through her senses: especially her sense of sight. Visual perception is made the paradigm for all knowledge-imparting experience.

Of course, Guba qualifies the imagery by stating that a value window influences what is seen. A window is added to the core scene; a window that distorts and limits the views it makes possible. Values are added to a more primordial scene; added from the outside. Guba further modifies the core scene to produce his portrait of critical research. Critical researchers look through their value windows with conscious awareness that what they see is distorted by their window of choice. Thus in his depiction of critical methodology Guba's imagery includes the complication of multiple windows and observers who are free to choose one window from the others.

But it is the core imagery that is of particular interest. And this core imagery involves three main components: an observer, something observed, and the process of observation. This scene separates the observer from what is observed in an essential manner, even though this separation is modified with the image of "window" and even though it is argued to not exist when Guba discusses constructivism. The primal scene backgrounds each modification: one has to understand it in order to understand the alterations Guba introduces.

The primal scene of perception also renders knowledge-imparting experience a basically passive and solitary event. True, the structures of the "window" might be built up from cultural action and interaction, but the knowledge-imparting experience itself is passive and solitary. At the *moment* of knowledge acquisition, we find a passive observer alone with her experience.

This core imagery of an observer who gains knowledge of objects and events through perception underlies everything else Guba has to say. To understand what Guba means by "value window" one must first grasp the core imagery associated with a solitary experience of passive perception and the distinctions pertaining to it. Guba's arguments against the separation of observer and observed (a feature of the constructivist position he adopts) require modifications of the same background scene, and in this way presuppose and are limited by it.

SOLITARY PERCEPTION AND THE TYPOLOGY OF METHODOLOGIES

The workings of this underlying originary scene of passive, knowledge-imparting perception becomes most telling when one looks at Guba's portrayal of the three other research orientations in his typology. Positivists are said to believe that the purpose of inquiry is to find out "how things *really* are," and "how things *really* work" (1990:19), and thus to be committed to a "realist ontology."

> Once committed to a realist ontology, the positivist is constrained to practice an objectivist epistemology. If there is a real world operating according to natural laws, then the inquirer must behave in ways that put questions directly to nature and allow nature to answer back directly. The inquirer, so to speak, must stand behind a thick wall of one-way glass, observing nature as "she does her thing." (1990:19)

Once again the dominant image is that of perception. Guba's idea of *realism* is constructed from this imagery: Realism means objectivism; it means the existence of objective things ("nature") that exist in independence of human knowledge. "Things" is supposed to mean perceivable *objects*, or, in most versions of realism, underlying nonperceivable entities and forces that give rise to perceivable entities. All that is *real* to the realist are objects and objective forces giving rise to them. But in actual fact, a realist is simply someone who believes that existence is independent of human knowledge: all existence need not be conceptualized as "objective." Guba's metaphor of an observer looking through thick one-way glass is a good representation of naive realism rather than realism per se.

As an aside, it should be noted that logical positivism was pitched *against* naive realism. Logical positivism was similar to phenomenology in at least one important respect: its belief that only perceptual phenomena, "sense data," can be known with certainty. It then diverged from phenomenology by building its philosophy on the objective side of perception alone, paying little attention to the subjective conditions of perceptual experience.

Postpositivists, according to Guba, recognize the distortions imposed by values on inquiry, but argue that "reality" works as a regulating principle on all possible interpretations. This is but a rearrangement of the same core imagery:

> The essence of this position is that, although a real world driven by real natural causes exists, it is impossible for humans truly to perceive it with their imperfect sensory and intellective mechanisms (Cook and Campbell, 1979:29). Inquirers need to be critical about their work precisely because of those human frailties. But, although one can never be sure that ultimate truth has been uncovered, there can be no doubt that reality is "out there." Realism remains the central concept. (1990:20)

Paradigmatics

Once again, Guba is using the root metaphor of passive perception to construct the concept of "real." What is "real" is "out there," corresponding to the distinction between subject and object as it structures perceptual experience. Then, when Guba discusses his favored orientation of constructivism, he will dispute the distinction between "out there" and "in here."

Once again, I must point out that realism does not necessarily entail the belief that all knowledge is of objective entities, nor that certain knowledge is at root perceptual. To say that existence is independent of human knowledge is not to say that existence is to be reduced to the object pole of perceptual experience, nor that perceptual experience is the paradigmatic form of knowledge-imparting experience.

The constructivist position, Guba's own orientation, is the only one Guba claims to "totally replace" the paradigm of conventional positivism. For the constructivist: "'Reality' exists only in the context of a mental framework (construct) for thinking about it" (1990:25).

The idea is that existence is not independent of human knowledge and experience. Guba does not actually elaborate about what he means by "thinking" and "construct" in the sentence quoted above. But one can see in his use of these terms that they are metaphoric extensions of the scene of passive perception. A "construct" is like a window or a frame that gives form to an otherwise featureless substance. Perceptual experience dominates the imagery.

Guba further explains the constructivist position and its belief in the fusion of existence with human experiences:

> "Reality" can be "seen" only through a window of theory, whether implicit or explicit....If "reality" can be seen only through a theory window, it can equally be seen only through a value window. Many constructions are possible. (1990:25)

It is true that Guba uses perception *consciously* as a metaphor to explain the constructivist position. But this metaphor seems to have worked as a double-edged sword by constituting, through metaphoric extension, the core concepts that Guba employs to describe the constructivist paradigm. In some places Guba claims that the same "facts" can always be explained with multiple theories: "No theory can ever be fully tested because of the problem of induction" (1990:25). Here "theory" is conceived quite traditionally as consisting of statements about regularly occurring, objectively perceivable, events. "Facts" are given, but diverse (inductive) theories can be used to explain them.

In other places Guba claims that "facts" do not appear without theory. This is at odds with the first idea, the idea that facts are somehow given but can always be explained through markedly different theories, none of which can be proven. In this second argument facts are not given, they too are constructed. The imagery is that of the construct, the framework, the window frame.

What are constructions made of? Guba makes his most telling comments by indirectly addressing this question when discussing the *interactive* nature of knowledge:

> Even post-positivists have conceded that objectivity is not possible; the results of an inquiry are always shaped by the interaction of inquirer and inquired into. There is no Archimedean point. And if there is such an intimate interconnectedness in the physical sciences, how much more likely is it that the results of social inquiry are similarly shaped? This problem of interaction is devastating to both positivism and post-positivism. First, it renders the distinction between ontology and epistemology obsolete; what can be known and the individual who comes to know it are fused into a coherent whole. Further, it makes the findings of an inquiry not a report of what is "out there" but the residue of a process that literally creates them. Finally, it depicts knowledge as the outcome or consequence of human activity; knowledge is a human construction....(1990:26, italics in original)

Important ideas here coincide with certain features of critical methodological theory: the connection of knowledge and social action, for example. And in general one must say that Guba is working with important and sound insights but trying to theorize them with contradictory imagery. His formulations still depend on the imagery of perception. Notice the distinction, for example, between "inquirer" and "inquired into" used in the first sentence.

Paradigmatics

How are we to understand this distinction if what is "inquired into" is the creative product of the inquirer? This recalls the old idea of the perceptual flux (see below); a basic substance that is given form only through culturally determined "windows." What is "inquired into" may be a formless flux, but within this core imagery it is still distinct from the inquirer. The interaction between inquirer and the objects of inquiry does not deliver the final blow to objective realism simply because to conceive of this very distinction is to suggest a difference between a realm into which one inquires and the inquirer. "*Inter*action" suggests that there is something to interact with.

With the root metaphor of passive perception Guba has set up straw figures to knock down by means of a "totally new paradigm." But Guba's "new paradigm" seems to be genuinely new wine poured into an old and inappropriate glass. "Ontology" refers to a theory of existence, not to the theory that all that exists is objective in nature. "Epistemology" refers to a theory of knowledge. A theory that displays the relationship of social action and interaction to knowledge does not automatically fuse epistemology with ontology. If we begin with communication, rather than with passive solitary perception, we will find that a distinction between ontology and epistemology is made with every meaningful act, in everyday life as well as in science.[2]

So, from the same image, the image of a solitary moment of experience in which an individual perceives items or events and feels certain that she knows them to exist as such, one can derive each of the four orientations Guba presents in his typology. With the addition of qualifying imagery, like those of the window and the inquirer producing external appearances, all four orientations appear as Guba describes them. Constructivism, at least as formulated by Guba, is the same scene of passive solitary perception but with one side suppressed.

---

[2] Habermas's theory of the three formal realms, presupposed as three ontological domains referenced with each meaningful act, applies here.

NEO-KANTIAN IMAGERY: PERCEPTION AND "THE FLUX"
The originary scene revealed here centers on our common experience of passive perception. This sort of experience is generalized and made paradigmatic for knowledge-imparting experience not only by Guba, but by many other philosophers and methodological theorists. Martyn Hammersley's scholarly study of methodological debates within sociology since the 19th century displays the strong influence that one philosophical articulation of this same core imagery has had on research methodology: neo-Kantianism (Hammersley 1989).

Neo-Kantians like Rickert and Wendelbaum conceived of reality in terms of a perceptual flux that congeals into perceivable units only through the influence of human values. As soon as one has a perceivable unit, a "fact," one has a set of values that brought out the form of this unit from the perceptual flux.

Some neo-Kantians took this imagery in the direction of realism, maintaining that abstractions from the flux can be made that correspond to independent ("real") features of the flux itself. Others took the same scene in an idealist direction to argue that human values are associated with universals rooted in ubiquitous human interests. Neo-Kantian philosophy is one of several influences on both the development of positivistic conceptions of social science and the development of Blumer's competing "naturalistic" methodology.

The concept of a formless perceptual flux will be the inevitable product of any relativist philosophy (like constructivism) that takes its point of departure from the scene of passive, solitary, knowledge-imparting perception. The "flux" is a metaphoric residue left after one side of perception, the objective side, is collapsed. It is collapsed, but it still plays the role of the object pole in perception, a universal "something" or "substance" that retains realist imagery.

PRAGMATISM, A GENUINE ALTERNATIVE
Hammersley's study displays the complex nexus of influences on 20th century methodological theory. Neo-Kantianism was only one such influence. Another influence, which in its essence fully

breaks with the originary scene of passive, solitary, perception, is American pragmatism. Hammersley devotes an entire chapter in his book (chapter two, 1989) to the influence of American pragmatists on methodological and sociological theory.

Pragmatism took an alternative point of departure, employing different core imagery. Hammersley has this to say of Dewey's choice of philosophical beginning:

> Primordially, cognition begins not from a world of objects but from a sense of a whole within which various discriminations can be made. Objects as stable and meaningful phenomena are constituted by observation and thought. This is not to say that they arise out of nothing, but is to claim that the way they appear to us is in large part the product of our perceptual and cognitive activities, conscious and subconscious. (1989:53)

One can recognize some formulations present in Guba's description of constructivism; that, for example, objects are the product of our perceptual activities, and the idea of a "whole" experience. But Guba's use of similar formulas would amount to a murky misappropriation from pragmatism were he to indicate direct influences from this school of philosophy. The same can be said about symbolic interactionism.

The core feature of the above quotation about Dewey is its focus on a different kind of experience: a holistic preconceptual experience in which a project of activity is synthesized with related objective references. From this different choice of beginning, interest is not immediately drawn to the production of perceptual objects to meet the requirements of an activity: it is rather drawn to the question of differentiation. What particulars differentiate from original holistic experiences? How are differentiation processes brought about? Why?

Now constructivists and various relativists will suggest that it is the subjective orientation, the values, of the actor that bring about differentiation. But wait a minute; isn't subjectivity one of things that differentiate out of primordial holistic experience? The subject-object distinction associated with perception will come after the fact, if we are to take seriously the alternative scene of holistic experience. Perhaps other things differentiate out of primordial holistic experience as well as the subject-object distinction. One cannot explain one category of differentiated experience with another category of experience that differentiates at the same time.

Dewey, James, and Pierce all worked with this alternative originary scene of action and preconceptual holistic experience. The notion that "ideas" pertain to human habits, rather than to universals involved with all perceptions, is one important articulation of the alternative scene. The idea that a theory of truth must be centrally concerned with the processes through which consensus is reached between people is another important articulation.

It was George Herbert Mead's philosophical work at Chicago, however, that best begins to answer the question of what constitutes the differentiation process that leads from holistic and implicit modes of experience to knowledge-imparting (symbolic) experience (Mead 1967). His work began to answer the question of what differentiates out of holistic experience as well.

The key idea is that experience becomes knowledge-imparting only through symbolic representation. Perception is not directly knowledge-imparting, nor is it *the* form of experience to examine, initially, in order to understand how experiences become represented symbolically. An illuminating point of departure must enable us to reach into the heart of symbols, signs, and representation. Efforts to theorize symbolic representation that begin with perception run into major problems. Mead gave us a theory of symbols that begins with interaction, rather than with perception. The ramifications of his theory are profound. Symbols and signs do not exactly "construct" perceptual objects, not in the sense of a pattern pressed against a flux. The paradigmatic form of a symbol is not something perceptual but rather the experience of action constituted by interactive expectations. Symbolic action *references* objects within contexts of communicative expectations. And symbolic action does not reference objects alone but always, necessarily, and simultaneously, references several other categories of existence—nonobjective categories that include subjective states and assumedly shared values and norms. Communication occurs first in Mead's originary scene, perception (as knowledge-imparting) is secondary to communication.

Mead's work therefore united the idea of initial holistic, undifferentiated experience, with an evolutionary theory of the symbol, placing communicative action into an originary paradigmatic position.

This modified originary scene was both so promising and so different from the scene of passive perception as to have led Jurgen Habermas into calling Mead's work a "paradigm shift" (Habermas 1987b:ch.5). None of the imagery associated with knowledge-imparting passive perception works within the alternative scene of Mead's special pragmatism. "Flux," "value-window," "theory-window," and so on, are not appropriate. There is still room for a realist ontology, in that existence need not be collapsed into human knowledge. The regulating rules employed in postpositivist realist theories originate in communicative imperatives rather than in a real physical world: but these regulating rules make it necessary to *posit* real categories of existence, including the physical. Regulating rules associated with objective existence also may include, as many pragmatists put it, the "resistance" of the physical world against various human endeavors.

Moreover, "reality" has an inexpressible characteristic that appears in pragmatist terms through the distinction between holistic and differentiated experience. Derrida's work on the concept of presence intersects with certain pragmatist themes here: holistic experience is always gone as soon as it is symbolized (see discussions of Derrida in the other essays of this book). In one sense predifferentiated experience is "reality," which cannot be directly captured in a conceptual or perceptual way.

MURKY BORROWINGS FROM PRAGMATISM

The original American pragmatists influenced Blumer and Chicago School sociology quite directly. Many theorists of the Chicago School worked with Dewey and Mead or were their students. Thus pragmatism exerted direct influences upon early qualitative research methodology in the United States. It played a role in Blumer's "naturalistic method," symbolic interactionist theory, and no doubt in contemporary versions of constructivist methodology.

However, authors like Blumer did not exploit the full possibilities of pragmatist insights. Less fundamental formulations from pragmatism seem to be conflated with the core imagery of neo-Kantianism in symbolic interactionist thought. Thus, Hammersley frequently notes ambiguities in Blumer's writings. At times Blumer made statements that sound very like those of sophisticated (postpositive) realists, at other times he made statements that sound very much like the beliefs of contemporary constructivists. Many sophisticated realists *and* many contemporary constructivists use modified neo-Kantian imagery that has the scene of passive, solitary perception at its core, modified through the introduction of qualifiers such as the "value window" and the "theory window." Despite rather sweeping statements about the social construction of knowledge and its connection to social action, knowledge acquisition is still conceived by these theorists mainly in terms of perception.

This state of affairs would explain the lack of attention paid to the role of power in noncritical methodological theories. Knowledge-imparting perception will not seem to be shaped directly by power relations unless it is understood to be a process that is secondary to communicative structures. When constructivists and other noncritical contemporary methodological schools do acknowledge the importance of power in their epistemological theory, it is usually via the imagery of something imposed on the experience of perception, conceived as external to perceptual processes themselves. The largely unexamined term "values" is usually employed to this end.

PASSIVE SOLITARY PERCEPTION BEYOND NEO-KANTIANISM

As mentioned above, neo-Kantians thought in terms of a perceptual flux that takes on form only through the influence of values. This is one version of the originary scene of passive solitary perception. Neo-Kantian thought had to be addressed in this discussion because its emphasis on values as the material through which perceptual windows are constructed directly parallels statements made by such contemporary methodological theorists as Guba. Neo-Kantian imagery has worked through both realist quantitative and symbolic interactionist methodologies to help shape the terms of our contemporary paradigm dialogue.

But neo-Kantianism was only one formulation rooted in the originary scene of passive perception. The scene of a passive observer, feeling certain of the existence of what she perceives, is not only core to neo-Kantian thought and positivism, it was also central to phenomenology. Phenomenology built off the same imagery in a very different direction. The same scene was central to physicalism and many other competing philosophical schools. The passive solitary perceiver has been paradigmatic to mainstream Western philosophy at least since the Enlightenment.

Critical theory developed in the 1930s, drawing upon thought initially produced more than a century before by the German Counter-Enlightenment. Counter-Enlightenment thought took various forms: German romanticism, objective idealism, and the praxis philosophy of Karl Marx.[3]

These points are important to my discussion in several ways. First of all, the scene of passive perception underlying so much of Western thought has been most profoundly attacked in recent times by Jacques Derrida and those postmodernists who have followed in the wake of his first works. Derrida's famous phrase, "the metaphysics of presence," is closely related to what I am calling "the scene of passive perception." In fact, "the metaphysics of presence" is a phrase that critiques as well as describes, and in this way subsumes "the scene of passive solitary perception." It was not the neo-Kantians nor was it the positivists who developed

---

[3] See Taylor 1979 for a discussion of Enlightenment thought and the traditions opposed to it. Bernstein 1971 is an exciting effort to compare the alternative of praxis theory with pragmatist philosophy as well as with trends in 20th century analytic philosophy. My essay "Power, Truth, and Method" devotes considerable space to the argument that praxis theory can and should be reformulated and then incorporated within critical theory and critical methodologies.

the most rigorous and convincing philosophical formulations based on the scene of passive perception. It was rather Husserl and his followers who accomplished this with philosophical phenomenology.

In phenomenology one will find astute, penetrating, and insightful descriptions of knowledge-imparting perception. Derrida's work began with the careful deconstruction of phenomenology. Since phenomenology is one of our best efforts to present a case for the primacy of knowledge-imparting perception, Derrida has given us one of the best critiques of this originary scene.

In addition, Derrida has devoted much of his career to producing deconstructions of most major Western thinkers, finding the metaphysics of presence everywhere, including the work of Counter-Enlightenment thinkers. Critical theory began by drawing upon the Counter-Enlightenment tradition. It sought to replace perception-based theories of reality and knowledge with theories that employed the concepts of praxis and dialectics.[4] Derrida's critique, therefore, could be used against critical theory itself, as Derrida would certainly maintain.

However, modern critical theory has borrowed, through Habermas, heavily from the work of American pragmatists in its development of a genuine alternative. The originary scene of Habermasian critical theory is very much Meadian, with important supplementations and refinements. In addition, we can add to this scene from the insights of Dewey and James: initial experience is holistic and undifferentiated. The differentiation processes that make holistic experience knowledge-imparting and symbolic can be explored with insights from Herder and other "expressivist" thinkers of the Counter-Enlightenment.

Two of the remaining essays presented within this book elaborate portions of the pragmatist scene: "Four Scenes for Posing the Question of Meaning" and "Power, Truth, and Method." Both, in diverse ways, present their own critiques of the metaparadigm that can be found underlying the so-called

---

[4] See Quantz 1992 for a good discussion of critical theory and its relation to critical ethnography; see Giroux 1983 for a summary of the original critical theorists and Ingram 1990 for a thorough philosophical overview.

paradigm dialogue. But the emphasis of these two essays is on positive formulations rather than on critique; the formulation of an originary scene that is a genuine alternative to the scene of passive solitary perception.

Essay Two

POWER, TRUTH, AND METHOD
Outline for a Critical Methodology

"WE ARE RIGHT!" OR "WE WILL WIN!"?
Some years ago I attended a meeting of the "Institute for Critical Cultural Studies," an informal group of faculty and students at our university. This particular meeting featured a paper on the Rosenberg executions. The presenter displayed subtle and insightful use of certain structuralist and poststructuralist analytic methods. Newspaper, magazine, and television "texts," produced during the trial of Ethel and Julius Rosenberg for spying against the United States, were carefully analyzed. The presenter was able to show how structural categories that are associated with narrative form (such as "hero" and "villain") were configured along with culturally thematic categories (such as "female") to construct the guilt of the Rosenbergs and to basically bring about their sentence of death. "Death by Text" was the title of the paper.

At the presentation's end a professor of sociology sitting near the front asked for more evidence to support certain points made by the author. Her reply piqued my interest. She said that either he would be "rhetorically convinced" by her presentation or he would not. She elaborated her point, saying that there are no standards of validity existing outside of rhetorical force, and that we need to think in terms of interpretation rather than in terms of truth.

The sociology professor attempted to extend the discussion by asking whether or not she believed certain "standards" were implied in the distinction between "persuasive" interpretations and "nonpersuasive" ones. Now my interest was greatly magnified. I looked forward to a discussion of the "truth" and "rhetoric" distinction: something that might bring to the fore issues highlighted in the famous Searle and Derrida debates. But unfortunately other members of the audience irritably and impatiently (almost angrily) intervened. They told the professor that he entirely missed the point by mentioning *standards*, and they managed to shift the discussion before the author could respond again.

I was disappointed. Apparently, the sociology professor had set himself up for perfunctory dismissal by the majority of the audience. His sin was to suggest a difference between "rhetoric" and "truth." He was quickly labelled a "modernist" who failed to understand postmodern principles. His voice was silenced within two minutes, and so, in effect, was mine.

Sitting quietly near the back, I reflected on the course that critical social theory has taken since the late 1970s, when my own involvement with this genre of intellectual work began. I had first become engaged with social theories of the critical sort as a social activist rather than as an academic. In activist circles, I realized, theory always did display a certain "rhetorical" dimension in that it served to legitimate the belief systems that all activists require for their hope, solidarity, and ability to argue against other voices in politics and the media.

Theory, for many activists, is frequently rhetorical in the modernist sense. Many activists do not take the time to carefully question their theoretical beliefs but rather accept them when they meet gut feelings. Theory is often used by activists on the basis of its fit with value orientations alone. Thus some of the social-psychological processes involved within activist cultures do seem consistent with historically modernist connotations of "rhetoric." Theory is ideology; a belief system used to maintain commitments, to maintain activist identities, and to quickly argue down opponents. Theory is persuasive for many activists, but it is not often the product of careful efforts to find "truth." This is because basic truths are already assumed by many of those engaged in trying to change society.

In modernist terms, "rhetoric" refers to forms of persuasion other than valid truth claims, and social activists often employ such forms. Postmodern views, of course, render the difference between persuasive force and "truth" totally spurious. All that truth ever is or can be is that which persuades (some) people.

Theory is a form of rhetoric for many social activists. But, I also realized as I reflected at the back of this room, activists could hardly put theory to these "rhetorical" uses if we did not believe that society is *in truth* unequal and that inequality and injustice are *in truth* morally unacceptable conditions. Our interest in theory is always conditioned by the assumption that inequalities could be truthfully described by some method of investigation that is not "merely rhetorical," not simply an assertion of power or persuasive influence. And our moral convictions are rooted in the belief that we hold to a set of values of universal benefit to human beings, not rooted in the interests of one group at the expense of another. The modernist distinction between truth and rhetoric is assumed to be valid by most social activists I have worked with, without careful philosophical explorations in this area.

Trickle-Down Effects

My activist friends and I during the 1970s believed that we were basically *right*, in our views about the nature of society and in our moral convictions. During the 1980s the influence of postmodern modes of thought came to challenge the conviction that one could be basically right. Certainly, reappropriation of the term "rhetoric" has taken place with great sophistication in some circles, so that its distinction from "truth" is not exactly the point of retrieving original senses of this term. But, as is the case with a great many terms and phrases first produced by postmodern thinkers, there has been an irritating trickle-down effect whereby postmodern vocabulary has become a series of buzzwords used with little understanding of their original formulation. One increasingly hears postmodern slogans uttered in naive and nonreflective ways: "there is no truth, only interpretation," "the subject is dead," "moral discourses are simply the masks of power," "truth is a regime."

A short time after hearing the paper on the Rosenbergs I attended a convention on cultural studies held in Austin, Texas. Between paper presentations I expressed some of my concerns to Richard Johnson, a former mentor from the Centre for Contemporary Cultural Studies in Birmingham, England. Richard remarked, as a sort of active listening response to my laments, that perhaps the old assumption of critical theorists—"We are right"—has implicitly been reformulated as "We will win" in many circles. Postmodern discourses sometimes sound like new versions of "might makes right," where "might," of course, must be relocated from the realm of powerful groups of people to the realm of "subjectless discourses."

In this essay I will return to the origins of critical ethnography to unearth certain tacit advances made there with respect to the relationship between power, truth, and method. Early critical ethnography, I will argue, retrieved and reformulated the concept of praxis in important ways. It located power in the culturally productive features of the human subject and thus implicitly suggested a relationship between power and method that remains to be fully articulated. I will also briefly review certain themes within postmodernism, both in order to trace a few influential slogans back to their origins and to argue that certain important insights have been illuminated in postmodern work that must be addressed in a methodology of any sort. The tacit reformulation of praxis theory in early critical ethnography addresses some of the same issues taken up by postmodernism, but with the suggestion of positive frameworks from which to think and act, rather than the depiction of logical aporias. Finally, I will relocate some postmodern ideas within a methodological outline that is cognizant of the complex relationship between power and truth yet does not reduce one to the other. To this end, Habermas's theory of communicative action will be supplemented and slightly altered through the incorporation of praxis theory: not praxis theory in its original formulation, but praxis theory as Paul Willis and other early critical ethnographers tacitly reconceived it.

POWER AND SOCIAL STRUCTURE: THE BIRTH OF CRITICAL ETHNOGRAPHY

Critical ethnography emerged as a genre of social research during the 1970s, a period characterized by major theoretical disputes in Western Marxism (Anderson, P. 1976, 1980). Early critical ethnographers were Marxist in orientation and accordingly developed their contributions to social theory within Marxist frameworks.

After only a short period of time, however, the early critical ethnographies of the 1970s attracted a fairly wide audience of social theorists (Apple 1979, 1983, 1993; Giddens 1979, 1984).

The success of the first critical ethnographies in gaining a wide audience can be partially attributed to Marxist debates that took place during the same period, for critical ethnographies demonstrated a solution, of sorts, to the "structure versus agency" problematic that was strongly foregrounded in these debates. Perhaps because the climate of those years foregrounded structure and agency to such a great extent, other insights embedded within those early critical ethnographies have remained rather covert. A tacit understanding of power, in particular, can be found in these works. This is an understanding of power that has not yet been fully articulated and exploited for its possible contribution to the debates on truth and method that occupy center stage today.

Power and Social Ontology

The term "social ontology" is no doubt risky in a period when "ontology" generally has become regarded as an outdated subject, a legacy of Western metaphysics that has been surpassed by our movement out of modernist thought toward something new. But I use this term because it helps to distinguish between the sorts of theorizing that took place in the 1970s and the sorts of theorizing that are taking place today. During the 1970s, concepts fundamental to any general understanding of social reality were enthusiastically discussed by critical theorists. The idea was that one could become clearer about terms like "social structure," "social action," "power," "class," and so on, largely through armchair theorizing. Terms like these could then be fruitfully employed as a sort of a priori framework with which to study particular features of social life, social change, microsociological interactions, and macrosociological relations. Thus, much of the grand theorizing that took place during the late 1960s and early to mid-1970s was sort of "ontological" in nature. It was an effort to elucidate "the assumptions about existence underlying any conceptual scheme or any theory or system of ideas" (Flew 1979).

The focus of these discussions was on "social existence" rather than existence per se; something like a secondary ontology.

The structure versus agency debates were about how to conceive the general structures of social reality, not about how to gain knowledge of it in any manner, empirically or otherwise. The question of power was framed during this period as an ontological sort of question, not an epistemological one. Postmodernism, which was making a big impact on French academics during this same period, had not yet entered extensively into the debates of Marxists and other critical theorists. Although Althusser's development of a structuralist interpretation of Marxism did fully address epistemological issues and connect them to ontological ones, his theories were hotly disputed mainly at the ontological level by other schools of Marxism.

The question of power, as raised in these battles of the 1970s, was tightly connected to the question of social structure and its relationship to human agency. Three major schools formed and fought it out with each other: Marxist-structuralists of the Althusser and Castells variety, Marxist-culturalists of the Raymond Williams and E.P. Thompson camp, and what might be called "traditionalists" or the "old," as opposed to the "new," left (Johnson 1979; Castells 1977, 1978; Thompson 1963, 1978; Althusser 1969, Althusser and Balibar 1970).

The controversies between these three schools of Marxist thought have been well summarized elsewhere (especially Johnson 1979), and I will here simply provide a highly condensed review, tailored to the question of power alone. Traditionalists uncritically employed the famous "base-superstructure" model in their social theory. This is a version of functionalism, in that all cultural, social, and political aspects of society were explained in terms of their functions for maintaining and reproducing the economic base. Human agency was not well theorized by this school though human agency was appealed to when the prospects for social change were considered. The main problem with this school was its lack of theoretical coherency. Functionalist arguments that intrinsically ruled out human agency as of explanatory significance were employed when critiquing society; agency arguments were used when calling for change. Power was not well theorized but was clearly associated with the social system when functionalist arguments were marshaled. Social change was to be brought about by human agents, implicitly locating power in human agency. But social change would only be successful on a revolutionary scale when the "right historical stage" of capitalism had been reached, locating power back in the social system.

Althusser's efforts to construct a structuralist version of Marxism were much more sophisticated than what may be found in most traditionalist work. Althusser followed the structuralist movement generally by ruling out subjectivity and human agency entirely as explanatory factors for understanding society and social change (Althusser 1969). Power was quite explicitly conceived as a structural factor alone. Althusser's work no longer enjoys the attention it once claimed, partly because of the cogent attacks launched upon it by other Marxists who saw the need to preserve human agency as an explanatory factor in social theory. Marxist-structuralism has, however, enriched critical theory ever since its emergence, particularly through its attacks on the base-superstructure model and its arguments in favor of the "relative autonomy" of the cultural, political, and social spheres from the economic one. A good deal of work on the nature of the capitalist state was inspired by Althusser and remains important to critical theory today (e.g. Offe 1984; Saunders, 1981, 1983; see also Apple 1993—especially page 169).

Marxist-culturalism refers to a fairly loosely defined body of historical studies conducted by certain British Marxists (Kaye 1984). E.P. Thompson was probably the most theoretically minded member of this group (Thompson, 1978). He attacked the base-superstructure model as well as Marxist-structuralism for their failure to recognize the importance of culture and human agency as explanatory categories. He wrote, for example: "*Social* relations of production are simultaneously economic, political, cultural, and moral" (Thompson quoted in Kaye 1984:236, italics in original). Such relations feature into "real experiences" of conscious human beings (Thompson 1963:10). For Thompson and, to a lesser extent, other culturalists, power is an intrinsic feature of human agency.

Humans create new cultural forms at all times. Power resides in the social system only insofar as the system impinges upon human agency through ideological influence and political, legal, and economic constraints. Every human act is an act of power that, however, takes place within pregiven conditions of influence and constraint.

Praxis Theory

Althusser insisted that the mature Marx who wrote *Das Kapital* had broken fundamentally with the early Marx who wrote the *Theses on Feurbach* and *The Economic and Philosophical Manuscripts*, among other things (Marx, 1977; Althusser, 1969; Althusser and Balibar, 1970). This idea was crucial to his arguments that the mature Marx had formulated an implicitly structuralist view many years before the rise of structuralism. The early writings of Marx clearly make use of a theory of subjectivity and human agency. They do so through Marx's use of the term "praxis."

Culturalists, on the other hand, insisted on the continuity of Marx's writings. Marxist-humanists like Raya Dunayevskaya (1989a, 1989b, 1992) share this view with the culturalists and explicitly argue that praxis theory runs through all of Marx's works although it became more implicit in *Das Kapital* (see Bernstein 1971). Certain passages in Marx's earlier work are often appealed to in order to support this thesis, particularly where Marx states that humans create their own history, but not within conditions of their own choosing.

Praxis theory is important to this discussion because I shall shortly argue that Paul Willis, in what I take to be the inaugural study for critical ethnography, *Learning to Labor* (1977), retrieves and reformulates praxis theory in implicit but crucially important ways. Thus we need to review some of the core themes within praxis theory.

The concept of praxis is discussed in some of Marx's early writings, particularly *The Philosophical Manuscripts of 1848* and the *Theses on Feuerbach* (Marx and Engels 1976: Vol. 5). Praxis was conceived at that time within the shadow of the still dominant Hegelian tradition. It was conceived of in terms of core Hegelian categories: alienation, objectification, and self-production. In Hegel's philosophy, *Geist* produces itself through expressing its implicit nature in objective forms. No objective form truly expresses *Geist*, however, and each expression embodies a contradiction that will lead to a new expression, producing a dialectical movement. The early Marx relocated Hegelian themes within the human subject. Humans, not *Geist*, express and objectify themselves. They do so, Marx believed, primarily through their work rather than through other modes of human activity. Furthermore, Marx limited the concept of work to actions oriented toward the physical world: actions that produce material products. Marx made these moves in a deliberate effort to escape from the idealism of Hegelian philosophy. Yet the emphasis on work and on action oriented to the physical world alone truncated the core insight in damaging ways. For the moment, let us stay with Marx to see what more he had to say about praxis, and let us ignore the grave limitations imposed on the concept through the emphasis on work. I shall return to the limitations later on by arguing that Willis overcame them.

Marx's basic idea was that human beings are motivated to realize their potentialities in work. By working to create products humans actualize their potentialites. The paradigm case, for Marx, is the work of the artisan who conceives of a useful product and then creates it in a skillful and artistic manner (see Habermas 1987a: ch. 3 for a critique). There is pride and satisfaction in such work as this. One "creates one's self" through expressive activity of this type, and human existence is a process of self-production.

Human beings are fundamentally motivated to express themselves in their work, but this requires certain objective conditions. We must be able to work so that the conception and execution of our products are united, to work so that the tools, materials, and productive infrastructure required are under our control, and to work so that the entire work process, including its division of labor, is under our control as well. Only if these conditions are met may human beings satisfy fundamental expressive needs.

By "expressive needs" I mean self-productive needs: the need to become a self, maintain a self, and grow as a self through expressive activity. If the above conditions of work are not met, as they are not for working-class members of capitalist society, then human beings will be in a state of "alienation." They are cut off from the products they manufacture because it is not their ideas they execute but those of their employers, foremen, and managers. They are cut off from the expressive process because they rarely complete the full productive activities required by factory-made commodities. The work process is fragmented into a series of menial tasks carried out on production lines. And, of course, capitalist workers do not own the products they produce (they must buy them with their wages), they do not own the tools they make use of, they have little or no say in the way production tasks are organized. This is "alienation." Alienation is harmful to human beings because it truncates praxis. Life is expressive activity, but under capitalism "life" has been severed from "work." Praxis needs are displaced from productive activity and ideologically displaced into the false hopes of consumerism.

Thus Marx really had an implicit theory of human motivation that went beyond crudely materialistic models. His use of the term praxis borrowed from ideas developed by Herder that Hegel had also borrowed but, of course, in a much different way (see Taylor 1979). Herder's view, called "expressivism" by Charles Taylor, was that human existence is an expressive movement from implicit potentialities toward their explicit manifestation. Herder, Hegel, and Marx seem to have formulated the same insight in diverse directions; an insight that reappears in twentieth century existentialism.

Praxis theory is a theory of human existence, a theory of the connection between "being human" and primordial structures of desire, need, and motivation. But the concept of praxis should not be limited to the artisan model of work alone. Herder and Hegel alike had broader, more insightful ideas about human existence and human motivation. Work is only one of many spheres for expressive activity. Praxis can be fulfilled in ways that do not produce a material product and in ways that are not directly economic in nature. Self-production and expression, above all, spring from a desire for recognition (as Hegel realized) and are internally tied to the social-communicative preconditions for the emergence of a self. Praxis is more about human-to-human relations than it is about human-to-physical world relations.

The core themes that are identical for Herder, Hegel, and Marx include the fundamental preoccupation humans have with respect to their identity, the incomplete and implicit nature of the human self that drives humans toward self-expression, the never-ending nature of this quest for the self through activity, and, finally, the dependence of such expressive needs on certain objective conditions—control over the conditions of one's life and work, the importance of autonomy to the expressive process, and the need for a community of equally autonomous companions as one's audience and source of recognition.

Critical Ethnography: Praxis as Cultural Production

Willis's appropriation of the concept of praxis emphasized many of these same core themes. The dependence of his analysis on a concept of praxis is less explicit in *Learning to Labor* than it is in his two earlier publications based on the same field study (Willis 1975, 1976), but it implicitly permeates *Learning to Labor* just the same. One of these earlier publications, *The Main Reality* (1976), argued that "the main reality" for the "lads" Willis studied was their socially constructed identities. The driving force behind the culture created by Willis's lads was their need to construct identities of which they could feel proud and through which they could gain and routinely maintain a sense of dignity. Teachers frequently argued with Willis's lads to try to convince them of the importance of schooling for their futures. But Willis showed that such arguments missed the point: actions oriented toward the construction and maintenance of positive identities were much more foregrounded in these boys' experience than actions oriented toward a future job. Willis's lads were cultural producers[1] first,

---

[1] Willis's theory of cultural production is more clearly articulated by Anthony Giddens (1979 and 1984). The idea is that all social action draws upon pre-existing cultural themes but also refashions them slightly. Cultural production is also cultural reproduction if reproduction is thought of as an iteration. The slight changes introduced in each iteration produce cultural drift. Giddens has

planners and goal-seeking agents second. The "main reality" was the culturally dependent identity.

In the immediate wake of *Learning to Labor*, other critical ethnographies were conducted that made use of Willis's model of human agency as cultural production and of his insights on social structure (discussed below). The origins of the "cultural producer" model of the human being in Willis's appropriation of praxis theory was not explicitly treated and, in general, fell further into shadows surrounding the concept of "cultural production." Careful examination of Willis's three publications during this period, however, clearly shows a sophisticated, if not fully articulated, treatment of the praxis concept.

Willis basically retained Marx's views about praxis and alienation but broadened the concept through a more encompassing model of human action. A crude, but appealingly brief, condensation of his analysis would go as follows. Human beings are expressive organisms essentially concerned with their identities. Identities are constructed and maintained, not primarily through work oriented toward the physical world, but interactively and thus culturally. This need not, in any way, downplay the expressive importance of work and of action oriented toward the physical environment. Most action oriented toward producing a material product has its meaning in relation to the culturally defined identities associated with such activities. The artisan achieves fulfillment through work because her products are appreciated and found useful by other human beings. Her products symbolize herself materially.

Marx's conception of praxis was based on the idea that one actualizes one's self in material products in some sort of essential way. The nature of the work process, of course, is entirely mediated by social structure (as in class structure) but the implicit standard by which Marx judged the structural conditions of work to be either alienating or not was a view of direct self-expression in actions oriented toward the physical world. Willis implicitly

---

formulated this as "structuration"—culture is simultaneously the medium and the outcome of social action.

challenged this idea by discussing the work and schooling process in terms of cultural milieu. No material product, in itself, is self-expression. Material products and work performance generally are self-expression in terms of how other people might recognize the worker *through* her work. Thus Willis's reformulation of praxis removed that category of action that is oriented toward the physical world from its paradigmatic position, and placed a more encompassing, but undertheorized, understanding of human self-expression in its place.

Willis did implicitly regard certain features of praxis to be essential and not culturally relative. These included the control one must have over one's own activities if they are to be self-expressive, and the drive of praxis needs to feature such control in all environments. When one's experience of work and schooling is not one of alienation, then actors are able to construct identities homogeneously and synthetically through *both* their work and the cultural milieu they produce (and reproduce) as part of the work process. In this case, praxis needs will be met simultaneously within the cultural and institutional realms.

When, on the other hand, one's experience of work or schooling is indeed one of alienation, then cultural forms are created, at least in the case of many groups, in opposition to the conditions of alienation. Praxis needs, in other words, will always be pursued in some relation to the goal-oriented tasks of one's institutional life. When such tasks are controlled by others, are menial, fragmented, and do not facilitate self-expression, then workers develop cultures that try to maximize what few opportunities for self-expression do exist in the tasks themselves (e.g., the pride taken by Willis's lads and their fathers in hard physical labor) and simultaneously meet praxis needs by resisting cultural forms associated with the authority figures of the setting: teachers, foremen, employers.

Praxis thus comes to embrace a broader conception of action. Goal-oriented action appears as just one dimension of cultural action more generally conceived. Action becomes a concept divisible into diverse categories, types, or dimensions, and *praxis becomes a concept of human expressive need that will seek to unify all such dimensions of action under the control of a self-actualizing, autonomous subject.* When social relations and institutional organization put the goal-oriented dimension of acts under the control of others and cut it off from the praxis of the workers, the workers pursue praxis needs in other ways, often through the construction of cultural forms that resist, critique, and otherwise challenge the alienating environment.

By expanding the concept of praxis toward a more complex model of human action, Willis located power within the human subject. All human acts are acts of power, and power is somehow linked to existential needs: needs to construct the self through actions under one's control. Willis thereby redeployed themes one may find in Marx's original use of the term praxis in a manner that is more consistent with the first formulations of the same basic idea in the work of Herder and Hegel. But he also retained the unique emphasis Marx gave to work environments and the sociological interpretation of "alienation" as a feature of class and organizational structure. Praxis refers to an essential drive to unify all dimensions of action under the control of a self-actualizing, autonomous subject: alienation refers to the ways in which social institutions capture control of one or more dimensions of action, usually the goal-oriented dimension, such that workers and students must construct themselves largely in opposition to the nature of their work.

The legacy of Willis, even in other early critical ethnographies (McRobbie 1978; Everhart 1983) initially foregrounded the model of "cultural production" without fully exploring the implicit relationship of this model to an expressive model of human subjectivity and action; that is, without explicitly recognizing the retrieval and reformulation of praxis theory in Willis's work. Critical ethnography became a genre of social research that unreflectively carried forth a contemporary version of praxis theory.

The Structural Side of Power in Early Critical Ethnography

Willis's work made its major impact not by explicitly formulating a new version of praxis but by showing how power works in and through human agency to reproduce social inequalities.

Critical ethnographies following Willis, like McRobbie's study of British working-class schoolgirls, adopted his model of cultural production not in order to articulate the implicit ideas about praxis embedded there, but rather in order to highlight more of the complexities and subtleties of social reproduction as it is "mediated" through cultural production. Social theory influenced by Willis (Apple 1979, 1983, 1993; Giddens 1984) also took up his resolution of the structure versus agency problematic rather than his tacit insights about the nature of human agency itself. The influence of early critical ethnography, then, has mainly been felt in our theoretical models of the structural side of power which, since Willis, has been thought of in terms of the conditions through which human agency is expressed.

The structural side of power has, since the advent of critical ethnography, been theorized away from structuralist or functionalist models. Many advances have been made. Michael Apple has demonstrated the autonomous but simultaneous intersections of class, race, and gender relations on the structural side of things (1983, 1988). Anthony Giddens has given enormous sophistication to the concept of "conditions of action" (1979, 1984). In all this work, structural power has been conceived in terms of human action and agency instead of in opposition to it.

There is much that can be said about the structural side of power, but this topic is not within the scope of this essay. Let me end this section by noting that human agency has been *assumed* in post-Willis critical theory but not explicitly theorized. Its connection to some of the original themes within praxis theory, particularly, has been ignored.

POSTMODERNISM

Now I must alter the focus of our discussion for a time by making some brief, dense, and necessarily limited remarks about postmodern views of power in order to set the stage for an outline of critical methodology. My effort will be to give the gist of a few themes found in Foucault and Derrida so that the origins of certain trickle-down buzzwords and slogans may be clarified. In addition, I wish to illuminate several important themes developed in postmodern writings that cannot be ignored by any methodology. This section will help to set the stage for developing an explicitly reformulated theory of praxis that has methodological significance.

Death of the Subject

Postmodernism has had two very major trickle down effects of relevance to critical social theory. The first is its attack on human agency as an explanatory principle, and the second is its attack on "truth." Michel Foucault and Jacques Derrida have been two of the most influential figures in the postmodern movement. I shall begin with Foucault.

Foucault was a postmodernist in the direct sense. That is, he explicitly claimed to have outlined the principal forms of modernist thought, to have shown how each such form reached a dead end, and to have helped lead the way into a new historical era: an explicitly *post*modern one. His work is diverse and it is well known that he went through a number of stages during the course of his writings (Dreyfus and Rabinow 1983). However, his *The Order of Things* has been particularly influential in giving sense to the term postmodernism (1970).

In *The Order of Things* Foucault argued that Western society has gone through a number of periods, each of which was characterized by a certain paradigmatic conception of "truth" and "knowledge." The modern period, which began in the eighteenth century, was the first period to emphasize subjectivity in its epistemological framework. But this modern period has been fraught with intellectual tensions because of the contradictions involved in trying to use a theory of human subjectivity as the groundwork for understanding truth and knowledge.

The contradictions Foucault had in mind concern two beliefs held simultaneously within the modern period: (1) structures of subjectivity are a *precondition* for all knowledge and, (2) it is possible to produce knowledge *about* subjectivity. Within the deep structures from which modern thought has formed, the subject must first exist for any form of knowledge to be possible and yet the subject appears simultaneously as just one of many objects of knowledge. Specific modern theories and philosophical movements could proceed only by suppressing one of these two beliefs constituting the modern worldview, or by seeking to resolve subject-object tensions with dialectical or otherwise self-referential modes of reasoning.

Foucault thought that three primary modes of dealing with the contradictions of modernist deep structures were formulated and worked out to dead ends by the middle of the twentieth century. Each mode of attempting to theorize about subjectivity without violating the dependence that all theorizing activities and their results have upon subjective preconditions and structures was characterized by a "double": the empirical and the transcendental double, the cogito and the unthought double, and the return and retreat of the origin double (Foucault, 1970: ch. 9). Within each double Foucault showed how various modern theories emerged and failed. Within the same double some theories emphasized one side of the terms (e.g., Hegel's emphasis on transcendence within the empirical and transcendental double) and competing theories emphasized the other side (e.g., Marx's emphasis on the empirical within this same double). Foucault argued that post-Enlightenment theories have exhausted the possibilities of their structural frameworks such that the modern period has come to an end.

Because it was the core location given to subjectivity in the modern period that produced the doubles and ensured the futility of all theories produced within them, postmodernism begins with "the death of the subject" for Foucault. Humanistic conceptions of the actor and thinker must be scrapped. Neither subjectivity nor agency may be employed as explanatory terms but emerge, rather, as the effects of something else. This "something else" was *power*. The movement away from subjectivity in the primordial structures of modern thought toward a conception of power as primordial is a movement from modernism to postmodernism.

Foucault's work suggested a postmodern methodology for the human sciences that does not depend on the concepts of agency or subjectivity as explanatory terms. His methodological efforts were first called the "archeology of knowledge" (Foucault 1970) and later, with some alterations, the "genealogy of knowledge" (Foucault 1979, 1980). Though these proposed methods differ in important ways, both make use of the concept of power. The idea is to uncover unconscious cultural conditions, presupposed within diverse "discourse-practices" that construct the conditions only then to mask their constructed nature, and that originate in multiple, nonunified, sites. One uncovers such conditions in a way analogous to the manner in which an archaeologist uncovers layers of deeper and older foundations when digging out the remains of an ancient city.

Foucault's writings, however, arguably fall within the same problematics he articulated with the theory of "doubles." Power has a covertly transcendental status in his work, while also appearing as the object of his analysis. More importantly, Foucault's effort to reduce truth to power cannot escape his own activities as a writer who writes to be understood, who writes his ideas so that readers will be convinced of their merit. The distinction between truth and power is intrinsic to all efforts at being understood or understanding another. Let us examine this a little more closely.

Foucault claimed that "truth" is always the product of certain discourse-practices whose conditions of possibility lay deep within the cultural unconscious. The conditions of possibility are constructed by these same discourses and then hidden, as constructions, so that they appear as essences. The idea of "sex" is an example. Discourse-practices about sexuality construct the concept of sex (as in ideas about essential prediscursive differences between males and females) and then mask their own act of construction.

Foucault's histories described, empirically, the rise of discourse-practices during various periods. Discourse-practices must not be explained with any assumptions about truth; to the contrary, "truth" is always something defined internally within some discourse-practice.

People employ concepts of truth always within a discourse-practice of some kind. Thus we cannot, for example, argue that the discourse-practices of psychology developed as better ways of describing psychological phenomena. Psychological phenomena did not "exist" until psychological discourse-practices brought them into being. To explain the rise of a discourse-practice in terms of its congruence with the reality of any phenomena it explained would appeal to absolute truths about which human theories form and with respect to which human theories improve. This is expressly not what Foucault wanted to do. All truth, he believed, is an internal effect of discourse-practices. Discourse-practices are prior to truths.

If discourse-practices do not rise and fall according to how well they explain "real" phenomena of which they are about, how can one explain them? Why did they rise at all, and why did they give way to new discourse-practices over time? Foucault answered by explaining the rise, change, and end of discourse-practices as the workings of "power." Yet power must be conceived of outside any connotations of subjectivity; the death of the subject must be upheld in postmodern methodology. Thus, to take an example, the power-knowledge connection cannot be here conceived of as an "ideology," imposed by a dominant group upon subordinate groups in order to serve dominant group interests. Insofar as "interests" are related to human motivations and desires, the concept of ideology presupposes subjectivity. And insofar as ideologies are viewed as distortions of reality, the concept of ideology presupposes real objective states of affairs to which truth claims are related. But postmodernism is organized around the death of the subject, and power is prior to truth claims and, thus, prior to objective states of affairs.

Hence Foucault had some idea of "anonymous power" that was the principal explanatory term in his historical studies of discourse-practices. To ask about the rise of a discourse-practice is to ask about the form that a particular strategy of anonymous power took; nothing else.

This is, very roughly, how Foucault reduces truth to power. Anonymous power produces discourse-practices and each of these, in turn, determine what the people of a certain era will take as true, false, good, and bad. Not only does anonymous power determine how "people" ascertain truth and falsity, it actually constructs subjectivity. Discourse-practices determine what is taken to be a human being during any particular era.

This view seems initially unappealing and unconvincing because of its dependency on the idea of anonymous power. Habermas succinctly captured the imagery in this comment on Foucault:

> The danger of anthropocentrism is banished only when, under the incorruptible gaze of genealogy, discourses emerge and pop like glittering bubbles from a swamp of anonymous processes of subjugation. (1987a:268)

But the deficiencies of Foucault's ideas can be more rigorously addressed. Foucault implicitly claimed the status of truth for his own work without recourse to "power." He claimed, at least implicitly, that his historical studies were in some way accurate, that his methodological formulations were somehow sound. Without such a claim there is absolutely no reason to accept Foucault's arguments. If his own work is also to be taken as an effect of certain discourse-practices whose standards of truth are simply products of anonymous power, then there is no obvious reason to accept his views. Foucault's views undermine any claim he himself can make for accepting his idea of truth over any other idea of truth.

The idea that truth and power are autonomous concepts, and that acts oriented toward understanding (including writing histories and formulating theories) presuppose this distinction, will be reviewed in sections following this one. Habermas has attacked Foucault quite eloquently using this notion (Habermas 1987a: chs. 9 and 10).

The distinction between power and truth, however, is not without complexity. I will argue later on that power *is* associated with acts oriented toward understanding but that this internal connection between power and truth must be captured through a reformulated concept of praxis. Foucault's views are primarily unappealing because he *reduced* truth to power, because he conceptualized power to be something anonymous and subject-less, and because he took anonymous power to be both what is *discovered* through empirical studies revealing a cultural unconscious and simultaneously what is *presupposed* in all knowledge claiming action.

The reader should retain, from this brief discussion of Foucault, an understanding of the origins of those postmodern slogans proclaiming the death of the subject, the total construction of subjectivity via discourses, and the basis of truth in power. The reader should also retain my assertion that potent arguments exist against all such formulations, if the formulations are presented in a totalizing manner. The idea that truth claims can be reduced to the workings of an anonymous power leads to contradictions.

The Metaphysics of Presence

Like Foucault, Derrida claims that Western intellectual traditions have reached a dead end in terms of their efforts to give us truths. Like Foucault, Derrida is postmodern. Unlike Foucault, Derrida's work does not suggest a method. His famous use of "deconstruction" is a sort of strategy rather than a method. Deconstruction never gives us any positive formulations, it rather displays the dependence of a body of thought on certain metaphysical assumptions that can *never be known as truths*. Most prominent of the metaphysical assumptions repeatedly brought to light by Derrida is what he calls "the metaphysics of presence."

Derrida's early presentation of the role played by "presence" in the presuppositions of great philosophers is extremely insightful and profound. His first books deconstructed Husserl's phenomenology of experience (Derrida 1962, 1973). Husserl had carefully analyzed the nature of experience and its various structures. Derrida followed Husserl's line of discussion very carefully in order to turn things around at the end, undermining Husserl's project.

Husserl based phenomenology on what he called "the principle of all principles": the certain knowledge one has of a phenomenon when one experiences it (Husserl 1962:141). When I see a cup before me I feel certain that the cup is there and unreflectively proceed with my stream of action assuming that the cup exists and has certain properties. A phenomenologist, however, carefully examines this experience of certainty and argues that what I can be certain of is not the *reality* or the *existence* of the cup but rather the reality of my *experience* of the cup. The cup may or may not be there (I could be dreaming, hallucinating, daydreaming), but the *phenomenon* of "this cup" is certainly there within experience. The phenomenon, at least, of what I take to be one *side* of a cup given to me from one perspective at one moment is certain within my experience.

This is certain knowledge: phenomena. This is the principle of all principles from which a theory of knowledge and truth may be built up by the phenomenologist. As primordial structures of experience and certainty are built up from the principle of all principles, the questions of existence and reality can be re-addressed: the concepts of reality and existence can be approached from "first principles."

Derrida showed, however, that this idea of being certain of experiencing a phenomenon depends on the idea of presence. To believe that the phenomenon is really *there* within experience such that one *knows* it to be there, is to believe that a moment or series of moments take place in which the phenomenon is purely and immediately present before the knower, the one experiencing it. Derrida then used Husserl's own analysis of moments and experiences to show that presence is never such a certain thing and can never be so.

The moment in which I (think that I) know a phenomenon is before me, tacitly references a prior moment in which it really was before me against a present moment in which my attention has shifted so that I know that I am aware of the phenomenon. One cannot experience presence in an unmediated, knowledge-imparting way. As soon as an experience of a phenomenon becomes something *known*, a movement has already occurred such that the phenomenon before us is really a "trace," a memory trace or impression left by a bygone moment of pure presence. The concept of having something present to us and the concept of knowing that something is present to us require temporal separation: they cannot be simultaneous experiences.

Try it out. Focus your attention on an object and see if you can freeze out a moment in which you simultaneously have it before you and know that you do. It is impossible. "Presence" is unattainable in pure form within experience and yet it is presupposed or implicated in experience.

Derrida famously argued that any object of conscious experience both *differs from* an original moment of pure presence always already gone by, and *defers to* this moment of presence as a ground of certainty. *Differing from* gives us the immediate past. *Deferring to* can be understood in two ways: as "deference" (the authority of the certainty one feels to be located in the moment of pure presence already gone by) and as "deferment" (the postponement of this certainty for the time in which another moment of pure presence will be experienced). No experiences directly give certain, undoubtable knowledge, because all experiences make knowledge differ from a presence always already gone. But experiences will implicate or "defer to" immediate, knowledge-imparting, experience as moments both always already gone and always yet to come. The idea of presence is necessary for experience but never reached within experience. The idea of presence is therefore outside Husserl's "principle of all principles" and can be nothing more than a belief. Therefore, Husserl's "principle of all principles" deconstructs.

Derrida argued that experience accordingly might be thought to have a "sign structure." Let us see how he made this argument. Signs are meaningful insofar as they represent or stand for something which they are not in themselves. "Tree," in itself as a sign, is either a set of conventional marks on paper (the written word) or a vibrational regularity of sound (the spoken word). "A tree" is something referred to by the written and spoken signs—words—and differs from these written and spoken signs. But the sign "tree" has meaning in that it stands for our concept of tree, which in turn is usually conceived of in some relation to our experiences of trees. There are three "things" here: the sign "tree," the concept of tree, the experience of tree. "Tree," as sign, has meaning through its difference from our concept or experience of tree and through its deference to an immediate relation between the concept and/or the experience of tree and the knower. The sign "tree" is a deferment of the experience of tree as concept or as empirical reality.

The concept of tree and its relationship to experiences of trees is not the focus of this discussion; whether the sign "tree" is taken to represent a concept or an experience or both, it must differ from what it represents. What it represents, meanwhile, involves the notion of "presence": either a "real tree" present to one in empirical experience or the "tree concept" present to one in thought. Concepts and empirical experiences both are phenomena. So it is the difference between a sign and the phenomenon it refers to that is the focus of analysis here.

Since "direct experiences" of phenomena have the structure of differing from a prior moment of pure presence and also of deferring to this prior moment in terms of the certainty of the experience, "direct experience" of phenomena has *itself* a sign structure. Signs differ from and defer to "direct experience." But "direct experience" also has structures of differing and deferring. Within direct experience a distinction between pure presence and "absence" is necessarily already made. This is the distinction between the "now" and the "just has been," a distinction one can understand when noticing the difference between a moment of purely having something before consciousness and a moment in which one *knows* that something is immediately before one. Knowledge-imparting presence cannot be a certainty because of this structure—differing from and deferring to—inhabiting it. And yet it is knowledge-imparting presence that is "deferred to" in Husserl's theory of signs. That is, knowledge-imparting presence is the "principle of all principles" for Husserl; our foundation of certain knowledge.

Now, Derrida used these arguments to *fully* deconstruct Husserl, which is to say that he used them to show that all the core terms we had to make use of in order to conduct the discussion of experiencing phenomena depend on some belief in the possibility of knowledge-imparting presence. Since this has subsequently been shown to be unreachable within conscious experience, all the concepts initially accepted, and all the new ones developed along the way, deconstruct.

For example, the logic of Husserl's own analysis of moments required use of the ideas of "retention" and "protention"—moments just past that somehow inhabit the present moment, and moments anticipated that also in some sense inhabit the present moment. Retention and protention alike bring an "absence" into the present moment. What is "retained" *was*, and what is "protended" *is not yet*. This is another way to undermine the concept of a phenomenon immediately present to consciousness, and to suggest the idea of a *trace* as intrinsic to experience. A trace is like a memory image deferring to a moment just gone by in which the "real phenomenon," of which we now only have a trace, was "really there immediately before us." A retention is a trace, and Husserl argued that the experience of a phenomenon requires a retention.

So it might seem that we could conclude: "Phenomena are really traces." But we cannot. All the logic and conceptual frameworks used to get to this point have deconstructed. If we try to conclude that all phenomena are really traces we will find we have assumed that a trace may be immediately known as such during a moment of knowledge-imparting presence. And we cannot do that. The same logic will just give us traces of traces of traces . ...

So the whole structure comes down and nothing remains from which we could make positive statements. Ultimately at issue is the concept of "presence," which Derrida takes to be a metaphysics. Belief in presence, which can be found in many diverse theories, epistemologies, and philosophies, is a dogma.

Desire and Power

I will now have to leap far ahead, leaving out many clarifying steps for want of space. Derrida's various works suggest an important relationship between desire, truth, and power in diverse ways. Let me be extremely crude and simplistic in order to give the gist of some of this. Partly because presence is an impossibility and experience is never a certain affair but is rather always riddled with uncertainties, and partly because the trace structure of experience defers to an experience of pure presence that cannot be reached, *desire is a fundamental structure of experience, knowledge, and meaning*. One of Derrida's many formulations of this idea is the following:

> There never was any "perception"; and "presentation" is always a representation of the representation that yearns for itself therein as for its own birth or its death. (1973:103).

Yearning—desire—is a structure of experience. All experiences will involve forms of desire that work back (as if) to a primordial form of motivation. Thus, by "desire" we must mean the very broadest senses of motivation. We must include fear, all forms of anticipation, all subjectively felt tendencies to move ahead in action or thought. Conceived in this very broadest way, experience is always laced with desire, or motivation, toward something *not yet here*.

This might be seen in the case of the "deference structure" of experiencing phenomena as certain knowledge. The certainty one feels is not really certainty that the phenomenon as such is right there now, but rather consists in a motivated sense that particular experiences could come next, or that particular thoughts could be formulated as true (such as "this is here right now"), or that particular actions could be taken in relation to the phenomenon with particular results. The certainty is actually displaced and is thus always colored by a particular motivation on the subject's part. Certainty is an experience deeply connected to expectation. And expectation is experientially related to some form of desire or fear: either directly (when what is expected is also what is desired or feared), or indirectly (when what is expected backgrounds, as an assumed condition, what is hoped for or dreaded).

Experience, meaning, and knowledge all involve motivation in this way, all anticipate future states and possibilities that are unknown, because they are "not yet," when anticipated. In some places Derrida writes of a fundamental "longing for presence" that structures all experience and meaning. We can understand roughly what is meant in terms of the structure of deference and its relationship to motivation as just discussed. The "longing for presence" is, of course, never fulfillable because "presence" is never to be reached. But, in some places in Derrida's work, we get a view of human existence that involves tacit awareness of fundamental uncertainties that one longs to make certain, futile though such longing is. Human assertions of truth, then, may be regarded as expressions of power in that they can be nothing more than assertions motivated by desire. Humans continuously assert "truths" that they cannot prove or know, due to the unreachability of presence. Humans assert because they are motivated to do so. Humans fundamentally want certainty, long for it, and express power in trying to feel it. Yet it is unattainable.

Now, this relationship between power, truth, and experience comes up in various portions of Derrida's writings. When it does, one is reminded of themes that are developed as theories of existence in the work of existentialists like Sartre, in Hegel's writings, in the work of Kierkegaard, and in Nietzsche's theory of the will to power. The longing for presence is related to the desire for recognition, the desire for security, the desire for self-actualization and self-validation. This is not a new idea and we may take Derrida's treatment of it to reflect an insight that other great thinkers shared. It will be an important idea in the discussion of praxis to follow. But one must understand that Derrida does not present the longing for presence as a theory of existence. Within his work as a whole this imagery is to be taken as another deconstructive move, not a positive assertion about the ways things are.

Just the same, our task is only to note Derrida's insight, to note that other great thinkers have also had it, and to note his special treatment of it for what that may clarify regarding the insight itself. We need not accept Derrida's location of his discussions of truth, desire, and power within his general strategy of deconstruction. In terms of what Derrida contributes to this insight, his suggestion that experience itself is always colored by motivation and that motivation can lead to assertions of power is a new way to look at an old idea. Experience has a sign structure. It is meaningful as soon as it is. And meaning in this primordial sense corresponds to motivation, anticipation, and power.

Experience is never knowledge without an assertion of power. All formulations of knowledge are underminable because of the metaphysics of presence upon which they depend. All such formulations, therefore, must be considered to be products of assertion, products of power, *claims*. I will relocate this insight within a very different framework a little later on. Claims are communicatively structured; human motivation includes a desire for recognition; truth and the presence problematic can be understood within a reformulated concept of praxis. I will elaborate in sections below.

A last point should be made regarding Derrida. Desire, power, longing for presence, and so on, all sound very subjective. Knowledge is reducible to the claims of a subject, to acts of power, to a "will to power," to a "will to truth." The imagery of the subject pervades these ideas as I have so far presented them: the subject experiencing desires, longing for presence, and asserting "truths" as a way of mollifying this longing. True, from Derrida this imagery appears only within more general strategies of deconstruction, such that the imagery itself deconstructs when the final Derridian moves are made.

But I have already said that we are free to examine Derrida's insights and to remove them from his deconstructive strategies. Do we have some insights about the nature of the human subject then? Taken outside the project of deconstruction, does Derrida's work suggest a potent model of subjectivity?

The answer is that even removing Derrida's discussions of desire, truth, and power from his strategy of deconstruction does not directly provide us with a theory of the subject. This is because Derrida has shown us that the deference structure of experience does not only defer to the object (as a moment of pure knowledge-imparting presence would reveal it) but also to the subject (as it would be in a state of pure presence). For Husserl, the subject is found at first as one "pole" to the experience of phenomena. Experience itself delivers a distinction between an objective and a subjective pole. But Derrida's arguments against presence apply at least as much to the subject as to the object of experience. The subject of experience is removed from experience itself, and is dependent on reflections after the fact. *Meaning comes before subjectivity, not after.*

Power, desire, and fear all appear to be more like ontological structures than like features of subjectivity in Derrida's writings. Desire, anticipation, longing for presence, are features of *meaning* rather than features of subjectivity. This insight too, will have importance for our effort to conceive of a critical methodology.

RECONFIGURING THE SCENE OF PRESENCE: ACTION, NOT PERCEPTION

Presence and the Scene of Solitary Experience

One interpretation of Husserl is that he pinpointed and subtly analyzed a fundamental scene from which a good deal of Western philosophy has been built up. This scene is one we all recognize: that of being alone, of seeing something before us or of having a mental image in mind, and feeling certain that this thing or image exists, along with its particular properties. From this feeling of certainty many competing theories of truth have been formulated: versions of empiricism, positivism, phenomenology, and idealism employ it.

The scene of the passive observer who feels certain about what she sees is also a covert background to many methodologies. The concepts of validity, truth, reliability, and induction, as used by social scientists, take their sense from a backgrounded scene of the lone experiencer who feels certain of the existence and properties of what she experiences.

The basic approach has been to take this common experience of certainty and from it articulate an explicit theory of truth. I see a red cup on the desk in front of me right now, feel certain that it exists, that it is here, now, and red; and I may be tempted to build up an entire epistemology on this sense of certainty. The movement is from feeling certain toward articulating truths. All such efforts to ground a theory of truth in the scene of lone experience, however, are suspect given Derrida's deconstruction of presence.

Reforegrounding the Scene: Action and Expectation

The scene of solitary experience is generally taken with perception in the foreground, in paradigmatic position, to give us a passive subject contemplating some object. Yet solitary experience always involves more than perception: it involves the continuous movement of thought and the experience of desire in ways that are just as primordial as perception and in ways that need not be framed as themselves perceptual. To say that when alone we experience a stream of thought or that we experience the coming and going of various desires is not the same as to say that we *perceive* ourselves thinking and desiring. To frame this scene as a scene of perception is already to theorize it. It is already to foreground or privilege one component of this scene; a component that is already an interpretation.

What happens if we switch things around a bit: retain the same basic scene but bring some of its background structures forth and let the foreground of perception recede so that a sort of gestalt shift results? This I will attempt to do now.

First let us note the importance of context to any perceptual experience. I see a red cup before me and feel certain that it is there, but do so, always, within some larger context. If the context is such that you are with me and I see the cup and then say: "How do you like the cup my wife gave me for Christmas?," then my certainty of the cup's existence as a cup, and as red, simply becomes one reference in a meaningful act made toward you. In this case the reference to the cup is not as foregrounded in my experience as is my expectation that you will say something nice about my gift. The truth of the cup's existence is assumed in my reference, and assumed to appear to you much as it appears to me. The cup becomes a reference that coordinates my meaningful interactions with you. To use a term favored by Husserl but used somewhat differently by him, the cup is a sort of "index" of a bounded set of expectations that I have regarding how you will respond to my statement (Husserl 1970).

I do not know precisely how you will respond to my statement but I do have implicit expectations that your response will be one of a bounded number of possibilities. The boundaries are indexed or symbolized partially by the cup and its properties. All the social and physical properties of "cup" are portions of the boundaries of my expectations. But within the context of the entire experience many other things index and symbolize the boundaries of my expectations as well: an expectation that we will engage in "chitchat," an expectation that you take my comment to reflect friendly feelings toward you, and so on.

Now, I have not exactly reforegrounded the scene of solitary experience because I have included you in the picture. By including you it was easy to draw attention to the importance of expectations and action in experience and meaning. I will shortly take our aroused attention to expectations and action right into the heart of the scene of lone experience itself. But I will first have to make some distinctions regarding the idea of "expectations."

Four Layered Categories of Expectation
Expectation of Action Consequences Alone

I have a cat whom I regularly feed milk from bowls, cups, and plates. Imagine this cat, whose name is Bessy, seeing this same red cup in my hand. She sees the cup, then meows eagerly and rubs up against my leg. We understand her; she expects me to put the cup down so that she can smell what is inside and lap the contents if they smell good. When she sees the cup we might say that she experiences a nonreflective sort of certainty that the cup exists truly, and that this confidence or certainty in the cup's existence is indistinguishable from her desire to lap milk and her expectation that I will put the cup on the floor. For *us* the truth of the cup's existence is distinguished from these things and we may say that this "truth" is a totally implicit reference carried by her actions; an "objective" part of the situation which, as "objective," escapes Bessy's explicit awareness.

The cup in this case is a reference that bounds possible *action consequences*. It is a feature of the horizon of Bessy's expectations. She expects that if she meows and rubs against my leg, she will be able to lap milk a little later on. The truth of the cup's existence is implicitly and remotely referenced by her expectation of getting milk. By extrapolation, *all* perceptual experiences of certainty will involve a reference to the object that bounds possible consequences of actions oriented to it in some way. The "properties" of the object, such as the property of the cup to hold liquid, to remain in place when lapping from it, to be cold, warm, or hot, perhaps originate as tacit and implicit features of more foregrounded expectations of action consequences. The more possible and diverse the actions and consequences we can experience when perceiving "cup," the more "the cup-in-itself" differentiates as a single object with certain properties. "Cup" is a reference that limits a horizon of expectations.

But expectations of consequences alone will not give rise to knowledge. They will only give rise to activities that are bounded through their orientation to the cup. For knowledge to arise, the experience of the object, in any way and with any foregrounded motivations and expectations, has to be *noted*. Once the cup is on the floor, my cat Bessy will move toward it eagerly, sniff at it cautiously when it is in smelling range, and then carefully test its contents with a few timid licks before lapping away in blissful abandon. When she spots the cup on the floor, she simply acts in expectation of possible consequences, and her certainty of the cup's existence is totally implicit, totally a tacit reference that is not noted or thought about.

This is the first layer of expectation: expectation of action consequences *alone*. It is not knowledge-imparting, only action-inducing.

Expectations of Action Consequences Mediated by Actions of Another

However, when Bessy sees the cup in my hand she has to *get me to put it down*. She meows and rubs against me in expectation that I will act in certain ways. The existence of the cup is thus also an implicit reference to her expectations of what I will do. It is a reference such that I, too, must be aware of the cup and share certain expectations regarding its "properties" in the same ways that Bessy does. Bessy does not, of course, think about this feature of her expectations. She is a cat. She simply acts in expectation that I will respond in a certain way. The shared experience of the cup between her and me is indistinguishable, within Bessy's experience, from her expectation that I will put it down and her desire that I do so.

But we may once again note that from our perspective an implicit "assumption" exists on Bessy's part: that she and I share perceptions of the cup. Implicitly and tacitly the "properties" of the cup are referenced as what is "the same" for Bessy and for me together. This is an objective feature of the situation, for us, that is not explicit, as "objective," within Bessy's experience.

By extrapolation, *some* perceptual experiences of certainty will involve references to the object that bound expectations of coordinated action between two conscious beings. Implicit in these expectations is a reference to "the thing-in-itself" as what is the same for both beings. And what is the same for both will involve expectations held by each being individually; expectations that are for each being concerned with the consequences of possible acts oriented toward the object.

This second layer of expectation, *expectations of action consequences mediated by the responses of other beings*, rests dependent upon the first.

This second layer of expectation also does not yield knowledge. Bessy is not concerned with noting the existence of the cup, nor even with noting the general routine of rubbing me and having me put food down. Probably within Bessy's experience no sharp distinctions exist between subjectivity and objectivity. I can be expected to act in certain ways when Bessy acts in certain ways toward me, sometimes in relation to mutually perceived objects bounded by their own horizons of expectation. But my experience of the cup is not a feature of Bessy's expectations; only my objectively consequential actions are. My objectively consequential actions, moreover, would not be much distinguished from Bessy's desires and expectations.

Tacit Intersubjective Expectation and Communicative Action

Now for the third category of expectation. Let us say that you are beside me once again and that it is you, not Bessy, who sees me holding the cup. You say: "Oh, could I have a drink from that cup too?" In a number of ways your act differs little from Bessy's. You desire a drink and expect me to cooperate with you to make a drink available. Consequences are foregrounded in your act and these consequences include my responses to your request. Like Bessy, you refer to the red cup in your act, but you use a *word* to explicitly refer to it. By using a sign to explicitly refer to the cup, the horizon of your expectations has taken on structures that were absent from the horizon of Bessy's act. Although it is your expectations of getting a socially mediated consequence that are foregrounded in your meaningful act, backgrounded in your act are expectations that I will understand "cup" in the same way that you do. Of course, backgrounded in Bessy's expectation horizon is also an implicit assumption that I understand her desires in some sense. But for you this expectation of understanding includes the implicit assumption that you could explain the word "cup" to me should I fail to catch on. A distinction between your desire, your use of symbols to express your desire, and my own privileged zone of experience and understanding structures your interaction with me in close to an explicit manner.

For you to employ language at all you must have learned it previously in your life, within interactive contexts in which understanding alone was often the main point. When a child uses a word incorrectly, it is pointed out to her. The lesson of language-teaching interactions will no doubt often foreground the consequences that incorrect uses of signs and symbols produce, but in the background is an important distinction: the distinction between correct and incorrect language use itself, aside from consequences. Languages and all sign systems conventionalize symbols across indefinite numbers of possible consequence horizons, so that expectations of understanding differentiate from expectations of specific consequences.

When this takes place, intersubjectivity is born. The expectation that another will understand your use of signs is constructed tacitly from the expectation that another will experience what the sign is about in the same way as one's self. This is intersubjectivity. The expectations associated with simply being understood, aside from consequences, tacitly assume multiple subjectivities capable of having common experiences.

So if I respond to your request for a drink from my cup by nodding my head and handing you a bagel, you will probably say something like: "No, no, I said *drink* from your *cup*." At this point you are acting toward me not merely in expectation of objective consequences to your act, but explicitly in expectation that I, as a subject like you, will *understand what you mean*. The foreground of your initial act: "Oh, could I have a drink from that cup too?" was your horizon of expectations associated with the consequences of your act: I will either say "yes" and you will get a sip, or "no" and you will not. But this horizon of expectation was frustrated because a backgrounded reference to the meaning of the word "cup," or perhaps "drink," or perhaps the entire linguistic stream including its prosodic form was not grasped by me.

This sort of expectation, *communicative expectation*, differs significantly from expectation oriented solely toward consequences. In this case the "truth" of the cup's existence, your certainty that the cup exists, enters into symbolic, and therefore intersubjective, experience. It is not totally implicit to the situation but tacitly is a part of the experience of the actors. It is backgrounded but comes to the fore if a misunderstanding occurs.

Now, and only now, does the object of experience become knowledge-imparting. It becomes such because it can be represented symbolically for memory and discussion. "What I just said was 'drink' not 'bagel.'" The objects of experience are available for memory, discussion, and contemplation because they are represented symbolically. When represented, however, they are immediately intersubjective in nature. They are represented only within boundaries of communicative expectations. Because you and I are able to talk about cups, drinks, and bagels, the truth of the existence of these objects appears as a tacit boundary-imparting reference of possible communicative acts. This reference tacitly includes the existence of a region of common experience (the object, the cup), the existence of two separated regions of experience (yours and mine) to which only one of us has access (you to yours and me to mine), and the existence of shared understandings (the meaning of "cup," norms about sharing and how to ask another to share).

So it takes at least two subjectivities to set the grounds to formulate the certainty one feels of the existence of an object into a *truth claim*. The subject-object distinction itself enters experience only through intersubjectivity. To formulate the existence of the cup as a truth claim presupposes at least two subjectivities with enclosed regions of experience, a zone of common experience, and a set of shared understandings. Without these things, "cup" does not exist autonomously from desires and expectations.

Explicit Intersubjective Expectation and Communicative Action

Lastly, suppose you see the red cup in my hand and you say: "My goodness that is a *large* cup, isn't it?" Here intersubjectivity takes a more foregrounded position than was the case when you asked for a drink. Your comment on the size of the cup is meaningful within a horizon of expectations that are primarily communicative in nature. Intersubjectivity is consequently highly foregrounded: I either affirm, qualify, or negate your claim about the size of the cup. Our common experience of the cup is what is referred to most directly: two subjects who are supposedly experiencing the same thing in the same way. Expectations of objective consequences have moved into a background position, but they are there. They have to be there for your act to be meaningful. "Cup" and "large" are themselves indices of implicitly understood action consequences oriented toward objects. Expectations of the consequences of multiple, possible, actions oriented toward the cup background the foregrounded claim that the cup has the quality of being large.

Now the issue becomes the actual existence of this cup and its properties. It is something about the true nature of the cup, assumed to be within the experience of two different subjects, that explicitly structures your expectations of my response to you.

In addition, your sense of certainty about the existence of the cup and its properties is tied to an expectation that I will agree with your truth claims about the cup. The role of "presence" in structuring your certainty of the cup's existence is less primary than the role of communicative expectations. The "deferred" moment of your sense of certainty is more directly involved with your communicative expectations than it is with the passage of time from moment to moment.

Summary: Communicative Anticipations Rather than "Presence"

So, to conclude this subsection, experience is knowledge-imparting only when it is intersubjectively represented. Intersubjective representation occurs through specifying the object of experience in relation to bounded sets of expectations. Intersubjectivity is reached through a hierarchy of expectations: from expectations of consequences alone, through expectations of how others will act in relation to the object, to expectations that others will talk about and ultimately experience the object in the same way as you do. Once intersubjectivity is reached, and a sign system such as language is developed so that actions oriented toward understandings and not just consequences may take place, the "object itself" and its "properties" may enter explicitly into experience. But they enter experience only in contexts of anticipation and expectation; in contexts of action and interaction. The "object itself" becomes a communicative foreground built up through background expectations of action consequences. The concept of "object-in-itself" is dependent on distinctions between shared experience, private experience, and shared understandings.

Thus the "object itself" has the sign structure Derrida attributed to experience, but this sign structure is illuminated here from a different angle. The object of experience has a sign structure because it is such only through expectations and anticipations of how an entire group of people will act toward it, talk about it, and ultimately experience it. An object of experience is differentiated from the experiencer only through intersubjectivity, only when represented within a horizon of communicative expectations. If I am to be able to transform an *experience of* into a *knowledge of*, I must simultaneously take the position of others in relation to my object of experience, and my "knowledge" is bound by expectations of how communicative actions that refer to the object would be understood by others. The more I try to reach the object of experience in order to express my certainty of its existence as a truth, the more foregrounded becomes my assumption that any anonymous member of a cultural group would experience the object as I do. Of course, I therefore cannot reach the object itself. The object itself must remain as the limit reference of certain communicative horizons. The more universally the audience is conceived, the more refined and explicit become the representations of the object and its properties: but I still cannot reach it. The expectation of the affirmation of others (their responses in congruence to my expectations) intervenes between the object and me. Differently put, the expectation of the affirmation of others references both the cup and "me." Subjectivity is born through communicative expectations at the same time that objectivity is.

The "cup-in-itself" is now an index, not of coordinated perceptions alone (as Husserl would have had it) but of communicatively structured expectations. "Differing from" and "deferring to" originate here from action projects and communicatively structured expectations. The "thing-in-itself" of perception appears now as an index of expectation horizons.

The Scene of the Lone Experiencer as a Special Case

What, then, of the original "scene" of solitary experience? Here it is: I am all alone, I see the red cup before me, and I feel certain that it is there and that it is red. I start to construct an explicit theory of truth from my feeling of certainty. What is going on?

Monological Theories of Truth

Well, reconfiguring the scene of lone perception to show that all perception is contextualized by a stream of action and expectation demonstrates the unusual nature of the core scene that underlies so many theories of truth. This scene is one in which perception enters into a stream of action and expectation in such a way that the experiencer contemplates or thinks about the object of experience by herself. When we note this red cup for contemplation or communication or memory, the action stream is purposeful and of a special category of acts. The cup must be represented with either an image or a set of words, and this occurs as the *next* act. That is, a feeling of certainty that the cup exists here and now is part of the motivation for a special kind of action that we call "perception" and that could also be called "representation." When we try to make the original experience of seeing into an explicit truth, into an item of knowledge, we must *act*, and this original experience becomes a *reference* of the act that must always already have just gone by. The pure moment of experience is referenced, not present.

In more usual situations, I would simply see the cup and continue with my stream of activities without noting it. Or I would see the cup and then pick it up to drink from it, or perhaps I would see it and speak to another person with reference to the cup. In these cases the feeling of certainty moved into different kinds of acts, some of which refer to the cup's existence and nature only implicitly. The feeling of certainty in these cases constituted expectations that make another act possible.

But by contemplating the cup, my next series of acts are explicitly symbolic, employing all four categories of expectation (as discussed above) in an intertwined manner. I am engaging in an internal "monologue," representing the cup for an abstract and internalized audience. The always already gone feature of experience appears here not so much because of the inevitable march of time but because I had to act, and act for the sake of an abstract and internalized audience, for perception to be "perception." To make my awareness an explicit awareness of this red cup I must employ horizons of communicative expectation even though this is done internally.

This is an importantly different way of understanding Derrida's arguments about presence. As Seung expressed it: "The primacy of temporal process is the heart and soul of Derrida's theory of signification" (1982:152). Our new perspective renders similar conclusions about presence and the desire structures of experience, but with an emphasis on acts rather than on time per se. It is as if time itself were born anew with each act. Action is primary, and communicative action is what gives birth to the problem of presence because communicative action is what makes signification, representation, possible.

Now if I contemplate this cup and then formulate an explicit theory of truth based on generalizations from my experience, I will construct an epistemology that Habermas calls "monological." It will be a theory of truth in which the solitary experience is emphasized. Because all efforts to make an object of experience explicit will involve communicative expectations, the resulting theory of truth will be based on a "monologue," a manner of talking to one's self. The object-in-itself becomes an issue only within horizons of intersubjective expectations. Monologues are possible only when *dialogues*, or "multilogues," have been internalized. It is partly by forgetting this that we arrive at Derrida's problem of presence, construed with time as an a priori structure.

Therefore, Habermas argues that many theories of truth, theories that depend on assumptions of presence, are misguided because they fail to recognize their dependency on internalized dialogues. They are theories that have forgotten the origins of thought in social interaction. They are limited and lead to contradictions of the sort indicated by Derrida because they tacitly depend upon dialogical models of truth. Derrida's own elucidation of the contradictions of presence also tacitly depends on a dialogical model of truth. This is Habermas's idea: modernity appears to have come to dead ends because of its dependency on monological modes of theorizing (see particularly 1987a: ch. 11, but also 1981, 1987b, 1988).

HABERMAS'S DIALOGICAL THEORY OF TRUTH

Reconfiguring the scene of the lone experiencer, the scene that underlies so many Western conceptions of truth and the scene that Derrida has deconstructed, has made it a secondary rather than a primary sort of scene. By the end of the discussion above, knowledge-imparting perception was rendered the status of an uncommon sort of experience that depends upon more common ones: experiences structured by action and expectation. There is no point in trying construct a theory of truth from a scene that is easily rendered derivative of more primordial scenes. We need a new primal scene upon which to build a theory of truth, one in which meaning is exchanged between at least two conscious beings.

Assumptions, Offers, and Claims

Habermas's "primal scene" would not be that of a lone subject who feels certain of a perception but would be that of two or more organisms communicating with each other. Let me illuminate core features of his theory through an example. This example is not as "primal" as it might be because it employs fully socialized adults of modern society. It is not "primal" in the sense of evolutionary origins of intersubjectivity and symbolic systems.[2] It is primal only in the sense that it is basic to notions of truth used routinely by modern adults.

Here is the example: You and I are at a meeting during which a most irritating paper is being read that employs naive postmodern slogans of the crudest sort. You are feeling frustrated and irritated. You glance toward me and find me looking back at you. You see me wink and smile at you. You feel better and smile back, casting your eyes toward the ceiling at the same time.

These are expressive acts, meaningful acts, though nonlinguistic ones. Clearly they can work only through signs: the wink, smile, and the cast of the eyes upward. More fundamentally, however, they must work through presuppositions and claims. My wink indicates that I assume you and I share similar experiences regarding this paper presentation. I assume you share a way of *typifying* this situation with me, that together we share a category

---

[2] Habermas actually discusses a sort of "primal scene" on pages 5 through 42 of Volume Two, *The Theory of Communicative Action*: (1987b). I discuss my own version of this primal scene as "originary scene three" in my essay, "Four Scenes for Posing the Question of Meaning" within this book.

in which to place the paper reading and adopt roughly the same judgmental attitude toward it. With my wink and smile, however, I *claim* that this situation should not be taken too seriously. "Let's not get too bothered by all this," I imply, "let's take this as mildly annoying but mainly humorous." I *offer* a position for you on my side of an "us versus them" situation. I assume you will understand that I feel friendly toward you. I claim to be the sort of person who does not succumb to postmodern fads and the kind of person who does not let annoying situations affect me too deeply. I offer a light, as opposed to a serious, interpretation of the setting.

Tacit *assumptions*, *claims* and *offers*: so it goes with all meaningful acts. To understand my wink and smile you must grasp something of the tacit horizon of claims, assumptions, and offers to which it makes reference. The difference between an assumption and a claim, a claim and an offer, has to do with *foregrounding*. Any feature of the horizon of meaning could in principle be foregrounded, and once foregrounded it is a claim more than anything else. This is because its dependence on the affirmation of another is "brought to the fore" when it is foregrounded.

With my wink and smile I *claim* that the situation ought to be taken lightly and I *assume* that we share a negative judgment of the setting. In principle, you could challenge either the claim or the assumption. You could tell me later on that papers such as these are no joking matter, challenging my *claim*. You could also indicate this challenge directly after my wink, by frowning. Or, later on, you could surprise me by arguing that this paper was very well constructed and profoundly important, challenging thereby one of my background *assumptions*. If you do the latter, a portion of the background horizon of my act is brought to the fore and shifted in status from assumption to claim. Of offers, assumptions, and claims it is the claim that is most fundamental to the dialogical theory of meaning. An offer and an assumption can always be revealed as, at bottom, a claim.

Three Categories of Validity Claim

Habermas's theory of communicative action makes much sense of scenes like this one of the wink. Habermas argues that all meaningful acts *internally reference truth claims*. Truth is internal to meaning. He uses the term "validity" instead of "truth" because the former term is more general than the latter and helps to emphasize the formal-pragmatic constitution of our truth, rightness, and sincerity concepts. That is, Habermas's use of the term "validity" emphasizes the communicative origins of truth and related concepts:

> A validity claim is equivalent to the assertion that the conditions for the validity of an utterance are fulfilled. Whether the speaker raises a validity claim implicitly or explicitly, the hearer has only the choice of accepting or rejecting the validity claim or leaving it undecided for the time being. (Habermas 1981:38)

Meaning is conveyed from one person to another via horizons of expectation. These horizons are bounded by tacitly referenced validity claims. The claims that tacitly accompany every act of meaning will always fall into categories, three of which will always be represented. I will list each category here and provide a brief illustration of it by referring to my example of the wink:

1) *Objective-referenced claims* characterized by the principle of multiple access. In the case of my wink, I assume that we both *see and hear* roughly the same things in this conference room. If you challenge me about this I could ask you to look again, or listen to an audiotape taken of the reading, or listen to reports from other people who were present at the time, or read my conference notes. In other words, objective-referenced truth claims are structured through multiple access to objects and events. The principle of multiple access structures objective-referenced truth claims. The objects and events at issue were not unique to my experience but shared with others present. They were recordable.

2) *Subjective-referenced claims* characterized by the principle of privileged access. In the case of my wink, I claim to feel friendly, humored, good-natured. If you challenge me about this I could not appeal directly to your sense of sight or hearing, nor to the sense experiences of others, nor to an audiotape, nor to lecture

notes. I could not appeal directly to anything involving multiple access at all. My feelings are part of my privileged realm of experience to which you do not have access. I can answer your challenge only by trying to convince you of my honesty in reporting my feelings to you. The objective features of my action may be appealed to as *indicators* of my subjective state, but it is always possible that I act in ways to disguise my real feelings and intentions. The principle of privileged access structures subjective-referenced truth claims.

3) *Normative/evaluative-referenced claims* characterized by ideas of what is good, bad, right, wrong, and proper. Habermas actually distinguishes between value claims and normative claims, but the latter, he suggests, originate in the former. Normative claims are basically claims about what all people ought to agree is right, wrong, and appropriate. Value claims are claims about what is good for me alone or for me and a small group of people. Normative claims can be articulated into "should statements": we should such and such and we should not such and such. Value claims do articulate into "should statements." The logical structures involved in supporting both sorts of claims, however, seem identical to me. No principle of privileged or multiple access applies in either case. For these reasons I put the two together as "normative-evaluative claims" (see chapter four, Carspecken 1996).

If one claims that people should not kill other people and one is asked to support this claim, then arguments will usually shift from "should statements" to claims about what is good and what is bad. Argumentation over normative claims seems to move toward value claims, and argumentation over value claims seems to move toward other value claims that logically entail the specific claims in dispute. Why shouldn't I kill another person? Well, perhaps because it is important to respect human life. Human life must be valued as intrinsically good. If I agree with that then I must logically agree that killing other people is bad—wrong. For both normative claims and value claims no realms of privileged or multiple access are appealed to; all that can be appealed to are other value claims in logical relation to the claim in dispute.

In the case of my wink, I assume that you and I share a way of judging and evaluating this hypothetical conference paper. If you challenge me about this by arguing for a different evaluation, I must fall back upon a less foregrounded portion of the horizon about my wink: my claim that some people (including you in particular) *ought* to evaluate this paper in a negative but tolerant way. Neither the principle of multiple access nor the principle of privileged access would structure my defense; only forms of normative-evaluative-moral argumentation could be used. In such argumentation I would have to persuade you of the worth of the values you most directly challenge by finding some *other* values upon which we do agree and by trying to derive my position on the values in dispute from these other values not in dispute. If one is to avoid the position of total moral relativism, one must assume that universal human interests exist such that remotely referenced value agreements can, in principle, always be found from which to argue for more immediately foregrounded moral claims. The principle of shared human interests structures normative-evaluative truth claims, and "shared interests" expand outward toward "universal interests" as larger and larger audiences are appealed to. "Shared interests" here should not be conceived in a utilitarian sense but rather in a manner cognizant of:

* the intersubjective constitution of individual selves,

* a hierarchy of human needs and motivations related to a theory of human development,

* an understanding that conditions for the autonomy and self-actualization of others are included in the conditions necessary for one's own autonomy, self-actualization, and self-validation.

Given these three formal categories of truth claims, it is easy to see that the scene of solitary experience usually prioritizes the objective-referenced claim and leaves the other two categories of claim untheorized.

In the rest of this paper I will use "truth" and "validity" as synonyms rather than reduce "truth" to the concept of objective validity claims, as is Habermas's own practice. Readers should understand my use of "truth" to be equivalent to my use of "validity."

There is much more that could be said about the three categories of truth (validity) claims, their origins and their structures. The nature of the normative-evaluative-moral claim is particularly controversial. I will not pursue these complexities in this paper but will refer readers to other sources. A good review of Habermas's three types of claims can be found in McCarthy 1978, chapters 2 and 4. The principles structuring normative-evaluative-moral validity claims are thoroughly discussed and debated in the essays of Benhabib 1992, and Benhabib and Dallmayr 1991.

Typifications and Identity Claims

Cultural *typifications* are used in meaningful interactions as both the pragmatic frameworks through which a situation is recognized as meaningful and as references. Cultural typifications are experienced in a singular fashion and yet synthesize all three validity claims. The typification "conference papers like this one," is a reference in my wink to you, and it also provides a set of assumptions we can both use in our interactions following the wink. If you accept my referenced typification, it then supplies an infrastructure through which we may interact. Validity claims of all three categories are synthesized in this typification. Objectively, the fact that a conference is taking place, a paper is being read, etc. are claims intrinsic to the typification. Evaluations of this paper are equally intrinsic: that it is one we should regard as silly, sloppy, frivolous. A range of expected possible subjective states also inhabits this typification: annoyance, irritation, humorous feelings, boredom, or feelings of superiority would all be possibilities. Cultural typifications synthesize normative, subjective, and objective categories in this way, but the categories of reference can always be unraveled through discussion and analysis. Typifications, however, have a singular and holistic quality in experience. It takes work to articulate the various layers and types of validity claim they imply.

In addition, there is the "identity claim" that all meaningful acts will reference, though with varying degrees of foregrounding. Identity claims are claims about personal identity that synthesize normative and subjective references in their foreground, but carry as well objective references pertaining to expected behaviors that are usually backgrounded. "I am the kind of person who does not succumb to postmodern fads" is a reference that requires a normative-evaluative category of "such-and-such kind of person, (evaluated positively)." An identity claim will always involve subjective attitudes, values, and capacities to which only "I" have direct access, *and in addition* will carry the assumption that other members of a cultural group will understand these subjective qualities and evaluate them as "I" do. Identity claims include references to "I regularly do such-and-such" and "I would never do such-and-such": a cluster of objective claims. Within the identity claim, however, subjectivity and normative evaluations are foregrounded and tightly synthesized. The identity claim is particularly important when considering the concept of praxis, as my discussion in sections below will attempt to show.

TRUTH AND POWER IN HABERMAS
The Formal and Pragmatic Properties of Truth

Habermas believes that all acts of meaning carry truth claims internally because meaning must be understood in terms of horizons of expectation, structured by intersubjectivity, that two or more subjects could in principle discuss when a misunderstanding occurs. Meaning *references* identical experiences and shared normative-evaluative agreements that may or may not actually *be* identical. Validity becomes an issue when multiple subjects attempt to mend misunderstandings by articulating and debating the intersubjective references involved.

Thus Habermas's theory of truth specifies the form of truth claims and notes their connection to meaning. It does not tell us anything about specific truth claims, nothing about the contents of any particular claim, except that all claims will involve the three categories which themselves specify the direction that arguments over specific truth claims will have to take. Objective-referenced claims must be debated through the principle of multiple access: repeated observations must be made. Subjective-referenced claims must be debated through attempting to establish support for the honesty of those making self-reports. Normative-referenced claims must seek shared normative-evaluative agreements and argue from them toward the norms or values in dispute. Habermas's theory of communicative action concentrates on the form of validity claims, not on the contents of specific claims.

With regard to the contents of truth, or validity, claims, Habermas gives us a pragmatic theory of truth. That is, a claim referenced to any of the three main categories should be regarded as true to the extent that it wins consensus. In a situation of total consensus the claim may be viewed as pragmatically true, which means that it is still "fallible" in principle, still open-ended. This is because future communities of human beings may reject this claim for reasons unforeseen by present communities. The pragmatic perspective on the contents of truth claims is a perspective that takes absolutely certain, explicit, and final truth to be unreachable. For Habermas, validity claims must be made in reference to the possibility of their absolute, or universal, validity (1981:58). But in practice this reference simply coordinates the debates and activities associated with the claim; it can never be verified in a once and for all manner.

The External Relationship Between Truth and Power

How, then, does Habermas conceive of power and its relationship to truth? He seems to work with an "external" and "internal" distinction similar to the one that structured debates between structuralist and culturalist Marxists, as discussed earlier. With respect to the contexts of action oriented toward reaching understanding, Habermas has emphasized an external relationship between truth and power. Power is that which distorts interactions oriented toward reaching an understanding. The archetypical case is that of argumentation, in which people seek to mend a disagreement or misunderstanding by arguing for their own position and by sincerely considering the arguments of others for contrary positions. Efforts to reach an understanding correspond here to efforts at finding truth. Power is placed on the outside of this process, as a distorting condition that must be reduced as much as possible if pure rational argumentation is to proceed.

The idea is simple and compelling. If you tell me that the red cup is large and I say that on the contrary it is small, our dispute is structured around the intersubjectivity of an objective-referenced claim. We could make repeated observations, we could introduce measurement procedures, we could discuss what we mean by "large" and "small" in objective-referenced terms. This sort of activity ought to end in a consensus between us such that pragmatically one assertion or the other will work for us as a truth, for a time.

But what if I reply to your comment about the largeness of the cup by pulling a set of brass knuckles from my pocket, placing them on my right hand, and saying: "No, this cup is small, *isn't it!*" You quickly reply: "Yes, yes, indeed it is!" Here I have compelled you to give me exactly the sort of response that under other conditions would have strengthened the pragmatic claim that the cup is small. But under this situation your response does not support my truth claim, for it was forced.

Now the example of the brass knuckles is, of course, extreme. What if you were eighteen years old and I was a famous fifty-year-old artist. You say, "What a lovely red cup!" I reply, "Not red, *carmine!*" You normally distinguish shades in such a way as to find "red" a better fit than "carmine" for this particular cup. But my status as a famous artist has caused you to suddenly doubt your normal usage of these two terms. Accordingly, you indicate agreement with my statement, "Ah yes, it is carmine." Here, too, a distortion has entered into the communicative setting but a more subtle one. You do not agree from your experience but from your deference to my status. You have not affirmed my comment from a feeling of certainty but, to the contrary, from a feeling of self-doubt that you conceal from me.

Power, Truth, and Method

The theory of communicative action treats power primarily in its external relationship to truth. No brass knuckles, no social inequalities, if the pragmatic requirements of reaching consensus on truth claims are to be met. The nature of communicative action itself *presupposes* social settings in which no force is used, all members have equal status, and all members are motivated only to reach understanding. The precise conditions for such an "ideal speech situation" are the following (see Habermas 1981:17-8):

* the presence of humans who share, for this moment, equal social status

* the presence of humans who are essentially equal in their autonomy and responsibility

* the presence of humans who are willing to be open to criticism and to discuss reasons rather than simply assert dogmas

* the absence of any force or coercion in the situation so that only the "force of the better reason" will bring about consensus.

Only consensus reached in settings possessing such conditions will provide the pragmatic truths we are after. Power must be neutralized.

Perhaps no social, communicative, situations are ever characterized by absolute freedom from constraints and distorting influences. Some situations do seem to approximate these conditions, but one can probably always find some distorting influences. For this reason Habermas has written of the *ideal* speech situation that is presupposed or referenced by every act of meaning but never fully reached empirically. Though he has given less emphasis to the phrase "ideal speech situation" in works following *Knowledge and Human Interests*, the idea is still fundamental to his theory of communicative action (see for example, *The Theory of Communicative Action*, Vol. 1, 1981:25).

The Internal Relationship Between Power and Action

When power is considered a condition of action, the emphasis is on its neutralization so that actions oriented toward reaching an understanding may result in pragmatically sound truth claims earning the consensus of a group. Power is that large category of forces that distorts the ideal speech situation referenced in every act of meaning. Coercion, ideological distortion, and the effects of social status would all be examples of this sort of power.

What of human agency and its association with power? Habermas's emphasis on power as a condition of action that distorts pure efforts to achieve rational consensus may obscure any location of the power concept within the components of action itself. But the "ideal speech situation" requires a neutralization of power, or an equalization of power, rather than its absence. Indeed, Habermas explicitly employs a positive concept of power when discussing action oriented toward consequences, as the next section will reveal. Subsequent sections will argue that power may be similarly located internally to action oriented toward understanding, via the concept of agency. There is both a constraining or structural sense to the concept of power and a generative sense. These two senses must be reconciled.

Power and Action Oriented Toward Consequences

Notice that pulling out a set of brass knuckles and using it to force you to agree with me that the cup is small is an *act* of power, not just a "condition." Habermas would agree with this. From the perspective of the communicative situation, my use of brass knuckles is a distorting condition operating externally. From the perspective of my act, power is an internally rooted quality. I pull out the brass knuckles to get the consequence I desire: a statement of agreement. My act is powerful to the extent that it achieves its goal. Habermas explicitly locates power as internal to action oriented toward consequences in several places in his large body of writings. It is clearly stated in his lengthy critique of Foucault (1987a: chs. 9-10). Acts are powerful when they succeed; when they bring about intended consequences.

The sense in which power may be understood as internal to action oriented toward consequences is this: Such acts are constituted by goals—they intend to make an intervention in the world and alter a state of affairs there. We call acts "powerful" when they succeed by their own standards; realize the goal constituting them. If such acts fail to realize their goals they are not powerful acts, but this does not mean they are without power entirely. They still make a difference, still effect a state of affairs.

This connection between power and action oriented toward consequences is internal. It is not the case that some acts have power (acts that are successful in fulfilling their constituting goal) and some do not (acts that fail to bring about their goal). It is only the degree of power that differs empirically. Anthony Giddens states that power is *logically tied* to action, because action always intervenes and "makes a difference" in the world. The concept of power, for Giddens, is linked to the idea of "transformative activity" through the notion of "capacity" (1979:69). Power is a capacity of the actor presupposed by her action. The concept of "actor," or "agent," presupposes this capacity. All acts presuppose power, therefore, and empirically it is only a question of *how much power* is expressed.

In his writings on Foucault cited above, Habermas points out that we consider *knowledge* powerful when it directs goal-oriented action successfully. For knowledge to be powerful, it must correctly represent reality. Knowledge capable of directing goal-oriented action successfully correctly represents means-ends relationships. Powerful knowledge is "true" knowledge. This is how Habermas criticizes Foucault's reduction of truth to power. Knowledge must be judged according to standards of truth that are conceptually separate from the power of acts to succeed. Otherwise the ability of an act to succeed would only depend on the will of the actor, not on the knowledge the actor employs in conceiving means-ends relationships. We regularly experience differences in the ability of diverse beliefs or theories to inform successful goal-oriented actions. These differences make sense only by assuming a conceptual distinction between truth and power.

This distinction between truth and power does not rule out an internal connection between power and action. All acts express power simply because all acts issue forth from agents who could have acted otherwise. Less powerful acts will be acts whose internally constituting validity claims fall short. The relationship between power as a capacity inherent to the agent and power as an empirically variable quality associated with an act's consequences is rather like the relationship between the illocution and perlocution of a meaningful act. Perlocutions vary empirically, but all meaningful acts have perlocutionary consequences. No perlocutions are possible, meanwhile, without illocutions. All acts presuppose power because all acts produce effects that depend upon the agency of the actor. No acts, as opposed to behaviors, could take place without agency.

Thus Giddens' idea that power is a capacity inherent in the concept of agency is consistent enough with Habermas's theory of communicative action. "Action," as opposed to "behavior," presupposes an agent. An agent has, among other things, the capacity to act: to make interventions in the world, pursue goals, and choose from alternative courses of activity. Power is logically tied to action itself and is not simply a condition of action that may be present or absent. As a condition of action, power can be neutralized, that is, equalized, in interactions oriented toward understanding.

Power and Action Oriented Toward Understanding

Therefore, power ought to play some internal role in action oriented toward understanding as well as in action oriented toward consequences. Habermas's position on this often appears to be that only actions constituted by goals have this internal connection to power, and goals are always referenced to objectivity. Purely communicative acts are often discussed by Habermas as special sorts of acts designed to repair disagreements so that humans may continue to coordinate their activities within a world of objects and goals. When misunderstandings occur, interactions between humans may temporarily shift into a special mode that foregrounds the motivation to reach an understanding. But the "goal" of such special interactions is to restore conditions in which people coordinate activities to meet their needs in a world of objects and physical forces. This can give the appearance of a secondary, parasitic, status for communicative goals. Bona fide goals seem to be associated only with acts oriented toward consequences, and communicative goals are thus means rather than ends. People seek understanding in order to better coordinate their efforts at pursuing objective, non-communicative, goals.

It is obvious, however, that human communication has made possible a fairly large category of human motivations that employ communication for intrinsic reasons. In everyday language usage, the concept of "goal" and the concept of "consequence" are not reduced to interventions in an objective world. In everyday life people often use the term "goal" to refer to things other than objective states of affairs. In everyday modes of communication it makes sense to say: "My goal was to demonstrate the soundness of my theory." No one would question a person's grasp of the English language if they were to make such a statement. Nor would one question a person's grasp of the English language if they were heard to say: "My goal is to *feel understood* by the administrators even if they won't reduce our work load." In everyday life the term "goal" and the related concept of "consequences" are often used in reference to nonobjective states and conditions. Humans often desire to be understood, to express themselves fully, to produce art, to display new ideas, ... all for communicatively *intrinsic* reasons. We act purposefully to satisfy such desires just as we act purposefully to alter objective states of affairs.

Many communicative acts have purely "communicative goals." Does, then, power enter intrinsically into more purely communicative acts, just as it does into acts oriented toward objective consequences alone? Of course it does, as it must if power and agency presuppose each other. We measure the power of an act oriented toward consequences according to the degree of success to which the act realizes its constituting goal. In close analogy, we can "measure" the power of an act oriented toward understanding according to the degree that it reaches its particular goal. Successful communicative acts are experienced as "powerful" or "empowering." We feel empowered when our poems, our performances, our art, our ability to understand and affirm others, are seen and appreciated. We feel empowered when others understand us, appreciate us, recognize us. Communicative action *alone* is required for such empowering experiences as these. This idea is entirely consistent with the theory of communicative action, though one will not find its significance emphasized or developed in Habermas's writings.

There are some important differences between "consequence goals" and "communicative goals" that require exploration before we may move toward a reconstituted theory of praxis. These differences correspond to alterations in the significance of power, as something expressed in all action, in the case of purely communicative action. Once these differences are articulated, I will argue that while power and truth are externally related when one considers the power that comes to play within the conditions of communicative action, power and truth also have an internal connection when one considers the communicative act itself. Power is both constraining and generative.

It is not difficult to reconcile a generative side to power with a constraining side, within the theory of communicative action, if one thinks of equalizing power rather than of removing it to produce the ideal speech situation. Nietzsche's insights about truth as a *will to power* can be preserved without making truth secondary to power, without reducing truth to power. Truth is always at bottom a truth claim, a "truth act," that is motivated intrinsically. Reading Habermas one might get the impression that people discuss truth claims only to repair misunderstandings so that objective-referenced goals may be better pursued, human cooperation restored. But people also *enjoy* discussing ideas, writing books, communicating with others. Communicative action has its own special category of uniquely communicative goals. Communicative action is related to human motivation intrinsically, and not just instrumentally as a mechanism for maintaining a system of coordinated action.

Praxis theory comes closest to capturing the motivation complex underlying purely communicative acts. Praxis theory puts power back into communicative action, capturing the human desire and need for self-production that only communicative acts can satisfy. But praxis theory as Marx presented it fails through its singular emphasis on person-to-objective world relations. A reformulation of praxis theory in synthesis with the theory of communicative action is therefore called for; something along the lines Paul Willis developed implicitly in *Learning to Labor*.

ACTION ORIENTED TOWARD UNDERSTANDING AS ACTS OF POWER

In the case of action oriented toward consequences, power is expressed as soon as the act is committed. But the degree of power we associate with such acts will vary according to how successful the actor is in realizing her goals. That is why objective truth claims, objective-referenced theories and beliefs, are said to be "powerful" when they consistently inform successful acts. "Knowledge is power" takes its meaning in this way. Medical science has produced "powerful theories" because such theories have enormously increased human abilities to realize goals. To call knowledge powerful is really to employ a metaphor; it is to ascribe agency to knowledge. Knowledge is powerful only to the extent that it facilitates agency.

In the case of action oriented toward understanding we similarly find that power is expressed as soon as the act is committed, but the degree of power varies according to how successful such acts are at achieving goals. People know when their purely communicative acts fall short of or exceed expectations. Successful acts that are purely oriented toward understanding result in an "empowered" feeling. Unsuccessful acts oriented purely toward understanding result in a feeling of diminishment.

There are important differences, however, between these two idealized types of act, between acts oriented solely toward consequences and acts oriented solely toward reaching understanding. Motivations involved in acts oriented solely toward consequences and acts oriented solely toward reaching understanding are categorically different. The goals of each sort of act also differ by category. Purely communicative goals often become clarified only after the act, whereas it is easier to preformulate the goals of acts oriented mainly toward consequences.

Let us take the example, once again, of using force to compel someone to agree with you. The act of compelling one, through coercion, or bias, or influence, to speak *as if* they agree with you falls into the category of consequence-oriented action. The consenting behavior produced in the other was consciously desired and is objective in nature (though as the objectification of a meaningful act). When interactions that are produced in a communicative situation involve power in the sense of bringing about objective consequences or objectified meaningful acts (e.g., forced statements of agreement), the communicative dimension of the action is distorted. Thus, power distorts communicative settings to the extent that the actions of various people have been objectified and made the desired consequences of goal-oriented acts.

The example of forcing another person to act as if they agree with you illustrates one of the important distinctions I have in mind. As acts oriented toward consequences, they are "powerful" when they succeed. As communicative acts, however, they fail to provide a sense of being understood, of being recognized, and, in these specific senses, they fail to empower. When being understood or recognized is our goal, the less the apparently affirming act of the other seems to have been coerced or compelled or influenced, the more it seems to have been freely provided, the more understood we are likely to feel. The more the one who affirms appears to be a free, autonomous, agent, the more certainly we will feel that we are understood and the more empowered we are.

Powerful acts of communication require equalized *formal* power relations between actor and audience. The goal is not to alter an objective state of affairs but rather to effect an understanding, a recognition, within another subject who is in principle free to disagree.

Human motivations associated with acts purely oriented toward understanding vary a great deal. One axis of variation would be discontinuous in nature and defined by the specifics of communicative goals. There are acts oriented primarily toward discoveries: bringing an original artistic or theoretical or factual discovery into articulation for the intrinsic delight this provides. Some acts, on the other hand, emphasize the identity of the actor.

I will say more about the second category of purely communicative action, the category in which identity claims are emphasized, a little later on. But it is appropriate to note its connection to human development here. Though acts constituted primarily by the motivation to assert the identity of the actor require equalized formal power relations between actor and audience to be successful, they can be expressed with the *desire* for differential power; to present the actor as superior to the audience. Acts motivated in this way are subject to a fundamental contradiction between the desire that motivates them and the formal conditions required for their success. This contradiction was well articulated by Hegel in his *Phenomenology of Spirit* (1967). In terms of human development, early modes of claiming a valid identity (which is dependent on the understanding rather than the objective actions of an audience) often take the form of asserting a self that is "more than" the audience appealed to. The impossibility of such a desire to reach its telos (because it would require an audience that is *not* subordinate but rather equal to the actor in its subjective capacities) can produce a developmental sequence in which new modes of claiming a valid identity arise. There is nothing comparable to this in the case of action oriented toward objective consequences.

Communicative Goals

The "goal" of action oriented toward understanding is not located in objectively observable consequences, it is located in nonobjective, subjective attitudes and states. Moreover, much action oriented toward an understanding has not clarified its goal (the specific understanding desired) until *after* the action is completed. "I didn't know what I really needed to say until I said it!" is not an uncommon remark heard in everyday life.

Now there are times during everyday life when individuals act communicatively only after mentally rehearsing what it is they have to say in order to perfect their communication. In these cases, which are not as common as more spontaneous communicative interactions, people clarify their communicative goals through a process of internalized communicative action, performed for the sake of an internalized audience.

Goals, particularly communicative goals, are not fully known until they are clarified through actions directed toward them. The experience of having a goal that directs an action and that is nevertheless not yet fully understood until the action is completed (a goal, that in fact, includes its own clarification within its motivating constitution) can be understood through part/whole and implicit/explicit distinctions.[3] Let us consider some typical experiences to make this idea more accessible.

Examples of the Holistic/Implicit vs. Delineated/Explicit Distinction in Action Oriented Toward Reaching Understanding

> *Example 1*: You are talking to a friend about something that interests you and in the process of talking find yourself formulating your ideas in what seem to be surprisingly clear and new ways. At the end of the conversation you feel quite excited: "I should write that down," you think. "I might forget it." You leave the conversation feeling energized and hopeful.
>
> *Example 2:* You are trying to express an idea you have to someone else and feel that each formulation falls short of the mark. "No, that's not it either," you finally say. "I just can't seem to express it in words."
>
> *Example 3:* You are about to teach a class, give a talk, act in a

---

[3] I discuss this peculiarity of communicative goals at length in the "Four Scenes" essay.

play, or take part in some other performative activity. You have an idea of how you want to pull this performance off but are not sure whether or not you will be successful. Your idea of how to pull the performance off includes a way *of being* that you need to enter into and act out: a sort of "persona" to adopt. Once the persona is entered into, the correct gestures, combinations of words, tones of voice, body postures and so on will come forth naturally, spontaneously, and appropriately. The trick is to get yourself into the right mode of being. Your sense of attaining the right mode of being, however, only comes from performing: from acting it out.

Example 4: You are with a new acquaintance and this person makes an unusual remark that you understand is intended to be funny. In fact it does seem funny to you but it also seems to call for a certain mode of response from you, not just a laugh. You understand, rather vaguely, what form your response should take (the approximate tone, inflection, length, etc.), but you also know that you just can't pull it off. You lack the words, lack experience with taking up the appropriate tone of voice and gesturing behavior that you realize would be required. In consequence you feel awkward; somehow inadequate. Without letting too much time go by you offer a weak laugh and a paltry smile to show that you at least understood the other's remark as funny. But you feel suppressed and "unseen" by the other person. "I'm just not that kind of a person," you think.

In the case of each example there is an interesting relationship between a prior, holistic, and implicit understanding of meaning, and actions that give that understanding explicit content. The content can be talk, or written words, or performances that involve gestures, facial expressions, and body movements. The subjective experience of holistic and implicit modes of meaning prior to their manifestation in symbolic action includes a feeling of uncertainty about their nature, significance, and validity. They have to be expressed if one is to become more certain of them. In addition, one can be aware of a gap between the expression produced and one's initial holistic understanding. Expressions can fall short of what is anticipated as well as exceed what is anticipated.

There is a distinction between communicative anticipations and explicit communicative acts that seems highly important for our investigations. What are communicative anticipations, and how are they related to the acts they constitute?

I put the last of the four examples in to illustrate the experience of understanding the acts of another in terms of the form of action they call forth from you, and yet not being able to correctly fill-in the form.[4] A full understanding of another will usually include the ability to act appropriately in relation to one's understanding. Yet it is not uncommon to understand meanings in terms of their holistic form without being able to manifest the action called for. It is not uncommon to understand the holistic form of an expression but only be able to provide a partially appropriate response. An incompetently "filled" form is an unsuccessful communicative act.

Monitoring Action

It is clear that people often act meaningfully, to either reach understanding or to produce expected consequences, when the holistic form of awareness described above does not precede the action. Often we begin to have this sort of awareness of our action *during* or *just after* the act. This is called "monitoring" action. However, if one monitors the meaning of an act either just before or during the course of acting it out, awareness of the act's meaning and significance comes in holistic and implicit form. Such awareness includes anticipations of what the act will be like in terms of what impressions it could make on others. Intersubjectivity constitutes monitoring and results in holistic/implicit modes of awareness. Intersubjectivity constitutes monitoring

---

[4] Husserl's concept of "forestructures" to perception may be relocated within an "action-first" phenomenology. My use of the term "form" here pertains to this relocation of "forestructures." This is extensively treated in the "Four Scenes" essay.

simply because monitoring one's own act amounts to taking the position of an audience with respect to it. When an act is completed, monitoring continues to give rise to holistic forms of awareness; not, however, of what the act will be like (for the act is finished) but of a clearer understanding of the impression it could have made on possible others. The form constitutes the act and is also clarified by the act through monitoring. For communicative acts, form is intersubjectively structured, tied to the chronic monitoring of meaningful acts.

Expressive Action and Recognition

So action oriented primarily toward reaching an understanding clarifies the specifics of its goal as it completes its course. It is also true that action oriented toward consequences often proceeds without an explicit symbolization of the goal in thought. But the goal of action oriented toward consequences alone is not cast in terms of understanding but in terms of producing alterations in the objective world. If one consciously thinks through the goal of action oriented toward consequences this event is itself communicatively structured, involving an internalized communicative action produced in reference to an internalized audience. Such thinking involves the same movement from holistic to more explicit modes of awareness: the clarification of the former through an act oriented toward understanding.

In the case of action exclusively oriented toward understanding, the clarification of holistic/implicit modes of awareness becomes an end in itself. This is why the underlying motivations as well as the goals of purely communicative acts are categorically different from those that accompany action for consequences alone. This feature of expressive action greatly distinguishes action oriented purely toward reaching understanding from actions oriented toward objective, or objectified, consequences. And it problematizes the relationship between truth and power in the case of such action.

Both types of action—action oriented toward consequences and action oriented toward understanding—are acts of power measurable by the standard of success: the degree to which a goal is realized. But how do actors determine the success of actions oriented primarily toward reaching an understanding, if the goal is clarified only through the act directed toward it?

The answer seems to be that actors will *recognize* their own communicative acts, if these acts are successful. They will also recognize a shortcoming in their act if it fails. How do actors recognize their successful acts as successful and spot those acts which fall short? Crudely put, actors experience either a match or a mismatch between their holistic modes of awareness and the impression their act delivers (through position-taking as well as through monitoring the responses of actual others) once it is completed. Successful acts bring about an experience of recognition because the explicit features of the act clarify a constituting form that the actor already understood implicitly or tacitly. This constituting understanding is closely tied, of course, to the concept of expectation. Among the many expectations constituting any meaningful act are always a cluster that anticipate what the act will bring out *for the actor*.

Premonitored Action

This is a crude but, I would argue, roughly accurate explanation of how we experience communicative acts as successful or not. It is crude because only a full phenomenological analysis of the meaningful act, conducted from first, second, and third person positions, could capture all that is involved (see the "Four Scenes" essay in this book for more on this).

We learn meaningful acts through socialization processes and day-to-day social interactions. We learn them holistically, not in all their complex objective details, but by grasping the singular impetus from which they spring. Such acts are constituted by expected responses that other cultural members will make to them as well as expected impressions that they will invoke within the subjective realms of other people.

Thus many acts are "premonitored" in their constitution. Imagine that someone smiles at you in a particularly warm and effective way, uniquely combining a slight turn of the head and a crinkle at the eyes with the smile. You feel very good and are quite taken by the manner in which this person conveyed such acceptance and goodwill. A day later you smile in much the same way at someone else, intending to convey the same meaning of acceptance. More accurately put, you smile in a new way for you, that *feels* as if it is much the same sort of smile you received the day before. It feels this way because it seems to bring out within you feelings similar to those that your friend brought out within you the day before.

Now, how did you learn the new smile? Simply by experiencing this other person smiling at you. You learned the entire complex action all at once, in a singular way, as a single impetus. That impetus is premonitored. When you experience the impetus to smile that way yourself, it is with a sense of how others will be impressed, or affected, by it—how they will "read" it. It is an intersubjectively constituted impetus. To learn how to act communicatively in one particular manner is simultaneously to learn expected impressions this act will produce in other people. Such learned acts are premonitored.

Monitoring one's own meaningful action is rather like bringing about, for oneself, the expected impressions constituting the act. It is like testing anticipations built into the action impetus, testing your ability to bring them off. It is quite possible that your effort to smile as you saw this other person smile will not work. You try it out but know, as soon as you have done so, that your effort fell short. The specifics of its falling short do not have a direct relationship to how your smile looks, because you don't see it (unless you try it out before a mirror). Rather, the specifics have to do with your subjective grasp of the impetus to smile in this way and your monitoring of the action as far as kinesthetic sensations allow. Your monitoring of the act failed to bring about the self-recognition that a successful execution would have.

To monitor an act is to engage in position-taking with respect to it during its course: to put yourself in the place of cultural others. But monitoring involves position-taking that is partial to the extent that the act itself has only reached partial manifestation. Simply becoming aware of an impetus to act involves monitoring it, but at very tacit levels. Holistic modes of awareness remain holistic and implicit in relation to the as-yet-uncompleted status of the act. Monitoring gains clarity during the course of an act to the extent that the act is completed. As the act completes itself the possible impressions it could make on cultural others become more clear. And the actor will have some idea, through position-taking (as well as through observing the actual responses of others), of how well the tangible act matched the anticipations constituting its impetus.

The Recognition Desire and the Socially Constructed Self

Recognition is the key experience that delivers a sense of success for purely communicative acts. Recognition, in addition, has roots in human motivation and human developmental processes. In the course of human life we not infrequently communicate with others primarily in order to feel understood, rather than to produce an objectively perceivable consequence. Any adequate theory of human motivation must include modes of desire that are primarily directed toward being recognized and affirmed by other people. Humans desire to feel a sense of dignity, to have high levels of self-esteem, to be understood. Intimate conversations are usually directed toward this end. So are the acts of writing poems, or philosophical essays, or doing well in one's career, or performing skillfully in interactions that display wit and insight. Many examples exist.

Successful actions of this sort result in a feeling of empowerment. This is because, at least partly, they result in a sense of being a free, autonomous, agent. The recognition one receives from successful self-expressive acts is an acknowledgment of one's status as a subject, as something beyond objective forms: a creator of objective forms.

Special Status of the Identity Claim

Hence the identity claim has a special status. It can be analyzed in terms of formal validity claims and the conditions necessary for them to be affirmed. But the identity claim is also a feature of human motivation. Insofar as every communicative act will include an identity claim as part of its constitution (at levels of foregrounding, backgrounding, and personal investment that vary enormously), the desire to be recognized as a self, an autonomous subject, is a core structure in all truth claims. Desire inhabits truth claims in this way. The connection between truth, a will to truth, and a will to power appears most explicitly with respect to the identity claim.

As many have realized, and as already stated above, a full experience of being a subject, of having agency and autonomy, requires recognition from other autonomous agents. This is because coercing acknowledgment of one's autonomy and agency brings at best a temporary, ultimately unsatisfying, fulfillment of the desire for recognition.[5] In addition, recognition must come from others deemed capable of understanding one's acts.

The ideal speech situation is presupposed not only by the pragmatic conditions for validating any sort of truth claim; it is presupposed as well by core components of human need and desire. A self-expressive act directed toward another person claims the autonomy and subjectivity of the actor. It is dependent, as a claim, on an affirming response. But such affirming responses will only count if the other is deemed capable of spotting a failure in the act, of providing a negating response if the act falls short. And the other, the audience, must be both free to do this and capable of doing it.

The desire for recognition is structured much as is the experience of recognizing one's own expressive actions. But the desire for recognition involves one more complication: the concern for having an identity, a social self one can respect, an identity as an autonomous subject rather than as an object.

The identity claim accompanies all meaningful acts, though it is highly backgrounded in some acts, is highly foregrounded in others, and is often intermediate in the concerns of the actor. Actors monitor their actions according to the identity claims they

---

[5] This is a strong theme, as is well known, in Hegel's famous chapter, "Lordship and Bondage'" in *The Phenomenology of Spirit*. See Hegel 1967:228-40, and Hyppolite 1974:143-56. Hegel was undoubtedly working with insights articulated through a much different framework by expressivist philosophers (Taylor 1979).

carry, and will often become quite explicitly concerned with their identities when people respond either negatively to their claims (in which case one can feel offended, diminished, embarrassed) or positively to them (in which case one can feel flattered, enhanced).

In some activities the identity claim is very much foregrounded. In these cases it becomes quite clear that the identity claim is structured by the part/whole relations already discussed for communicative action in general. One is less clear about one's identity (its nature and worth) before acting self-expressively than one is afterwards.

Power, Truth, and the Identity Claim

We are nearly at the end of this discussion about action oriented toward understanding. The identity claim has fundamental importance in such action. The insight that a truth claim is also a claim to power is related to the connection between identity claims and human motivation. The uncertainty of the self, its dependence on acting, continuously, in communicative ways and its dependence on the affirmation of autonomous others, can make the identity claim appear to be mere self-assertion, a claim to power. Successful acts that are strongly invested with the need to construct an identity feel empowering. In this section I wish to further explore the relationship between identity claims and power.

People are motivated to construct social identities and to maintain them. They are motivated to successfully construct positively evaluated identities when this is possible, but will act simply to get any sort of acknowledgment of their status as agents rather than objects if forced to. Children who are consistently ignored by their parents will often act in ways to provoke punishment (and thus acknowledgment of their agency) rather than continue to feel like "nothings." Better to be a bad girl or boy than to be nothing at all. Better to have some recognition from others, even if such recognition is for a negatively evaluated self, than no recognition at all.

Successful self-expressive acts feel good. They feel good in the body. They are energizing, sometimes thrilling. And they are associated with a feeling of empowerment. Humans are empowered, in this sense of the term, through successful self-expressions.

How are we to understand this feeling of empowerment that accompanies successful expressive action? It is related to the identity claim. Unsuccessful actions of this sort result in a feeling of vulnerability and diminishment. Included in the identity claim is the claim to one's status as a free, autonomous agent. This is the source of power in successful acts of self-expression.

At the same time, an identity claim is a *truth claim*. One seeks self-knowledge through identity claims. One is after the confirmation of one's existence as a subject with various qualities but, above all, one is after the confirmation that one is simply a subject who is more than any objective form; who is a locus of pure agency. And this requires recognition from another subject. Being a subject is being beyond objective forms and qualities. It is being a locus of power, creativity, and freedom. It is being a source of ever new expressive activity. To be a subject is to be more than the explicit actions one performs.

Now the issues are complex here and I do not want to become any more embroiled than I already am in difficult philosophical problems. The issues are complex partly because humans differ in the ways they pursue identity claims and differ in the extent to which they invest themselves in them. The pursuit of identity varies in form according to culture and according to developmental (maturational) stages. Many of us are content to gain regular, consistent, affirmations from others of a fairly static (but respected) social identity. We maintain such identities through routines of daily life and the consistent responses these routines bring from others. The recognition desire can be met at quite limited levels.

But it is possible to invest heavily in the recognition desire and seek to satisfy it in a totalizing way. This possibility is built into the desire itself. When indulged in, a basic contradiction becomes revealed that ontologically underlies the recognition need and the ephemeral social self. This contradiction is important to understand when attempting to understand the nature of truth.

The Ever Elusive Self

One can gain and maintain a sense of being a particular kind of person through constant activity, but one can never gain totally certain knowledge of what one is. Self-expressive acts will result in a feeling of being recognized and of recognizing one's self when expectations that constitute the action impetus appear to be realized. But for a number of reasons, self-recognition can only be approximate and temporary. The recognition drive is quite strongly oriented toward actual others who would have to be fully free and autonomous agents, as capable of negating one as they are of affirming one. One can never know for certain, however, what actual others experience of one's own self, because of the principle of privileged access. One has to gauge the responses of others through quasi-objective indicators: what their action reveals of their subjective states. This is always necessarily uncertain. And for basically the same reason, position-taking with an internalized audience will also always be uncertain. In addition, one can never be sure of the capabilities of other actors to fully recognize, or understand, one's self. A totalizing pursuit of the recognition drive will never succeed through self-expressive acts.

The truth sought after through expressive acts cannot ever be attained in knowledge. Yet it is a form of knowledge that is sought after: self-knowledge, as dependent as all forms of knowledge are on consensus—on affirmation from others. The self is the product of a desire that can never be totally satisfied. It is a desire for a type of truth, the truth of one's own subject-being and existential worth.

The limit point of intersubjectively constituted truth claims is the *identical experience* of two or more subjects. The impossibility of reaching this limit point as a certainty is most accentuated in the case of the identity claim. What is referenced is an identity between a holistic, potentially unlimited, sense of being a subject beyond all objective form; and the recognition (and thus validation) of this sense from a worthy (and thus potentially unlimited) other. This can never occur with certainty for epistemological reasons (the principle of privileged access). It is also an ontological contradiction insofar as the self is constituted both as a delimitable form when seen from the perspective of an other, and as a nondelimitable source of pure agency, a locus from which infinitely variable creative acts may issue forth.

In Mead's terminology, the self is both an "I" (locus of pure subjectivity and agency) and a "me" (a delimitable form understood only from the perspective of others). The recognition desire is a desire to become certain of the unlimited nature of the "I" from the perspective of others, a desire to construct an unlimited "me." But no "me" can be unlimited.

Derrida's insights about presence and its unreachable quality transfer over into the dialogical model of truth most directly with the subjective reference and the identity claim. It is not surprising to read, in Gayatri Chakravorty Spivak's commentary on Derrida, a formulation about the self that would seem to come right out of expressivist philosophy:

> ... to recognize that one is shaped by differance, to recognize, that the "self" is constituted by its never-fully-to-be-recognized-ness ... (1974:xliv).

The self is constituted by an ontological difference between self and other, a difference that reflects the distinction between the "I" and the "me," and a difference that also defers to an impossible state of presence: a state of presence in which two subjects gaze without any barriers (with "full access") at each other's depths and simultaneously oscillate between each other's positions to know each other and each self at once.

The "longing for presence" appears within the dialogical paradigm as a longing for self-knowledge. It is a longing for total self-knowledge that is also total self-actualization. The social self is infused with longing for self-actualization and yet can never be actualized communicatively or symbolically. Any totalizing search for the self that employs expressive action as its means will founder on a contradiction that is ontologically at its heart. Given the inescapability of the identity claim, its unavoidable attendance within every communicative act, this core contradiction inhabits truth claims of any sort. Truth claims are always partly components of an entire world claimed by the actor that gives the actor's self meaning and validity. And yet the desire to find affirmation from others for this world and this self, others who are themselves autonomous and pure subjects and, thus, in some ways beyond the boundaries of these claimed worlds, is also always part of the motivational complex. The desire for self-recognition is rife with contradiction.

But do remember that human beings are generally satisfied with nontotalizing pursuits of the self, with consistent experiences of partial recognition, with maintaining a basic sense of dignity. The ontological contradiction at the heart of a totalizing search for the self is well represented in a diversity of literature, predominantly in existentialist and spiritual literature. But it seems to greatly impact the lives of only a few human beings, at least in explicit ways. It tells us much about the ultimate issues that cluster around "truth" and "knowledge." But understanding the limited pursuit of a sense of dignity and respect is most helpful for examining everyday life empirically.

The limited pursuit of recognition needs makes sense of a point made by Anthony Giddens in his social theory: that human beings display the tendency to establish interactive routines to meet what he calls "ontological needs" (Giddens 1979, 1984). "Ontological needs" seem best interpreted, within the framework of this essay, as products of the need for consistent acknowledgment that one is a subject. And this is usually met through maintaining a limited set of respected social identities.

AN OUTLINE OF POWER, TRUTH, AND METHOD FOR CRITICAL METHODOLOGY

In my view, a reformulated theory of praxis employed to supplement Habermas's theory of communicative action is the best way to address the relationships between power, truth, and method. This is a promising road to critical methodology. To fully supplement the theory of communicative action with a reformulated theory of praxis, a theory of act constitution is called for that is cognizant of part/whole relations, of human motivation, of the experience of recognition, and of the fundamental importance of the identity claim. I have explored act constitution and its relationship to our concepts of truth and meaning in other publications that include the "Four Scenes" essay in this book.

In this final section of the present essay, however, I will come indirectly to these same issues through deriving the methods of inference that Habermas's theory suggests for any methodology in the social sciences. Each method of inference I discuss below will involve the power-truth-action relationship in some way. Praxis comes into the picture when noting the form of these various relations. The connection between praxis theory, power, recognition, and valid inference procedures appears most explicitly in my discussions of intersubjective recognition and cultural power below.

Objective Referenced Claims: Method, Truth, and Power

Objective-referenced truth claims are structured by references to intersubjectively identical experiences of a world to which there is multiple access. Methodologically, objective-referenced truth claims enter fieldwork in two distinctive ways: from the third person position peculiar to the researcher and from the first, second, and third person positions routinely taken by the subjects of study. Unless one's fieldwork is conducted on a cultural group that is vastly different from that native to the researcher, it will mainly be the third person position peculiar to the researcher that will require fixed attention. That is, if researcher and researched roughly share basic ways of talking about a *physical* world, objective references routinely made by the subjects of study will not usually be emphasized in the analysis. Studies of Inuits, Chomoros, Navajos, and so on, require attention to ethnoscience and thus to fundamental differences between how the researcher and how the researched name and explain the world of multiple access.

Within the third person position peculiar to the researcher, field records and interview transcripts must be explicitly considered in terms of the principles of objective-reference, the principle of multiple access in particular. Procedures have been explained elsewhere (Carspecken and Apple 1992; Carspecken 1996). They include use of multiple recording devices in the field, use of member checks, use of a low inference vocabulary, and use of a "bias check" with peer debriefers. The principal truth claim is that such-and-such took place as described. The inference procedure involves observation and measurement most fundamentally.

The best the social researcher can do to support her objective references is to show evidence that as wide an audience as possible, representative of diverse cultural groups, consents to the record as it is written and/or recorded. The best the researcher can do, in other words, is to follow the formal structures of the objective-referenced claim as much as possible in order to deliver a pragmatic (and thus fallible, open-ended) case for the contents of the field record: the record of what took place.

Power comes into the picture in an external way. Efforts to follow the principle of multiple access are efforts to approximate the ideal speech situation, in which formal power relations are equalized, and to keep objective references separate from subjective and normative references. In other words, objective accounts must be formulated against a background of the barest of normative assumptions to which the widest cultural groups may consent. If I say "this cup is red," I foreground an objective reference but employ background normative assumptions regarding the meanings of "cup" and "red." These background normative assumptions, however, are likely to win the consent of a very large group: they are "low inference." If I write: "At 12:32 the teacher entered the classroom," the same principles hold. A universal audience should in principle agree that the teacher came into the room at this time. If I write, by contrast, "The teacher lapped, doglike, from a ridiculously large cup," I have abandoned the principle of multiple access by using a high-inference vocabulary that clearly fuses objective and normative-evaluative validity claims. It is unlikely that a large audience would consent to my statement, particularly if the teacher is included!

The idea is to avoid putting either the researcher or the subjects studied into a privileged position of power; to keep formal power relations equalized. Use of a low inference vocabulary is an essential practice.

Normative Referenced Claims: Method, Truth, and Power

Things become more complicated with the next two categories of claim. Methodologically, the same two different perspectives hold for normative-evaluative claims as hold in the case of objective-referenced claims. Such claims are involved within the first, second, and third person positions routinely taken by the subjects of study and involved with respect to the peculiar third person position taken by the researcher.

On the one hand, the researcher must make normative inferences from her field record. She must reconstruct and articulate the normative references made by her subjects of study. That is, she must capture normative references made from the first, second, and third person positions that are routine to the people she examines. On the other hand, normative horizons already familiar *to the researcher* will come into play; both when she makes her inferences to reconstruct the normative-evaluative claims of her subjects, and when she writes her report for other people to read. The third person position peculiar to the researcher carries its own normative-evaluative horizons and these must be treated carefully. They are what may produce distorting biases.

The inference procedure employed to reconstruct normative-evaluative references is hermeneutic in nature. Observation and multiple access are not the structuring principles. Hermeneutic inferences require entering the first, second, and third person positions routine to the subjects of study as much as possible so that an insider's perspective is attained (Carspecken and Apple 1992, Carspecken 1996). The researcher must become a virtual participant. Once this entrance into an insider's position is attained, normative and evaluative references can be articulated.

Power must be located externally to truth through the equalization of formal power relationships, such that one's reconstructions are as accurate as possible. "Accuracy" is judged by the degree of consent that one's articulations win from the subjects who are studied. So, member checks, comparison of interview and observational data, group discussions between researcher and researched, and so on must be used to strengthen the claim to accuracy (Carspecken and Apple 1992, Carspecken 1996). Using these procedures approximates the ideal speech situation by equalizing the power relations between researcher and researched as much as possible.

Intersubjective Recognition: A Distinctive Category of Inference

Now for the big question: assuming that power relations between researcher and researched are equalized as much as possible so that the ideal speech situation is approximated, what conditions other than power and influence structure the processes by which members may or may not consent to the articulations of the researcher? In the case of objective-referenced claims the principle of multiple access answers this question. Repeated observations with multiple observers and devices can strengthen the objective-referenced claim, that is, strengthen consent to the record, if an ideal speech situation is approximated. This is the case whether one is a "realist" (believing that cultural consensus about what is objectively the case is structured by "real" properties of "real" things existing outside one's knowledge of them) or a "constructivist" (believing that such consensus occurs because remotely backgrounded agreements within the horizons of objective references actually "construct" the physical world).

But multiple access does not give us an answer with respect to normative-evaluative claims. No number of repeated observations, or of group discussions on the meaning of object terms, will support a normative-evaluative referenced claim. What factors structure consent to normative-evaluative truth claims within conditions approximating an ideal speech situation?

Habermas does not push this issue very strongly, but he does show us where a stronger push could be made. Actors agree about normative-evaluative truth claims when they recognize a personal interest in them. That is as far as Habermas takes us: consensus will occur when a single set of normative-evaluative claims wins the recognition of all parties involved without influence or coercion. If this occurs without influence or coercion, the normative-evaluative claims can be nothing other than shared by the group of consenters; to be "universal" within this group. The claims about what is right, wrong, good, bad, and proper are consented to in an "all for one and one for all" manner. Such recognition is intersubjective because it is a process of "noting," of framing the claim from the position of others. It is "intersubjective recognition."

But what is the nature of intersubjective recognition? It is not like perception as perception is usually conceived, for it involves the spark of familiarity, of seeing something clearly that one has already known in an unclear or implicit way.

Recognition Is at the Root of the Hermeneutic Inference

To answer this fully we will have to move into the last category, subjective-referenced truth claims, because recognition has everything to do with the interplay between subjectivity and normativity. When recognition occurs, an intersubjectively noted value or norm is experienced in match with a subjective state. One finds one's self affirmed within a normative articulation that by nature is claimed for an entire group. This will be further discussed in the section below about subjective-referenced claims since recognition involves both the normative-evaluative and subjective categories simultaneously.

Before proceeding to subjectivity, let us note that the hermeneutic inference employed by the social researcher to reconstruct normative-evaluative claims is itself founded on recognition. The researcher is in a position to articulate the normative-evaluative claims of others only when she can recognize them as her subjects do. This means that her own cultural horizons must be altered through contact with the cultural horizons of those she studies: the hermeneutic circle must be entered and employed repeatedly to bring about the insider's view (Palmer 1969; Carspecken 1996: ch. 6).

Once an insider's view is attained, tacit normative-evaluative claims will be recognizable to the researcher in the same way as they are to her subjects. Often they will appear as distortions: as reflections of unequal power relations between the people she is investigating. To spot the distortions, the researcher must be able to recognize the claim to universality referenced by each particular normative claim considered, and to note the failure of the norm or value to meet its own claim to represent mutual interests of the entire group. Distortions will serve as indicators of cultural power; of structural power manifested through ideology.

Thus power also enters the category of normative-evaluative truth claims in an ontological way. It is part of what one must *find* in the setting under study. It can be found within the normative-evaluative horizons of the culture being studied when the reference to universality necessarily carried by all normative-evaluative claims is spotted as a sham. In Habermasian terms, normative-evaluative claims necessarily purport to fulfill an interest universal to all members of some cultural group. When this limit claim of universality is experienced as falling short, cultural power is at play. If one cannot fully recognize one's self, one's own interests, within an articulated norm or value, then one would only consent to this norm or value because of the play of power. The concept of "interests" must not be limited to material interests. "Interests" also exist with respect to social-psychological needs, and praxis needs in particular (see Carspecken 1996 for an extended discussion). Cultural power, or ideology, works most forcefully by limiting the roles, and thus the repertoire of identity claims, available to members of a group.

Subjective-Referenced Claims: Method, Truth, and Power

The social researcher must be able to reconstruct subjective-referenced claims as her subjects of study themselves produce them. The researcher must also be cognizant of the fact that her own act of doing research and writing about it will carry references to herself; her intentions, qualities, capacities, and identity.

The principle that structures subjective-referenced claims is that of privileged access. When reconstructing the subjective references of other people, one must do so through the acquisition of an insider's view of the normative-evaluative realm so that subtle nuances of subjective reference may be picked up. A combination of long engagement with the community being studied and use of in-depth interviews are helpful to this end. Evidence for the validity of subjective truth claims must be built up through comparisons of self-reports with observed behaviors, and through comparisons of self-reports given in some settings with those given by the same people in other settings (Carspecken and Apple 1992; Carspecken 1996).

Additionally, when writing a research report, social investigators must be aware of their own identity claims and how they may influence what is written. As explained more thoroughly later on, researchers must be prepared to become "wounded" through their work (McLaren 1992, 1993); to allow their contact with others to threaten and perhaps alter their usual ways of conceiving of themselves. The researcher must strive for honesty at the deepest levels, and frequently this will induce states of anxiety, anomie, and self-doubt.

The *inference* procedure involved in subjective-referenced claims once again rests upon recognition. There is no multiple access to subjective states. The process by which we gain impressions of another person's intentions, states of awareness, desires, feelings, and so on, involves position-taking. As soon as subjectivity is represented in any way, explicitly or tacitly, it becomes intersubjective. One gets an idea of what another person intends or feels by implicitly sensing what one would feel or intend oneself when acting in the perceived manner. Subjective references carried by the acts of others must be recognized as subjective states one could feel oneself.

The implications of this are enormous. We ourselves can become aware of our own subjective states only through reflection and thus through representing our subjectivity to ourselves via cultural symbols. This means that subjectivity becomes something to discuss, something to infer, something in any way to note only through intersubjectivity. Derrida's deconstruction of presence spills over into Habermas's formal scheme quite directly when it comes to the category of subjectivity. Our own awareness of how we feel, what we think, what we intend, and so on comes after the moment of experience. Our awareness, our "privileged access," is always once removed from moments of experience always already gone. Thus in an important sense subjectivity is indeed a social construction, because privileged access to experience occurs only through internalized audiences; internalized monologues that are really dialogues between ourselves and an abstract audience. Subjectivity is an effect of cultural symbols as soon as it is something about which one can be aware.

But in an equally important sense, awareness of our own subjective states carries some internal standard by which one manner of naming the feelings we just had seems better than another. This is why recognition is at play. We must be able to recognize our subjective experiences, always already past as soon as we become aware of them, through the names and images that arise to structure our awareness of them.

The distinction between subjectivity and intersubjectivity is absolutely crucial to subjective-referenced claims. Subjectivity is not wholly the effect of social relations and cultural forms. It is given through a play between them and raw, unmediated, subjective experience always already gone. Though always already gone, unmediated experience of one's self is always referenced in every act of self-awareness. It is implied but unreachable, much the way Derrida argues that presence is implied but unreachable in experience. It works as a standard by which to evaluate the extent to which cultural terms for representing subjectivity match our experience. We must recognize what is always already gone in our subjective experiences through the intersubjective forms that give us self-awareness. The "trace" of subjective experiences that are always already receding does not logically deconstruct within the dialogical paradigm. Rather, the trace of unmediated subjective experiences informs our forestructures for those symbolic acts that would represent them. Some combination of trace and cultural form constitute the forestructures of symbolic acts.

Let me give an example. Within many cultural groups inhabiting the United States, males are not supposed to experience hurt feelings. It is more manly to "feel pissed off" than to feel hurt if one is insulted. Male consciousness-raising groups have challenged this traditional cultural form. The cultural form of the rational nonfeeling male has made it hard for men to recognize genuine feelings of psychological pain. Within various men's groups men often feel quite liberated when they are able to say their feelings are hurt rather than react aggressively to a hurtful event or remark. The new cultural form, "man feeling hurt for good reasons," serves as a label for subjective states that had been mislabelled by the cultural form of the macho male—"man feeling angry." Naming a subjective state is more than a semantic process of finding a good word, it is a process of finding an appropriate pragmatic label or role.

Why does it feel liberating to be in a group that offers a new label (new in the sense of being culturally legitimate)? Because the new label better matches a presymbolic subjective state. More traditional male cultures frequently prevented men from recognizing how they "really" felt. Yet how anyone really feels is inaccessible, even internally, until it is represented by a cultural form, a label of some sort. This is why a combination of trace and cultural form constitute the forestructures of symbolic acts representing subjectivity. The cultural form is intersubjective but refers to a subjective state, already gone by the time the state is named. It is only through such forms that even self-awareness may discover subjective states. Yet we have empirical evidence in support of the belief that subjective states are not merely social constructs. If subjectivity were only a social construct, consciousness raising groups of all varieties would have no basis. No one would feel liberated, experience greater self-understanding, or recognize themselves more fully within one cultural group as opposed to another. Though always something like a trace that escapes direct access, raw subjectivity features within experiences of match and mismatch, recognition and misrecognition, whenever feelings and intentions are symbolically represented.

The Internal Connection Between Power and Communicative Action

The above discussion further clarifies arguments made earlier about the internal connection between power and communicative action. Power is internal to communicative action particularly through subjective references. The match between a subjective state and its intersubjective representation feels empowering. Human beings desire it. In communicative settings there is very often a desire to be recognized by other people. There is a desire to have one's intersubjectively framed representations of oneself affirmed by others. A subjective state is framed through horizons of expectation as soon as it is represented. Much action is motivated primarily by the desire to satisfy that sort of expectation: expectation of recognition. Humans do not only desire consequences, they desire affirmation of their identity claims.

Hence the very inference procedure fundamental to normative-evaluative and subjective truth claims, *recognition*, is a motivated one, a feature of desire. And what is this if not *praxis*? By "praxis" I mean, of course, the concept as reformulated by Paul Willis—the desire to express and thus actualize one's self through cultural production.

PRAXIS AND CRITICAL METHODOLOGY

Praxis as reformulated in early critical ethnography is methodologically important in three major ways. First of all, critical social researchers need to be aware of the "praxis needs" of the people they study. Praxis is an explanatory concept. It allows us to understand why people construct the cultures they do, why the ideas and values people are able to express are tied to their construction of identities in order to meet existential needs (Carspecken 1991, 1992). When social relations of inequality place the goal-oriented dimension of action under the control of others and thus alienate it from the praxis of subordinate populations, cultural forms are produced that construct identities of dignity in spite of and often in opposition to the institutions involved (the workplace, school, home). Normative-evaluative orders are produced to maximize affirmation of the self, to bring about affirming modes of recognition in spite of and often in opposition to the goal-oriented portions of action controlled by others. Praxis is the motor that drives reproductive loops of the sort Willis discovered, and that Apple and other theorists have described.

Praxis is also the motor that fuels social movements through which people strive to change the system.

Secondly, social researchers do what they do in order to meet their own praxis needs. The researcher must realize that her reconstructions will carry tacit normative-evaluative and subjective claims of their own, will be part of the way she claims a valid identity for herself as part of her praxis. No analysis will be strictly neutral because all meaningful acts, including those catergorized as "science," carry evaluative claims and carry identity claims of the analyst (or scientist) as well. The researcher must be very careful not to let her own pursuit of praxis distort her analysis of field data. The best way to exercise such care is to make one's background claims very explicit in some way within the research report and also to present these claims to peer debriefers, ethnographic auditors, and the subjects of study themselves for discussion.

The distinction between truth and power is ontologically sound but as a limit case that structures all communication. This is an ideal distinction presupposed by all communicative acts. All acts, including communicative acts, are acts of power. But the conditions in which a truth claim is supported through the consensus of its audience must be as free of inequalities in power as possible. The social researcher will probably always assert her claims within conditions that fall short of the ideal speech situation because empirically power is rarely equalized. But the social researcher must strive to keep truth and power as separate as possible. This means that social researchers must strive to be honest on all levels.

Let us distinguish between "objectivity" and "honesty" here. Critical research is not "objective" in the usual sense of this term; it is not "neutral." It judges as well as describes social reality. One can state that a certain social situation is exploitative, demeaning, and out-and-out wrong without "being subjective." Habermas's three categories of validity claim must be honored in these sorts of assertions, however. Portions of a research report will be mainly objective referenced. Other portions will be mainly normatively referenced. One must separate one's arguments according to the formal categories of truth claim and employ validity requirements specific to each category. One must strive to be honest in one's write-up (a subjective referenced claim), to report events as they occurred with as little normative-evaluative interference as possible (an objective referenced claim), and to judge the situation in terms of experiential matches between members' interests and the necessarily universalizing value claims carried within their culture (the normative-evaluative claim). The requirement of being honest is of course not the same as "being objective." But, as will be shown by my third and final point about praxis and methodology, being honest is often very difficult.

Praxis and Epistemology: Inferencing from Exemplars

The third methodological point I wish to make regarding praxis is that the praxis concept enters deeply into the epistemology of a critical field project. The inferences that must be employed are incomprehensible without the reformulated concept of praxis. I have already discussed the importance of recognition in inferences made from qualitative data. Recognition, in turn, is related to the role played by exemplars in critical inferences. Critical ethnographies seek to illuminate the general in light of the highly particular. How is that possible? The concept of praxis helps us to understand.

In day-to-day life, people create meaning and gain impressions of meaning from others through exemplars. One acts meaningfully and claims an entire order of values and norms, plus an identity, plus a structure of "kinds of identities" into which one locates one's self, plus an implicit theory of society, *all at once.* Others understand the act by holistically recognizing the vast order of claims it implicitly carries. They find a position for themselves there and either reject it or affirm it or modify it when acting back. Meaningful acts always possess this quality of the exemplar. They exemplify entire ways of being and suggest many possible ways of acting consistent with these ways of being.

Meaningful acts are always examples of what it means to exist within a particular view of life. People communicate and learn through exemplars of the most universal implications. This is why it is possible to sort of catch-on to an entire subculture after witnessing just a few typical acts. After catching-on one can invent completely new acts that members of the group will recognize to be consistent with their culture. A world, not just a few specific acts, has been learned.

The theory of praxis explains the motivational features involved in exemplars. One invests or stakes one's self in one's acts of meaning and the world of claims they carry. Meaningful acts are exemplars of entire worlds that offer places, identities, for others to occupy. One often, perhaps usually, reacts to the normative and identity claims of another not so much in terms of their specificity but rather in terms of what world they exemplify. One's reaction to the various claims carried by the meaningful acts of others is frequently based on the extent to which and the manner in which one recognizes one's self within the entire world these claims exemplify. Praxis is about acting so as to recognize one's self through one's acts.

Praxis is the motor behind learning and communicating through exemplars. Claims made by others will be more readily accepted the more the world they represent offers a place for the identities one is used to assuming. Claims made by others will be more readily rejected, or reframed, or misunderstood the more the world they represent threatens one's accustomed identities by having no place for them or by having places of negative currency for them.

It is no different for the critical researcher. What one sees in the field will effect one existentially. To honor the three categories of validity claim that structure meaningful action and knowledge, the researcher will have to be open to feeling threatened by her field experiences. If she is not open in this way, power may act through her privileged position as the one who writes about others, as the professor or the professional, to distort the representation of what is there. When this sort of distortion occurs it occurs at the expense of those studied. To avoid this, one must be prepared to be threatened and to change through one's fieldwork; to be wounded (McLaren 1992). One senses a place for one's self in the meaningful acts of other people that might threaten the habitual ways in which one constructs one's self. If the researcher is not prepared to be wounded, she will not make inferences true to the validity requirements of normative, intersubjective reconstruction.

Once open, once willing to be wounded, the researcher becomes capable of reconstructing the implications of exemplars toward the very boundaries of their horizons. This will inevitably produce reconstructions of the most universal sort. When combined with systems analysis[6] it will illuminate concepts of power, action, social structure, identity, and social organization at their most abstract levels. Praxis theory thus underpins a principle method of inference employed by critical ethnographers: the reconstruction of specific exemplars toward their most universal levels of implication. In a sense, the universe is indeed reflected in every drop of dew. But one must examine many such drops, and the complex relationships between them, before one can begin to grasp all that is reflected by each.[7]

SUMMARY AND CONCLUSIONS

This essay began by asking whether critical social researchers can still claim to be *right*, objectively and morally, rather than be reduced to simply claiming that they will *win*. I have argued that we must still strive to be right. Postmodern slogans and buzz-words have thrown many critical researchers into confusion over the issue of truth. Truth has become regarded as merely the effect of power in some circles, as just an interpretation in others. I sought to trace some of the origins of these ideas to the work of

---

[6] I did not discuss systems analysis, a key feature of critical social research, in this essay. Systems analysis does not directly employ hermeneutic inferences but depends upon their prior use for cultural reconstructions. The validity requirements of systems analysis are outlined in my book on critical ethnography (1996: chs. 12-3). The less direct way in which praxis theory informs systems analysis is hinted at in the last essay of this book: "Five Third Person Positions."

[7] I do not mean to exclude systems analysis from the idea that exemplars enable critical social researchers to draw generalized conclusions from highly particularized studies.

Michel Foucault and Jacques Derrida. I have employed Habermas's theory of communicative action to argue, like him, that truth cannot be reduced to power. Truth is internally related to meaning; presupposed in universal ways with every meaningful act, and distinguished from power in essential ways.

I have also outlined the supplementation of Habermas's theory of communicative action with a reformulation of praxis theory. Power is both generative and constraining. It has a structural side and a side tied to the concept of agency. Most fundamental is its logical connection to the agency concept, and thus to the concept of action itself. Structural modes of power are best theorized in terms of action contexts—constraints and resources—within which agents must act.

Derrida's critique of presence, I have argued, is more subtle and has more implications for critical methodology than Foucault's efforts to reduce truth to power. But his critique of presence can be recast from the scene of solitary experience to the scene of acting meaningfully. With the shift from a monological to a dialogical paradigm, truth becomes a pragmatic reference. It remains an uncertainty but a bounded one, such that "truths" may be formulated and regarded as stable as long as they win consensus through the conditions specified by Habermas. The three formal categories of validity claim establish boundaries about every articulation that purports to be "true."

Postmodern authors usually write about truth in totalizing ways. By contrast, pragmatists argue that truth is always fallible. But of course pragmatists would then have to agree, and for the most part they do agree, that the truth of pragmatism itself amounts to nothing more than a set of fallible claims. And this, too, is a sort of totalizing claim. Pragmatist theories are meant to be appealing, plausible, and useful; but ultimately they are as fallible as anything else. Pragmatists will frequently handle the acid test of philosophy, the question of how a philosophical view might address its own status as a claim to truth, through the principle of fallibility. As long as the theory seems plausible and works, let us assume it to be true while always remaining open to changing our minds.

Thus we may regard the theory of communicative action to be a self-consciously fallible theory. The acid test—how does the theory of communicative action explain itself—would be answered along pragmatist lines: if it is plausible and works, let us continue to employ it. But why should we? Why should anyone accept this idea of universal fallibility? Can the pragmatist appeal *only* to the plausibility of her view? Is she not articulating tacit understandings she that believes all of us share, such that we might recognize their explicit formulation in pragmatist theories like the theory of communicative action? Is not recognition appealed to once again here, with respect to a theory that (in my version) includes a theory about recognition?

These are ultimate sorts of questions. They are totalizing. Within the framework of this essay the question of totally certain and final truth really becomes a question of whether or not the desire associated with praxis could ever be fully satisfied. Praxis is essentially the drive for recognition; the drive to construct one's self as a fully recognized and affirmed subject. A totalizing truth claim can only be supported, like any other, through intersubjective recognition. Since recognition can be demonstrated only by the externally observable acts of another subject, the reference to absolutely identical experience in multiple subjects can never be reached outside of a religious experience. The theory of recognition provides yet another perspective from which to understand the principle of fallibilism and deepens the significance of this pragmatist principle.

Derrida's insights remain totally relevant and of the profoundest significance. The final certain redemption of any claim to truth is infinitely postponed. Within the dialogical paradigm sketched here, postponement is inevitable because intersubjective recognition is an unreachable limit case. We have inevitable fallibilism because of the structures of intersubjective recognition. Truth is always going to be a truth *claim*. It is always going to be a truth *act*. Truth acts are communicative acts with communicative goals. I have argued that a special feature of communicative goals is that the more intrinsically motivating they become, the more they are tied up with existential needs and desires. Truth acts are indeed products of a will to truth, a will to power, a will to knowledge.

The postmodern wish to relativize truth to power fails, however, through its acceptance of a monological paradigm. Within the dialogical paradigm the will to truth presupposes self-to-other relations characterized by formally equalized power relationships. Truth is always an act of power, a will to truth, but one that always and everywhere must obey the structures of communicative action. This is why criticalists can claim to be right, and not just to win. The formal equalization of power relationships plus the special structures of each type of validity claim provide standards for assessing truth claims. Truth is not reducible to power for this reason. Truth and power are equiprimordial structures, internal to meaningful action.

And so the relationship of power, truth, and method is complex but not unmanageable. Truth is not reducible to power; yet power is the spring from which all claims to truth flow forth. The more we conduct research with a universal community of equals in sight, the more empowered we all will be. Specific, practical, totally comprehensible principles and procedures may be followed to avoid the dangerous conflation of truth and power. Critical methodology must never reduce *being right* to *winning*.

Essay Three

FOUR SCENES FOR POSING THE QUESTION OF MEANING
Phenomenology, Form, Feeling-Body, and the Origins of Intersubjectivity

To ask, "What is meaning?" is to invite general problems of self-reference. "What is meaning?" amounts to asking the meaning of meaning, presupposing thereby some of the answers one wishes to seek. The situation is not unlike the one opened by Heidegger when he asked what Being is. Strategies must be adopted when exploring the meaning of meaning that allow for the necessity of presupposing the form within which an answer will manifest as soon as the question of meaning is posed.

When I first seriously attempted to explore the nature of meaning, I simply proceeded with a phenomenological analysis of meaningful action. I attempted to unveil the structures of meaningful acts as we experience them from the second, first, and third person positions. At some time during my work on this phenomenological project I realized that although I might be clarifying structures of meaningful acts through my phenomenological explorations, I was not answering the question of what meaning is. Certainly I was elucidating possible answers to the question, but I was also revealing new questions about meaning that cannot be answered through phenomenological modes of investigation.

Therefore, when I completed a draft of my phenomenological study on meaningful acts, I became interested in the act itself of asking what meaning is. To question meaning is to act meaningfully. My own phenomenological investigations made this abundantly clear. The question can be asked, moreover, in different ways. The question is only intelligible against some presupposed background structures, as all acts of meaning work through contrasts between foreground and background. I continued to write my manuscript, but this time I posed the question of meaning against three distinctly different backgrounds.

The results of my phenomenological investigations themselves had suggested alternate ways of posing the question of meaning. Three backgrounds, three additional ways in which to ask the question of what meaning is, captured my interest most strongly.

Each background capable of making the question of meaning intelligible appears most immediately to me as an image cluster. The image clusters give sense and direction to the question. I adopted the word "scene" to represent the image cluster after reading Henry Staten's book on Wittgenstein and Derrida (1984), in which I found a good fit between Staten's conception of scene and my own experience of imagery when making sense of any meaningful acts. Phenomenological analysis itself is scene dependent, and my three additional investigations of meaning give a total of *four* scenes against which to pose the question of what meaning is.

Hence the title of this essay, "Four Scenes for Posing the Question of Meaning." The essay is a condensation and partial reworking of my unpublished and unfinished book *The Phenomenology of Meaningful Action*. This essay has four main sections, each concerning one scene against which the question of meaning can be asked. The first scene is background to my phenomenological project. In this essay I have greatly shortened my larger work to present a mere sketch of meaningful acts from a phenomenological perspective. I do not actually investigate the background that makes my phenomenological explorations possible but rather concentrate on the phenomenological results. Portions of the background employed when doing phenomenology are revealed, sometimes implicitly, in later sections of the essay, when I discuss the relationship between my phenomenological sketch and my work within the other scenes.

The next three scenes are investigated more as scenes in themselves. The nature of meaning is explored through them, but so is their very structure, partly through contrasts to the other scenes. I call the three additional scenes that are presented subsequent to the phenomenological sketch "originary scenes" for reasons explained below.

This essay should be regarded as a strategic investigation of meaning that is preliminary in nature. Because asking what meaning is amounts to asking the meaning of meaning, to presuppose from the start something of what one seeks, it is necessary to be very strategic in one's approach. I try to build arguments and descriptions along certain trajectories that can later be put into question *as* trajectories. A central feature of my strategy is to investigate meaning in four different ways, and to juxtapose each study with small sections of comparison and contrast introduced at appropriate moments. I say more about my general strategy in the overview.

OVERVIEW

A Phenomenological Sketch of Meaningful Acts

My general strategy, then, consists of the following. First, I provide a rough sketch of meaningful action considered phenomenologically. I begin with our experience of receiving an impression of meaning from the act of another. Hence the second and third person positions will be taken initially as starting points. As the analysis proceeds, it becomes necessary to shift to the first person perspective and consider the experience of acting meaningfully. My larger work carefully addressed the epistemological issues raised by such a mode of inquiry and supplied much more detail about the nature of action than can be included here. For this essay I am constrained to merely present a series of selected statements without an explicit treatment of the epistemological framework from which they were derived. I can only hope these statements will appeal to the readers' own preunderstandings of action and meaning enough to regard them as plausible.

Three Originary Scenes for Posing the Question of Meaning

Second, from the phenomenological analysis three "originary scenes" against which to pose the question of meaning will be indicated. Henry Staten used the term "scene" to indicate a meaning-imparting context, grasped holistically when a meaningful act is grasped: "A 'scene' as I am using the term might be as little as a phrase or as much as a whole culture" (Staten 1984:83).

"Originary" is a term from phenomenology that suggests a ground, foundation, or origin. The concept of an "originary scene," therefore, is that of an image cluster or image sequence capable of (1) illuminating the origin of some of the structures we discover through the phenomenological analysis of meaningful acts, and (2) casting the epistemological stance of phenomenology itself in a new light. Phenomenological analysis foregrounds description; originary scenes facilitate explanation. An originary scene is basically a paradigm in holistic form. It makes an image, an image cluster, or an image sequence foundational to a series of reflections that seek to illuminate, integrate, and explain features of experience. The experiences of concern here are those typical to meaningful action.

Phenomenological analysis itself depends upon an originary scene but this dependence can only be revealed, given my chosen strategy and textual organization, *after* results from phenomenological analysis are presented. Moving from phenomenological analysis to the consideration of three originary scenes will help to reveal the ways in which phenomenology itself is scene-dependent. Phenomenology is not all that it claims to be; it is not simply a description of "what is." That is why the originary scenes discussed in this essay problematize the epistemology with which this essay begins. Hence the title of this essay numbers our scenes as four rather than three: the scene that underlies my phenomenological sketch and the three originary scenes uncovered by this sketch.

In this essay, when I refer to "scene one," "scene two," and "scene three," I am referring to the *originary* scenes, in the order they appear, and not to the phenomenological sketch. "Scene one" refers to the scene of form and the flux, not to the phenomenology of meaningful acts.

Textual Syntax

The three originary scenes follow the phenomenological analysis in such a manner as to generate insights into the nature of meaning given by the syntax of the four main sections of this chapter. That is, each scene explicitly explores issues that are only tacitly addressed by both the other scenes and the phenomenological analysis. Each scene is vulnerable through its dependence on a beginning, but each scene roughly addresses in an explicit way various factors necessarily implicit in the other scenes.

The syntax involves moments of deconstruction, one scene often imploding the "originary" claims of the others. By moving through each scene in turn, a syntax is created that is rich with insights on the nature of meaning. One can thus picture the essay as a whole to be something like a circle of links, the connections between each link amounting to implosions. Spray from each implosion intersects with spray from the others, and insights are experienced at these intersections. Insights are guides to action and thought and may only serve originary, or foundational, purposes if one is willing to construct yet more scenes, knowing that they too could implode.

The alert reader will consequently notice that the organization of this essay suggests a fifth scene, as it must: a scene I have just interpreted through the metaphors of the circle, chain links, and implosion. This is another image cluster; one that roughly determined the organization of my essay. But the idea is to understand this fifth scene as subject to the same deconstructive strategies used explicitly on the other four. Our fifth scene is not meant to be originary. Readers will understand more of this as they move through the pages ahead.

Originary Scene One: Form and the Flux

Each of the originary scenes I have chosen to consider appears to be at the bottom of certain discourses on meaning. One I have titled "form and the flux," which is an implicit scene in much work on the question of meaning when it is posed as a question of the relationship between a sign and its referent. The question of the relationship between a sign and its referent has generally been approached through analyses of perception. Phenomenology, structuralism, and poststructuralism (as well as positivism and physicalism) have all developed their widely diverse arguments with a scene of form and the flux in the background. In the case of poststructuralist work, the "flux" (articulated in many diverse ways: "substance," "essence," etc.) is canceled. But poststructuralist work is nevertheless dependent on scene-one metaphorics in acknowledged, explicitly deconstructed, ways.

Originary Scene Two: The Feeling-Body

The next scene I consider is called "the feeling-body." This scene is more prominent in Eastern thought than in Western thought (Anandamurti 1968, 1978, 1987; Sinari 1974; Vahiduddin 1974). However, there is a contemporary literature on "embodied meaning" that presupposes scenes congruent to this one. Within phenomenology, the later work of Husserl (1970) and the writings of Merleau-Ponty (1962) both address certain portions of this scene. In ethnography, the work of Peter McLaren (1992, 1993) has been particularly insightful and promising. Thus, although this scene may appear to be the strangest of the three to most readers, that is partially because most readers will have been raised in Western cultures.

Originary Scene Three: The Origin of Intersubjectivity

The last scene I consider is "the origin of intersubjectivity." By *intersubjectivity* I am referring to prereflective structures that (1) take the existence of other subjects as a given, and (2) constitute experience through the process of position-taking with other subjects at various levels that begin with a primordial form of position-taking always already completed. Part of our sense experience of an object, for example, is the prereflective understanding that its objective features are available to other subjects much as they are to ourselves. Part of our experience of a feeling is the prereflective understanding that the feeling is not directly available to other subjects but must be indicated to them through body postures, gestures, or words. Objects and feelings are intersubjectively constituted.

Intersubjectivity is not the same as *transsubjectivity*. We can theoretically consider experiences that all subjects share, whether they realize that they do so or not. This would be transsubjectivity. The transsubjective experiences need not be intersubjectively constituted. Intersubjectively constituted experiences, on the other hand, need not be transsubjective. Emotions and feelings are intersubjectively constituted as soon as they are recognized, because such recognition delivers their quality of being outside the direct access of others. Others may or may not experience identical or similar subjective states. Emotions and feelings may or may not be transsubjective, but they are intersubjective as soon as they are recognized.

Intersubjectivity can be examined through the phenomenological investigation of everyday experiences of meaning but doing so continuously runs into "premonitored" action impeti that simply occur to actors in the stream of experience. That is, the impetus for a meaningful act will arise for an actor in an implicit, holistic, way, and is then either acted out or articulated into thought, or ignored for another impetus. The premonitored feature of many meaningful action impeti is an intersubjective feature; it is a part of the constitution of the actual impetus through the perspectives of a second or third person audience. If we phenomenologically examine such impeti, we discover the pregiven audience and a preanticipated set of possible responses, preconceptually understood when the impetus is understood.

Meaningful action impeti, in other words, are for the most part intersubjectively constituted even before they are recognized. They are premonitored. We can ask from where such pre-understandings of audiences come, ask where the origins of intersubjective constitution might lie, but we must employ nonphenomenological modes of investigation to illuminate possible answers. The question of the origin of intersubjectivity introduces the frameworks of human ontogenesis and phylogenesis. Both frameworks are incompatible with a strictly phenomenological method.

Phenomenological strategies, moreover, depend on mental acts of recollection and reflection, which themselves appear to involve preunderstood audiences if subjected to phenomenological examination. Hence for two reasons, one concerning the contents yielded by phenomenological analysis (the premonitored impetus to act) and one concerning the process of phenomenological investigation itself (the processes of audience-dependent recollection and reflection), the question of meaning points toward an originary scene that is not given within the direct experience of meaningful acts. While I will treat scenes one and two as special modes of phenomenological and deconstructive investigation, I will treat scene three with an opposite sort of approach that begins with assumptions about a shared, objective world.

Scene three will be limited, in this essay, to the phylogenesis of symbolic communication, ignoring important processes pertaining to ontogenesis. The phylogenetic scene will be sketched from two perspectives, one taking the work of George Herbert Mead (1967) as its point of departure and the other emphasizing small portions of Georg Hegel's (1967) philosophy. I rework portions of Mead's theory considerably, but attempt to present Hegel's work only for the sake of gleaning some of his important insights.

A Model

Finally, in my concluding section I will roughly and loosely bring things together into a model/sketch of meaningful action useful to social researchers. I have really made this last section of the essay a weak sort of gloss, referring readers to my book on critical ethnography (1996) for a tighter presentation that includes illustrations of its use and diagrams of its various components. On the one hand, this model of meaning is to be of use. I use it myself in qualitative research and teach students to use it. It lends itself to creative acts of meaning interpretation and does not prescribe procedures nor fix anything too permanently. It is a model, not a representation, of meaning.

On the other hand, this model must itself be understood as an act of meaning. The model includes a self-conscious claim that it is not meant to be taken entirely at its face value. It is self-referring because it incorporates the essentially deconstructable features of all acts of meaning within its body. It can be used to deconstruct itself, if that is what one wishes to do with it.

I will suggest that the insights generated by this essay on meaning involve implicit understandings that no explicated model can fully capture and that may be used to argue against any effort to formulate a model. Yet the model itself helps to clarify the way in which the general category of "models of meaning" can be undermined, and simultaneously is useful for those whose work involves the inference and articulation of meanings.

Thus, the model sketched out at the end of this chapter points both forward and backward. It is a sort of complex symbol for an implicit understanding of meaning that can be used to construct positive assertions about the nature of meaningful acts as well as to argue against any final certainty in one's conclusions. It is both highly useful and self-undermining, depending on the interests and concerns driving its appropriation.

The final section of the essay, which roughly sketches out a model of meaning, is not at all meant to be an answer to the question of meaning. It does not synthesize the major arguments of this essay into a conclusion. It does not produce an end, fulfill a telos, tidy up loose strings. I emphasize this here, and will do so again at the beginning of that final section in the hope that no reader will take my final comments very seriously. What I take to be valuable in this essay is what occurs within its body.

Recommended Reading Strategies

This essay is very dense, and is sure to put some readers off rather quickly. I would therefore like to inform readers that my discussion of each scene can be read independently of the others. This is true, at least, minus the analyses at the end of each scene that compare the manner in which various issues appear within diverse scenes. Each major scene was written with a different style, and readers might find some of the major sections more readily intelligible than others.

A PHENOMENOLOGICAL SKETCH OF MEANINGFUL ACTION

This section is a mere sketch of essential points that have been selected from many points that arise when considering meaningful action phenomenologically. As mentioned already, the epistemological issues associated with a phenomenological inquiry into meaningful action could not be explicitly addressed in this relatively short paper. The three scenes that follow this phenomenological exercise do illuminate epistemological issues begged here, but I do not always make this explicit.

I begin the phenomenological exercise with what is common to a second and third person position with respect to a meaningful act, the positions in which one receives an impression of meaning from the act of another. I move into the first person position at an appropriate place in my list of points.

1. *Meaning Is Prior to Objectivity:* When observing a social interaction or taking part in one, meaning is focal to the experience of a second or third person. Objective details of the act (what one sees, hears, possibly smells or tastes) are *apperceived* (ap-perceived, "perceived with," out of focus, analogous to peripheral vision in relation to the center of visual experience). Objective features of the situation are not foregrounded, they are not experienced "first" and then "decoded" for meaning. Rather, objective perceptions will only become foregrounded after the meaning of the act has been grasped, and then only if one has a purpose or project that requires such foregrounding. When one has such a project to pursue, objective factors are differentiated, via reflection, from a prior holistic experience as one set of components implicated by its meaning.

If a neighbor greets you as you walk toward your car, you understand the situation holistically as a greeting. The identity of the neighbor as someone you know; the distance between you and the neighbor; the specific words used by your neighbor; the body movements, facial expressions, and gestures of your neighbor; and all other objective characteristics of the situation are backgrounded within experience.

1.1 *Perception Is Secondary to Understanding*: Therefore, the question of sense perception and its relationship to meaning appears *within a phenomenological analysis of meaningful acts* as a second-order question. Indeed "sense perception" could be described as an effect of certain categories of internalized action, meaningful action that foregrounds an object pole in order to explicitly draw the attention of another to it. To "merely perceive" the objective features of a meaningful act addressed toward one, is but one way to internally communicate, internally act with meaning, toward an abstract audience.

To explicitly notice that your neighbor has, say, thrust her arms up and out while greeting you is to internally act just after receiving her salutation. The internal act is a prediscursive form of "She has thrown out her arms" or "You have thrown out your arms." It is a communicatively structured act of noting features of the situation open to multiple access that could be allowed to evolve into a fully communicative act expressed toward a third person party or toward the woman herself.

2. *Meaning Unifies the Act*: Any meaningful act can be analyzed as a behavior and as such broken down into an indefinite number of sensory components, from the perspective of the second or third person. The sense perceptions of various body movements and vocalizations can be noted in this way. But these sensory components amount to part of the apperceived context of a single act. "Perceptual acts," internalized communicative acts that foreground sense experiences, can delimit apperceived sensual elements and make them thematic. But perceptual acts will either take place within a project of activity that deliberately ignores meaning as the meaningful acts of others take place, or just after meaning has been grasped through reflection. Without a project that insists on sense perception only, a meaningful act is experienced as a singularity. The singularity of the act comes about through its meaning. Therefore, a meaningful act is *constituted* by its meaning.

When your neighbor greets you with "Hello neighbor!" you experience this as a single act. Subsequent reflection could break this singularity into many discrete moments and components. But subsequent reflections are also meaningful acts with their own singular qualities. If you broke your neighbor's greeting into all its various objective components you would be engaged in a special project of some sort for some reason. If you were taking an ethnography class, for example, and were required to write down all the objective components of behaviors you encounter in your everyday life you would be engaged in a project of this kind.

2.1 *An Act Has a Single Point*: In the stream of action one is impressed by *points* made by the actors. Focal to the experience of another's meaningful act is the sense of a single overriding point. The meaning is the point from which the actor comes; where she is "coming from." As David McNeill says in his work on gesture, utterances and nonverbal speech acts move from a "primitive stage" of global, synthetic, and imagistic unity through several stages of delineation (1992:1, 20, and elsewhere). The "point" of an act is also its origin in a unitary, global, synthetically multi-dimensional meaning.

McNeill uses the term "idea unit" in a similar way to my use of the term "point" (McNeill 1992:27). From the second person position, the "point" is usually grasped before any of its delineated details are explicitly understood. Even when a meaningful act is meant to have more than one meaning, as in a pun or a sarcastic remark, the multiple meanings derive from, and also deliver, a single point. The point in this case is the full pun or the full act of sarcasm.

The greeting of your neighbor is experienced as having a single point. The best articulation of this point is the act itself within its full context. You could attempt to recreate it if someone asked what your neighbor's point was. You could recreate the act in its context as best you can, and see whether the one to whom you are explaining the act "gets it." But other methods of articulating the point are always available. You can talk *about* the act in order to explain it to someone else; for example, "She was just being friendly, and didn't want to engage in a long talk with me."

3. *The Single Point of an Act Bears Multiple Meanings*: The single overriding point made by a meaningful act is holistic and implicit. It is what is first understood. One can appropriately respond to the act of another before one articulates the meaning of this other's act in either words or thought. If one does try to articulate the point of an act, one then engages in a new form of meaningful action: let's call this category of meaningful action *articulation*.[1] And when one engages in this sort of activity, articulating the meaning of someone's act, one discovers a multitude of meanings that work together to deliver the overriding point.

As said above, the most direct representation of your neighbor's greeting would be to recreate it in its full context. Articulating the meaning of the greeting as fully as possible in words, by talking about it, will delineate multiple meanings that were merely implicated by the point of the act.

For example, if someone asked you to explain your neighbor's greeting you might say, "She wanted to be friendly, but not to engage in a long conversation. She seemed to suspect that I would wish to get to my car without much delay. She expected me to say 'Hi' back. She suspected that not to say 'Hello' to me would indicate that something was wrong, because we always greet each other like this outside our homes." All of these meanings, and many more, were implicated in this greeting. All such meanings are grasped at once, as the point of her act. The point of her act bore multiple meanings.

3.1 *Moment-Totality, Component-Totality Relations*: The multiple meanings of a single act are implicated by the overriding point

---

[1] "Articulation" is used in this essay to refer to acts that make use of language in an effort to fully delimit meaning through a sequence of representations. "Expression," on the other hand, is used to refer to the acting out of an impetus. Expressive acts will generally contain an articulated content that, however, is surrounded by implicit, nonarticulated, references.

that is experienced as a totality as well as a singularity. Each articulated meaning amounts to a "moment" or a "component," of this totality.[2]

The point of an act is constituted by an array of meanings. Various types of array are simultaneously involved in the constitution of meaning, and the arrays themselves could be discussed as "moments." We can examine arrays externally and internally. Externally, we can analyze a meaningful act in terms of differentiable components exhibited through the actor's behavior. Speech acts embody their meaning through the juxtaposition of the rather linear linguistic utterance with holistic, less linear, gesticulations that usually possess a more immediate relationship to the "point."[3] All analyzable segments of the behavior that houses a meaningful act, such as the relationship between gesture and utterance and the relationship between semantic units, facial expression, and prosody, work together to bring about a singular impression of meaning from an array of moments and parts.

Internal arrays are patterned moments and components that must be tacitly grasped in order to grasp the point of the act. These arrays structure the act's meaning rather than the behavior housing the act. There are intentions, allusions, values, norms, identities, role sets, and all sorts of structures that must be grasped simultaneously when understanding an act.

---

[2] I will not make much of the difference between a "moment" and a "component" in this essay, but rather will just use both terms together to cover all the possibilities. A "moment" is an analytically derived aspect of meaning that depends upon the array of other moments for its special contribution or analytic sense. A "component" is an analytically derived aspect considered on its own, as if its contribution to the point of a meaningful act works externally. Usually a phenomenological analysis of meaningful acts will give us moments rather than components. But actors themselves can emphasize certain portions of a meaning array so as to give them some autonomy; to make them function as components more than moments.

[3] The lack of any gesticulation in some meaningful acts usually contributes to the point of the act through the suppression of possible gesticulations. Both actor and those addressed or observing the act understand the lack of gesticulation as an absence that contributes to the meaning. The absence of gesticulation would generally work as a positive reference within the internal arrays that constitute the act's meaning.

External arrays, when analyzed, give clues to the internal arrays. Consider the following meaningful acts from your neighbor:

a) She says "Hello" in a drab tone of voice without much body movement

b) She says "Hello" loudly and with sharp, short, tones, hands on hips

c) She says "Hello-ooo!" with arms outstretched.

Each act has a different point and the difference between these various meanings could be explained after the fact and through analysis and reflection, partly by drawing attention to the different, objectively discernible, moment-totality relations, or component-totality relations involved. Saying "Hello" with hands on hips differs from saying "Hello" with hands flung outwards. The difference in the array of behavior houses a difference in array of meanings.

The point of (a) could be, "I'm polite but don't much like you."

The point of (b) could be, "I am angry with you; I expect something from you."

The point of (c) could be, "You don't seem to like me but I am friendly just the same, and I will not give up on you; you should be friendly to me too; I am not angry with you even though you don't treat me well."

3.2 *Many Possible Moments and Components*: There are always many ways to articulate a single impression of meaning received from the act of another. Grasping a single overriding point does not result in a single way of articulating the meaning of an act in words or gestures. Each articulation is an interpretation since each articulation casts the overriding point somewhat differently. Articulations never exhaust the point; they always seem partial.

If your neighbor greets you with "Hello guv'nor," using inflections that reference sections of the British working class (when your neighbor is American) while tossing her head slightly from side to side, how would you articulate the point of her act? Perhaps: "She is being friendly and humorous. She is expressing affection. She doesn't expect me to engage in long conversation, but just laugh and say 'Hi' back."

Okay, but is that all? "Well, also, she is referencing an interaction we had yesterday when I said, 'How's it going, Doc?', and she is expressing some intimacy, or a desire for a little intimacy between us."

Anything else? "Well, yes, but it's hard to put into words. If I see her tomorrow and say, 'Hello, Doc' again, that would miss the point. I think that this is supposed to sort of close off something I started yesterday. Next time we meet, I should stop and talk with her a little. An invitation is involved. And there is more but I can't really articulate it all. I'm not even sure she would agree with me about all of what I've just said."

The point of a meaningful act can be articulated in many ways, each of which is partial and each of which interprets.

4. *Meaning as Forestructure*: Each possible articulation one could produce to explain the meaningful act of another, however, may be roughly judged as adequate or inadequate. The overriding point of the act is a forestructure from which articulations may be made. A "forestructure" is a "sketch-in-advance" of the articulation; it is a *pragmatic horizon* that bounds possible articulations. The boundaries are not, however, explicit or distinct. They are like a horizon in that they recede if you try to pursue them or delineate them, for doing so amounts to trying to articulate the boundaries and this casts forth new forestructures.

The relationship of forestructure to meaning is somewhat analogous to the relationship between a generative grammar and the infinite variety of sentences it makes possible.[4] But we must

---

[4] This relationship of forestructure to meaning is also analogous to the relationship of "rules of well formedness" to "strings" in number theory. See Hofstadter 1979:181-3.

take this similarity only as an analogy. For reasons presented below, meaning is in some senses identical to forestructure. *Both the "rules" and the "content" constituting a meaningful act are claimed together and embodied in the act itself.*

To understand the greeting made by your neighbor is to have forestructures from which to act or think. The many various articulations you could formulate of the meaning of your neighbor's greeting are so many ways of filling in foresketches. When you do articulate the meaning of your neighbor's act, thereby interpreting it, you have some sense of how accurate your interpretation is. You probably would not interpret the greeting by saying: "She wants me to change my trousers," unless something within your personal history with this neighbor and something about your trousers, known to you, would suggest that interpretation.

When you do attempt to give an accurate articulation of the point of her act you are able to tell roughly how close or far off you are: "She wants some intimacy in our relationship. Well, not exactly *intimacy*, but something like that." The point you have grasped provides you with forestructures that will guide your efforts to articulate the act's meaning and provide a sort of standard by which to judge the accuracy of your articulations.

5. *Meaning and Uncertainty*: The meaning of an act must be uncertain for two reasons: (1) it is uncertain in that it is a forestructure from which many interpretations are always possible, though bounded. It is implicit and only suggestive of modes of explication, not determinate of them. (2) Meaning is also uncertain because one is never sure one has the correct impression of the overriding point. Often one notes two or more possible points. Sometimes one feels subjectively certain that one understands the point of an act but then alters this impression when observing a subsequent act. Understanding a meaningful act is not a certain affair even though experiencing the act as a singularity suggests a single point. No articulation will capture or exhaust its point completely. Moreover, one is usually faced with several possible points.

So, to return to the example of your neighbor's greeting, it is quite possible that you would explain her act with something like the following: "She is expressing good intentions, and maybe also making a ploy for a little more intimacy between us. But maybe not. Perhaps she is just being friendly and is not seeking any greater familiarity between us. I am not absolutely sure." This explanation provides two different possible points.

6. *Subjectivity and Uncertainty*: The uncertainty that accompanies the understanding of meaningful acts is partially structured by subjectivity; by the condition that the actor has access to portions of her act to which the one addressed does not have access. The subjective state of the actor is indicated by her act of meaning and yet closed off from certain knowledge. This is generally understood prereflectively. It is often the main principle that generates the experience of several possible points to an act of meaning. Each possible point is distinguished from the others by possible experiences the actor might be having of her own act that are closed off from the direct access of the one acted toward.

The subjective/objective distinction rests upon a distinction between privileged and shared access. Getting an impression of the meaning of an act includes getting an impression of the subjective experience of the actor.

You might feel certain that your neighbor is expressing friendly feelings toward you but not be sure whether a bid for greater intimacy is part of the point or not. This gives us two possible points, both singular in nature but both analytically differentiated only by the question of how the actor is experiencing her own act.

6.1 *Meaning as Impetus*: Thus, the overriding point of an act includes an impression of the impetus that stirred the actor to act. The overriding point of the act of another amounts to a grasp of the "primitive form" of the act (McNeill 1992:33) as the first person experiences it prior to, and/or during, its external or internal "evolution" (McNeill 1992:40). The actor has access to the impetus of the act in ways that the observer does not. But an impetus to act is experienced from the first person position in an implicit and holistic way. It is a fusion of motivating feelings and preconceptually grasped anticipations of the nature of the act and the consequences the act will bring about.

Let's say someone asks you what your neighbor meant when she greeted you. The most direct way to get the meaning across is to find a similar impetus within yourself and act it out. If the person you are trying to explain the situation to shares as much context with your neighbor as you do, attempting to repeat the act would most closely capture the meaning by directly acquainting this person with the original act's impetus (as you grasped it). "What did she mean when she said 'Hello-ooo!'?" "She meant 'Hello-ooo!'"

6.2 *An Impetus Is Not an Intention*: The observer may note features of the impetus to act that the actor tried to suppress or was not conscious of, and convincingly point these out to the actor. An impetus is not the same as an intention. For example, one can act while feeling fear, tones of which are featured into the impetus and are noted by the observer but unacknowledged by the actor. In addition, one can act out an impetus that feels inappropriate to what one intends.

An "intention" is a secondary structure: the result of internally monitoring an impetus to act, a result of its "internal evolution" (McNeill 1992:40). An intention seems to be the degree to which an actor invests herself in the impetus to act. Meaningful action impeti reference intentions but are not directly constituted by them. Intentions are like a learned language that is greatly malleable but never identical with what we call agency. The actor's intentions are referenced by acts as one portion of a set of claims.

If your neighbor says "Hello" with sharp tones and hands on hips, you might believe something is wrong. You say back, "What's going on, Mary? Are you angry with me?" It is possible that she could then answer, "Oh, no! Sorry! I didn't intend to sound that way. I'm glad to see you but I am furious about a phone call I just received from my 'ex.'" The impetus of the act was not the same as the actor's intention, and in this case portions of the impetus were actually at odds with the actor's intention.

As another example, if your neighbor greeted you with "Hello guv'nor," you could ask her, "Are you bidding for a little more familiarity between us with your greeting?" An answer of "yes" or "no" would influence your interpretation of the original greeting by giving you more certainty about her own experience of her act. If she said "yes" or "no" you might decide that you have learned what her real intentions were in acting toward you. The real case, however, is probably that she has simply invested herself within one impetus as opposed to another. The intention is a claim carried by an impetus rather than a fact. Instead of saying "yes" or "no," for example, she might reply to your question with: "Well, I'm not sure. I did feel unusually warm toward you when I greeted you."

The impetus of a meaningful act, as experienced by the actor, is not identical with the intention of the actor. An intention is a claim when considered from the second or third person positions, and it is an investment when considered from a primordial first person position.

7. *Impetus as Forestructure—Acts Interpret Their Own Point*: An impetus to act is experienced by the first person, the actor, much as the forestructure of the impression of meaning is experienced by the one trying to articulate the point of an act, or to act back appropriately. It is a forestructure for the actor as well as for those addressed by, or observing, the act. An actor can experience an impetus to act just prior to acting, but only in an implicit, holistic, preconceptual, manner. Acting from the impetus is a way to interpret it; to fill in a foresketch. That is why we sometimes surprise ourselves during or just after acting, why we often feel more clear about the meaning of our impeti after acting from them. Acts interpret their point.

Let's imagine that your neighbor says, "Hello guv'nor" with an imitated British working class accent and slight tossing of the head. You get the point as including friendliness, affection, and humor.

Now the analysis will shift from her act to your experience of your own act back. You experience an impetus to act back that has forestructures calling for a similar accent and a similar use of vernacular terms. You find yourself acting to fill in this foresketch but what comes out is "Toodle pop! I mean *pip*! Toodle pip!, ha ha."

You surprise yourself first of all because the form "toodle [pip]" comes out, which is perhaps close enough to the form of the foresketch but a phrase alluding to the wrong British social class. You surprise yourself secondly because "pop" was actually spoken within the form instead of "pip." So you probably feel a little clumsy and awkward. The impetus was appropriate, but the explicit act was not, for two reasons (wrong social class referenced, and wrong word spoken). The impetus was a forestructure that you incorrectly filled in.

8. *Meaning as Impeti to Act Again*: Meaningful action impeti have the quality of forestructures. Impressions of the point of a meaningful act made by another also have the quality of forestructures. This is no mere coincidence because the meaning one understands from the act of another appears to be an array of impeti for new acts. The impression of the point of an act made by another is an impetus cluster for new acts of our own. The forestructure of the impression of meaning is in some sort of relationship to the forestructure of the original act.

From the third person position, the impression of meaning that an observed act yields is a set of impeti for articulating the point; talking about the meaning of the act. From the second person position the impression of meaning one receives from the act of another is usually an impetus to respond appropriately to the act; a forestructure of acting back toward the actor. All such impeti to act again have the quality of forestructures and therefore do not prescribe acts of response or acts of articulation in their details. They rather provide various horizons for acting again.

Once you grasp the point of your neighbor's greeting, or decide on one of several possible points, you are in a position to act in three categorically different ways. You have forestructures on hand to respond back to the neighbor, to talk about the greeting, and to imitate the greeting. Action impeti are on-hand. Your grasp of the point consists of impeti to act yourself.

8.1 *Meaning as Acting Again within Three Modes*: The impression of meaning received in either second or third person position allows for three categories of acting again. One can (1) repeat the act as the first person acted it, (2) respond to the act appropriately as the second person would usually do, (3) articulate the act in thought or words as a third person would do. From these three primary categories of "acting again," or understanding an act, come various secondary categories of acting again; for example, deliberately responding inappropriately.

Your neighbor says "Hello." To grasp the point of this greeting is to understand the forestructures of imitating her act, responding to her with something like "Hi," and telling someone else what she said and what it meant. All three modes are involved in grasping the point of the act. Your grasp of the act is an impetus cluster. You might not be able to fill in the various foresketches skillfully, but you understand their basic form.

9. *Action Monitoring*: As one acts meaningfully, one monitors the act from various perspectives: as the person addressed by the act might experience it and as various abstract or concrete, present or absent audiences might experience it.

If your neighbor says "Hello" and you respond with "Hi," as you respond you gain impressions of your own act as others might experience it. As you say "Hi," in a friendly manner, you probably gain an impression of how your neighbor will experience your returned greeting. You probably also gain a view of the act from the perspective of an uninvolved observer.

When you said, "Toodle pop!" you probably realized that you had the wrong word while it was being uttered from your mouth. Your ability to monitor your act allowed you to experience it as others would, notice that the wrong word was used, and quickly act again to remedy the situation.

9.1 *Action Impetus Monitoring*: The impetus to act meaningfully can also be monitored, without acting the impetus out. Action impeti:

> a) can be partially rehearsed in thought, instead of acted upon (activity proceeding from a first person perspective on the impetus, but in first person thought)
>
> b) can be partially considered in thought as it would impress the one addressed by the act (activity proceeding from a second person perspective on the impetus, but in first person thought), and
>
> c) can be partially considered in thought as it would appear to a general but absent audience (activity proceeding from a third person perspective on the impetus, but in first person thought).

In other words, the impetus itself can be "monitored," considered within one's privileged realm of experience, from a first, second, and third person position, through a mental rehearsal. This can occur through an indefinite number of levels of explicitness. That is, the act can be rehearsed with all the words thought out, or with a few words thought out and images or feelings representing the rest of the act, or solely in terms of images and feelings.

Your impetus to respond to the neighbor can be inwardly "rehearsed," so as to monitor its partial, internalized, expression. This can occur at very low levels of explicitness, in which some prekinesthetic sensations and vague imagery emerge within your subjective realm of privileged access. It can also occur at fairly explicit levels in which the words you would use actually take form in thought—you might even subvocalize them. You could also adopt a third person perspective on your impetus, allowing it to be expressed as an observer would perceive it. And you could also adopt the second person position to imagine your act as the neighbor might experience it.

9.2 *Monitoring as New Impeti Differentiated from an Original Impetus*: Monitoring an act is not a process by which a free consciousness observes and considers an act, but rather the eruption of new impeti to act that are differentiated from an original impetus. Monitoring often begins while an impetus is in the process of being acted out or mentally rehearsed. As an impetus evolves into action, one can experience new impeti in relation to portions of the forestructure of the original impetus.

These new impeti are often chained. One can, for example, experience the sort of impetus to act back that the person addressed by one's act may feel and then, in chained formation, experience an impetus to respond to that anticipated response (i.e., before one has completed one's act and thus before the person addressed has acted back). One can experience an impetus that corresponds to the remarks about your act that a nonaddressed observer might make, and then experience a chained impetus to act in relation to those virtual remarks.

Thus one often experiences an impetus to act just after completing an action in order to forestall an anticipated misunderstanding, to receive anticipated affirmation, to support a portion of the forestructure against which an objection is expected. But all such new impeti differentiate from the original impetus in a preconceptual manner and prior to the articulation of such categories as "objection," "affirmation," "misunderstanding."

Your neighbor says, "Hello!" in sharp, short, tones and with hands on hips. You respond with, "Well! hello!" in an equally angry manner. But as this comes forth you monitor it from a third person perspective that you commonly assume and with respect to which you usually construct your identity. Your response seems mean and totally lacking in high-mindedness from this perspective. So you immediately act again, as soon as your angry response is finished. You now say, "Oh, sorry Mary, I'm not really angry with you. Why are you angry with *me*?"

9.3 *Premonitored Action Impeti*: A great many action impeti have a premonitored quality. They are *constituted* by the expected impressions they will make on the one addressed and on observers. Actual monitoring processes that take place during the course of expressing an act or during the course of a mental rehearsal clarify the premonitored moments of the original impetus.

When your neighbor says, "Hello-ooo" and you respond by laughing and saying "Well, hello-ooo," it is as if you are acting out one part of a play. Your act has an audience already built into it. It is premonitored.

Premonitored action impeti are related to the concept of "typifications" discussed in other sections of this essay.

10. *Interactive Syntax and the Temporal Horizon*: The impression of meaning one receives from the act of another depends in part on the action that has occurred just before, and the action that is expected to occur just after. Interactions possess a syntax. From the second and third person positions, the impression of meaning includes an impression of how the impetus is experienced by the actor in light of what occurred just prior to the act. The actor refers to prior action with the present act. The reference to prior action is part of the constitution of the act, part of its point.

From the first person position, monitoring occurs with the eruption of new impeti that are temporally differentiated from the act in progress. A second act of clarification, for example, references the first act. Even a second act that seems to radically "change the subject" takes an important part of its meaning in relation to the act just completed.

This amounts to a syntax of interaction, foreshadowed holistically as a temporal horizon to the act. The syntax of interaction is a syntax of "points" and is autonomous from other levels of syntax, such as the syntax characterizing languages; sign languages, and verbal language interspersed with language-like gestures, pantomimes, and emblems (McNeill 1992:37). The syntax of interaction itself involves moment-totality relationships: from the first person perspective, the point of a single act bears relation to a "project" in which possible sequences of future acts are referenced holistically; from the second and third person positions an impression of meaning will include a holistic grasp of the "project" through which the actor constructed her particular act.

Your neighbor says, "Hello guv'nor." You respond with "Toodle pop; I mean, toodle *pip*, ha ha." Your neighbor now says, "Ha ha, so what's new, friend?" The meaning or point of this last act is highly dependent on the temporal syntax. Your neighbor has made light of your unskilled response and changed the style of interaction, thereby communicating full acceptance and friendly intentions. References to the previous two acts are constituents of the third act.

Your neighbor also indicates an expectation that you will respond again but probably within the new, nonhumorous, style she introduced. References to immediately past actions and to expected future actions partly constitute the point of her last act. A syntax of interaction is a constituent reference within the point of the meaningful act. The neighbor's project initially appeared to be that of a short series of humorous, affectionate interactions. It changed slightly with her last act, the project now being that of maintaining a short series of friendly and affectionate interactions but without the humorous style.

11. *The Spatial Horizon of the Act*: The impression of meaning one obtains from the act of another is also related to the physical and social surroundings within which the act takes place. Part of the impression of meaning is an impression of how the actor construes the act in relation to the physical setting in which it takes place. The spatial horizon of an act forms one realm of pragmatic reference, one region of the moments unified by the point of an act and a project of action.

You can expect your neighbor to be aware of the fact that you are outside your home and moving toward your car. How your neighbor construes the spatial features of your interaction will be an important part of how you understand her. Her construal will either be referenced in her act or not. If she says, "Hi! Back to the rat race I see," you could take it that she has noticed your movement toward the car. If she says, "Hi! What did you think of the President's speech?" while moving slowly toward you, you could assume that she is giving little significance to your movement toward the car. You might then place a hand on the car door while saying, "Gruesome! Catch you later."

12. *The Impetus Prior to the Act*: An impetus to act meaningfully can be experienced prior to acting it through, monitoring it, or thinking explicitly about it. One can become aware of several possible impeti to act, for example, and act on one impetus rather than its alternatives. One can become aware of an impetus to act meaningfully and of its alternatives, without monitoring it or contemplating it. One can become aware of an impetus to monitor an act in progress without allowing its expression. One can bring an impetus to act to the threshold of acting it out, without then crossing over that threshold into activity.[5]

You could experience an impetus to respond to your neighbor with "Hi," but feel in such a great hurry as to ignore this impetus and simply rush to the car. You could experience an impetus to justify your use of the word "pop" instead of "pip" by explaining that you had been thinking of soda pop just before the greeting. But instead of expressing this impetus, you inwardly monitor it from the second person position and experience it as unnecessary and too defensive, so you do not express it. You could experience an impetus to keep thinking about your response to the neighbor, so as to uncover more possible "points" readable from your act, but pull your attention back to concentrate on what your neighbor will do next.

In all of these cases, action impeti are experienced prior to their

---

[5] I will not elaborate this point, but the alert reader will notice that it is a feature of the phenomenological method for examining action impeti. This assertion thus begs questions directly associated with the epistemology of a phenomenological inquiry. Phenomenological reflection appears to be a specialized form of what I have been calling the "monitoring" of action impeti.

expression and something like a choice is made whether to express them or not.[6]

12.1 *Preconceptual Awareness of the Impetus*: An impetus to act meaningfully will arise within awareness in a preconceptual way. It will first arise as a forestructure that may then result in either gross motor activity, or in monitoring activity (internal considerations from first, second, or third person positions), or in a newly foregrounded alternative impetus. Such awareness is preconceptual in that the impetus to act meaningfully will be that of a forestructure; a holistic, implicit, and in this sense *pre-understanding* of the act entailed by the impetus and of the consequences possible from a manifestation of this act.

The examples given just above included rushing to the car instead of saying "Hi," waiting for your neighbor's response instead of justifying your own misuse of words, and concentrating on your neighbor instead of thinking through all the possible meanings of your previous act. Each involved a quick, preconceptual, holistic, awareness of an impetus followed by a sort of choice. The impetus in each case was experienced in synthesized images and body sensations. The awareness was preconceptual.

12.2 *Preconceptual Awareness as Feeling-Configuration*: The impetus to act meaningfully can be phenomenologically examined as it first emerges in awareness. This is thematizing; "freezing," the impetus within awareness and examining its appearance. When this is done one discovers an impetus to be a feeling-configuration

---

[6] I write "something like a choice" in this sentence because the concept of "choice" is rather dicey. Very often the word "choice" is used to mean making a decision after a process of careful reflection. I am trying to capture a process that usually occurs without deliberation such that the impetus "of most experiential weight" is acted from. Whether we would wish to call this a sort of low level choice or call it something else is an issue on which I am as yet undecided. The section on George Herbert Mead explores some of the issues related to this question.

that is constituted by moment-totality relations on the level of feelings and images.[7]

Your neighbor begins to describe, at length, an article she read earlier that day. You experience an impetus to interrupt, explaining that you need to get going. You do not express it, and rather than listen to your neighbor, examine the impetus. There is a sensation in your right arm and hand, which would have moved up toward your neighbor in a "stop" or "halt" sign had the impetus been expressed. There are sensations in your throat and mouth which would have uttered, "Sorry, need to go." Your head was about to shake back and forth and you can feel sensations there as well. This would have been one act; the words and body movements would have been expressed in a coordinated manner. Vague imagery represents the act as a whole and is somehow experientially close to the body sensations.

Stopping the impetus and retaining awareness of it *first* delivers a general impression of the singular point to be made, felt in the body. *Second* comes the configuration of sensations distributed about the body.

12.3 *Three Shades of the Feeling-Configuration*: An impetus to act meaningfully, if frozen preconceptually for examination, displays a configuration of body sensations, a mode of I-feeling, and preimagery.

> a) The configuration of body sensations is a form of proprioception (Heil 1983): awareness of a state of sensation located within the body. Included in these sensations are what I call "prekinesthetics": sensations in those regions of the body that would move when the impetus is expressed. A "tight feeling" about the stomach, a certain awareness of the lips and cheeks, an "expanded feeling" in the chest, are all examples.

---

[7] This idea is related to, though not identical with, Merleau-Ponty's discussion of "preobjectivity" and body sensations. See Merleau-Ponty 1962, Introduction and Chapter One.

b) The I-feeling mode is revealed as closer to the actual impetus than the proprioceptive configuration. The latter differentiates within awareness as multiple sensations that, however, are linked or patterned in relation to the singularity of the impetus. The former, the I-feeling mode, is what unifies the proprioceptive configuration. It differentiates within awareness prior to the proprioceptive configuration. It is just prior to awareness of bodily sensation. It is a singularity, a way of being, an implicit identity. It is like ripples on a surface of water in that it is already going away when one becomes aware of it. It appears as the fading sensation of a former fusion of awareness and impetus.

c) Preimagery is also a part of the preconceptual awareness of an impetus to act meaningfully. It is pre-imagery because it is suggestive of visual images without focus, rather like peripheral vision or some forms of dream imagery. If made focal it takes on more definite boundaries but is still not as distinct as a concrete visual experience. It is *felt*. It contains "places" for the actor and those to be acted toward. The preunderstandings of both the act and a social context surrounding the act are included. Preimagery contains all this holistically, preconceptually, and as a mode of feeling rather than as a focal image.[8]

You are walking toward your car, you notice your neighbor within your peripheral vision, you hear her greeting, and you simultaneously understand the point of her greeting. Here is a possible impetus you might next experience in frozen form:

---

[8] David McNeill (1992) believes that an "image" arises within the subjective realm first, which, one could assume, represents the meaning of the forthcoming act true to its holistic origins if drawn or otherwise directly represented. However, fully explicit images do not precede acts within the consciousness of the actor. Rather, a special form of acting (externally or internally) from the same impetus would be required to make an image explicit. Thus my use of the term preimagery.

* A sort of tightened sensation along the side of your body nearest to your neighbor.

* A set of proprioceptive sensations that could be called prekinesthetic, felt in those portions of your body that would move if the impetus were to be expressed. These correspond to movements that would turn your head and trunk toward your neighbor while starting to speak. Many parts of your body serve as locations to these sensations.

* Some preimages associated with the above feelings that involve the movements that would come and the words that would be uttered. These preimages represent the movements that correspond to your act and the way the act would appear to your neighbor and others if they were observing. They are preimages because they are out of focus and abstract rather than vivid or concrete.

* A deeper sensation that grounds the unitary, singular, quality of the above sensations and imagery. This is a *way of being through the act* associated with this impetus. This is a sense of yourself as embodied within this one act. This is the I-feeling mode.

All together, this is a configuration because it consists of many parts unified by the singularity of the impetus. The experience of a unity is given through the "deeper sensation" mentioned just above—the "I feeling mode."

13. *Impetus as Symbol of a Symbol*: To examine the impetus of a meaningful act we had to freeze a preconceptual awareness and then phenomenologically examine it. This means that preconceptual awareness had to be made thematic. As soon as it is described as a proprioceptive configuration, preimagery, and an I-feeling mode, it becomes conceptual. This was a phenomenological strategy but it was a process that itself adds to the construction of what is revealed in awareness.

The feeling-configuration emerged with its three components—proprioceptive and prekinesthetic configuration, I-feeling mode, and preimagery—as something that points toward what was prior. What was prior was a single I-feeling state in which awareness was fused with an impetus to act. Thus it becomes "frozen" for examination, thematized, only by becoming a symbol for a prior state. What I am calling "impetus" is therefore a symbol, for it points *backward* to what was but is going-gone. It points backward to the singularity of the impetus to act. It suggests a prior fusion of awareness and impetus that has just broken apart through taking the phenomenological stance.

If we contemplate the singularity of the impetus, rather than its differentiated parts (proprioceptive configuration, etc.), we find ourselves contemplating a memory. There was an impetus, within which our awareness had been fused. This impetus is yet another symbol. It is a state of fusion in which awareness and impetus to act were one and yet were pointing *forward* toward the act. There are two symbols: one of a state already going-gone, and one of an act to come.

Both symbols are inhabited by desires. The discovery of the feeling-configuration symbol amounts to the discovery of a "pointing backward" that is a desire to recollect what just was; the state of fusion. The suggestion of the fusion state comes next, as a product of recollection. As such we find a symbol of what will come if we freeze things no longer but surrender to the impetus and allow it to act through us. This second symbol, which comes to us as being prior to the feeling-configuration symbol of which we became aware first "points forward" not as a desire to recollect but as a desire to surrender and allow the act to manifest itself. Each impetus has its particular desire, or promise. One is constituted by the desire to recollect a former state, the other is constituted by the desire to fulfill a telos promised by the original impetus to act.

Consider the impetus to tell your neighbor that you have to go, you cannot listen to her description of an article or a speech because you don't have time. Phenomenologically freezing this impetus allows an inner examination that reveals the body sensations, the preimagery, and the I-feeling mode described in a section above. These various moments and components point back to an original unity, and it is the I-feeling mode that captures that unity most closely. But the original unity itself is not revealed by your phenomenological investigation. That unity would have allowed for no phenomenological investigations because your whole being was fused within its moment. There were no differentiations that could have supported both the impetus and your awareness of this impetus. Thus the configuration of sensations, preimagery, and I-feeling mode represents a moment gone by. The configuration is a symbol pointing back to a lost moment.

Through the I-feeling mode it is possible to retrieve something like the original impetus to either act out the impetus or to continue the phenomenological process. The impetus is a symbol of the act it would give rise to: interrupting your neighbor. A desire is intrinsic to it. All impeti symbolize what would come, if they are acted out, and all are inhabited by a desire to act. Thus, thematizing them reveals a symbol that points forward, yet the thematized components and moments are not really the impetus. They can only be, in configuration, a symbol pointing back.

13.1 *Symbol as Desire*: The impetus to act was a state of desire, a mode of desire. It was a symbol that we find as such only through a second symbol with its own mode of desire: the desire to recollect the former symbol. Phenomenological strategies will always amount to the differentiation and objectification of a prior state and thus to a recollection that is conducted with its own forestructures, its own modes of desire. When applied to an impetus to act the resulting object of awareness is also a desire; a desire to move forth in action.

Desire is in both cases fused with a mode of I-feeling. In such a state one feels a certain promise. The preunderstanding of what is to come is a promise, a temptation, an anticipation within which an I-feeling is embodied.

14. *The Point Behind Is a Vanishing Point*: The effort to phenomenologically recollect the point of an act by reflecting on the impetus gives us only symbols of symbols. Moreover, when we are aware of the symbol pointing forward as it is given to us in phenomenological investigation, we find it differentiated in our experience only through the projection of new forestructures: those provided by a new impetus, a new desire attributable to the processes of reflection and recollection. When we are phenomenologically aware of an impetus as the symbol pointing forward we have already interpreted it against a new set of concerns. We have "looked backward" at the point behind the feeling-configuration symbol but cannot see or feel in an immediate way what is there. It appears as an anticipation, a desire, but is interpreted only through a new mode of anticipating and desiring.

Efforts to reflect further in order to purify the point behind only produce yet more forestructures. Trying to look backward amounts to new modes of acting forward: acting forward internally. The point behind is a "vanishing point." We never have an impetus to act purely within our conscious awareness.

15. *The Point Ahead Is a Vanishing Point*: Thus, to summarize and extrapolate: The meaning of an act is holistic and implicit. It is a forestructure from which to act, an impetus to which the actor surrendered. It is a forestructure from which to act again. The actor surrenders to an impetus but often also monitors and alters it while acting. The actor clarifies the impetus through the act. But the actor is left only with new impeti at the end of the act because clarification turns out to be but an extended repertoire for acting again, only an alteration in the actor's present concerns, desires, and not a final explication of the meaning of the act as such. Those who observe the act and are addressed by the act understand the meaning only through new impeti to act again from their respective positions, one of which might be the impetus to talk *about* the meaning of the act. The clarification of the meaning of an act for second and third persons is only an alteration in their concerns and their modes of desire constituting new possibilities to act.

The point of an act is a vanishing point for the actor; never fully and finally explicable as such through acting. Or, to say it otherwise, "explication" means alterations in one's present concerns, one's possibilities for moving on with activity. Among the new possibilities are ways in which the point just made could be "recollected" as a restatement of the meaning. But this involves new forestructures, new interpretations.

The point of an act is a vanishing point for the second and third persons; never explicable as such through responding to it with an effort to fully articulate its meaning nor with an effort to provide an appropriate response to the actor. Or, to say it otherwise, one "understands" another when one feels able to carry on with acting in relation to her, or one feels capable of speaking about the other's act with words.

From all perspectives, the point of a meaningful act is a vanishing point. It is a reference to an almost thinglike form that can never be apprehended as such.

Three Originary Scenes Suggested from the Phenomenological Sketch

The above phenomenological sketch is meant to be nothing more than a rough outline. It allows me, however, to pose the question of meaningful action against my three originary scenes in a more precise manner.

1) *Form and the Flux*: How is it that we can become preconceptually aware of an impetus to act? When we become aware of an impetus to act we are aware of a symbol; a desire to recollect. When we recollect we become aware of a prior symbol that is a state of desire pointing forward as a state of anticipation. It is a symbol of what is to come. Each symbol is a "form"; a sort of preobject to awareness with boundaries; forestructures. How do forms arise before awareness and what is their nature? How is it possible to be aware of form and what is awareness? What is prior

to form, what is "flux"? Asking these questions amounts to asking about meaning against the scene of form and the flux.

2) *The Feeling-Body*: How is it that an impetus to act, and thus a meaning in its implicit, holistic state, involves a proprioceptive configuration? What is the relationship between a proprioceptive state and what I have called the "I-feeling mode"? What is an I-feeling? What is the relationship between desire, I-feeling modes, and proprioception? To ask these questions is to pose the question of meaning against the scene of the feeling-body.

3) *The Origin of Intersubjectivity*: What makes possible our capacity to act out an impetus from first, second, and third person positions? The preimagery of the impetus includes a pre-understanding of an entire social situation: how is this possible? The uncertainty of the impression of meaning one gains from the act of another is rooted in the ability to sort of imagine the experience of an impetus to act from the first person position when in the second or third person position. How is this possible? The state of desire which is the impetus to act includes a promise, a preunderstanding of how one will feel after an act that is dependent on the responses that others will provide to the act. This suggests a preunderstanding of the act's audience. How is this possible? To ask these questions is to pose the problem of meaning against the origins of intersubjectivity.

ORIGINARY SCENE ONE: FORM AND THE FLUX
Form and Perception
The scene of form and the flux goes something like this: Imagine a chaotic, patternless, flux in which no form, no differentiations of any kind, are distinguishable. A lone subject somehow comes to perceive an orderly world, inclusive of both "outer" and "inner" forms and inclusive of the specifics of this subject's own nature. How does form emerge from the flux?

Once we can understand the way in which form is perceived and known, we can accordingly analyze how signifiers, such as words, come to stand for, or represent, form. This scene is generally arrived at through considerations of the relationship between signifiers and "forms," which then lead to the question of what form itself consists of and what makes it possible.

According to Staten (1984:5), "form" has been taken to be the primary connection between being and knowledge of being in most Western philosophy since the time of the classical Greek philosophers. Form has been taken to be what is self-evident, and certain knowledge must therefore build from direct experiences of form. The primordial relationship between knowledge and being is posed in a passive way in this scene: the self-evidence of form is given through an experience of reception, perception, immediate impression.

Thus perception is foregrounded in this scene. Perception is made the principal problem. Husserl developed the concepts of "horizon" and "forestructure" in his analysis of perception. I used these concepts extensively in the phenomenological sketch of action above, but transposed them from the contexts in which Husserl applied them to the context of meaningful action. The significance of the transpositions will become clearer through a consideration of Husserl's own usage of these terms.

Perception and Forestructures

For Husserl, perceptual form is given only against a set of tacit expectations projected forward in consciousness. We are not totally surprised in the course of ordinary perceptions, for example, because generally forestructures bring the form out for us in some sort of match between object and expectations. When we are surprised, forestructures are quickly rearranged. Thus many commentators on Husserl (e.g., Caputo 1987) emphasize the fact that Husserl did not believe in purely given, purely present objects of perception. What is "given" is always a "given-as," an interpretation. Objects (forms) are only possible within forestructures that preinterpret them. As Caputo says, this suggests a "hermeneutics of facticity" implicit in Husserl's work (Caputo 1987:57).

Husserl, however, wrote as if consciousness had a two-layered structure, such that reflecting backward on, or recollecting, a perceptual experience could indeed reveal pure forms of presence: The forestructures themselves could be revealed in a direct, uninterrupted way to consciousness. That is to say, though Husserl described perception as a hermeneutics of facticity, he treated the forestructures of the hermeneutic process as if they were directly, noninterpretively revealed to consciousness. It is particularly here that Heidegger, Merleau-Ponty, and especially Derrida have deconstructed Husserl's theory of perception. As Merleau-Ponty wrote: "I never actually collect together, or call up simultaneously all the primary thoughts which contribute to my perception or to my present conviction" (1962:61). The forestructures of perceptual experience can be no more revealed to consciousness in an immediate way than any other object of which we are aware. When we examine forestructures phenomenologically, some process of objectification occurs and *new* forestructures are involved in the objectification: forestructures used to objectify other forestructures.

Presence, Protention, and Retention

Derrida's critique of Husserl has become particularly influential during the past two decades. Using his strategy of deconstruction, Derrida reveals that the theory of signs as propounded by Husserl, particularly in his early and middle periods, rests on a theory of perception (inner and outer) that depends on the idea that it is possible to have something immediately present to consciousness. For Husserl, the focal object of perception is already hermeneutically interpreted by forestructures, but the forestructures themselves are supposedly available in immediate presence.

The ground for sign usage, according to Husserl, is the nature of perception (in the broadest sense; perception as the experience of any phenomenon). Yet when Husserl's theory of perception is carefully examined we find that this ground for a theory of sign usage itself possesses a sign structure. It is not really a "ground." To put Derrida's argument in a most decontextualized and truncated way, perceptual experience is always inhabited by deferment and absence and never by pure unmediated presence.

Derrida makes this point in a number of ways, and I will consider only his influential deconstruction of Husserl's theory of internal time consciousness.

Husserl argued that objects appear before consciousness in an experience of the "now"; the present. This experience of a "now," he claimed, is characterized by both *retention* and *protention*:

> I am speaking now of the alteration of *perspectives*. The perspectives of the shape and also of its color are different, but each is in this new way an *exhibiting of*—*of* this shape, *of* this color. Something similar to this can be studied in every modality of the sense-perception (touching, hearing, etc.) *of* the same thing. In the course of alteration they all play their role as exhibitings, now being interrupted, now beginning again; they offer many types of manifolds of exhibitings, appearances, each of which functions precisely as an exhibiting *of*. In running their course they function in such a way as to form a sometimes discrete synthesis of identification or, better, of *unification*. This happens not as a blending of externals; rather, as bearers of "sense" in each phase, as meaning something, the perspectives combine in an advancing *enrichment of meaning* and a *continuing development of meaning*, such that what no longer appears is still valid as retained [i.e., retention] and such that the prior meaning which anticipates a continuous flow, the expectation of "what is to come," [i.e., protention] is straightway fulfilled and more closely determined. Thus, everything is taken up into the unity of validity or into the *one, the* thing. (1970:158, italics in original)

Merleau-Ponty discusses this issue as follows:

> The present still holds on to the immediate past without positing it as an object, and since the immediate past similarly holds its immediate predecessor, past time is wholly collected up and grasped in the present. The same is true of the imminent future which will also have its horizon of imminence. But with my immediate past I have also the horizon of futurity which surrounded it, and thus I have my actual present seen as the future of that past. With the imminent future, I have the horizon of past which will surround it, and therefore my actual present as the past of that future. Thus, through the double horizon of retention and protention, my present may cease to be a factual present quickly carried away and abolished by the flow of duration, and become a fixed and identifiable point in objective time. (Merleau-Ponty 1962:69)

There are therefore at least two ways to understand the horizons of retention and protention in the experience of a "now." First, as made clear in the Husserl quotation, the "now" as usually experienced is located within a temporal flow associated with an object of consciousness. Previous phenomena associated with this object, and associated with it as exhibitings "of" this object, are in one sense lost to the past as soon as they arise, but in another sense they are "taken-up" and synthesized with ongoing phenomena, new exhibitings of this object, which is the "index," as Husserl calls it, of the correlation of perspective-specific experiences. In the flow of time about the experience of a durating object, new possible phenomena are protended as well.

The Merleau-Ponty quotation provides the other major way to understand retention and protention. To be in a state of perception, to experience a durating object before consciousness, is not only to be aware of an object but to be aware that you are aware of it. And this means that we are aware both of the object and of this object as distinguished from a brief period just gone by that is retained within the single experience of the object "now." I notice a pen on my desk but as I am aware of it I am also aware of a moment just gone by when it (must have) appeared to me. There was a first moment of simple awareness and a second moment of awareness of being-aware-of-the-pen. This reflection occurs every time we think of the now or discuss it. It is an objectification of something prior and the structures of retention and protention enter essentially into this objectification.

Retention as Absence and the Sign Structure of Experience

Derrida works within the general framework that produced these conclusions to take matters in a very different direction. The "now" experience of this pen does not retain anything, is not the result of any process of "taking up"; it rather symbolizes an absent moment. It "stands for" an experience just gone by in which the pen first appeared to me. It is thus itself like a "sign." What Husserl called "retention" is really absence. What we mean by the "now" is corrupted by the trace of something no longer "now"; something that *is* not now.

Husserl thought of signs in terms of the difference between an experience of presence ("real presence," complicated by his interpretive notion of facticity and his two-level theory of consciousness) and the presence of a sign to consciousness that represents (in German, *vorstelle*) this originary experience. Objects are revealed to consciousness through such originary experiences, experiences of "real presence," which then can be represented with signs (language, symbols, images). Moreover, at the heart of any stable object of knowledge is the possibility of limitlessly repeating its representation, its sign, with each such repetition standing for the "same" thing—the object. The concept of form, then, is that of a stable thing, available to originary experience taking place in a "now." The "now" is always inhabited by forestructures of retention and protention, and any sign that represents the object could in principle be repeated an infinite number of times, with the stability of the object in the experienced "now" grounding each repetition. The objectivity of form is related to the indefinite number of possible repetitions that could be made of its representations. Each repetition of the sign means the same thing because of this ground: the stability of the object (referent) given immediately through real presence.

Derrida indicates the reversal this logic takes when retention is conceived of in terms of absence:

> With the difference between real presence and presence in representation as *Vorstellung*, a whole system of differences involved in language is implied in the same deconstruction: the differences between the represented and the representative in general, the signified and signifier, simple presence and its reproduction, presentation as *Vorstellung*, re-presentation as *Vergegenwartigung*, for what is represented in the re-presentation is a presentation (*Prasentation*) as *Vorstellung*. We thus come—against Husserl's express intention—to make the *Vorstellung* itself, and as such, depend on the possibility of re-presentation (*Vergegenwartigung*). The presence-of-the-present is derived from repetition and not the reverse. While this is against Husserl's express intention, it does take into account what is implied by his description of the movement of temporalization.... (Derrida 1973:52, italics in original).

Thus it is repetition that constitutes the present and not the reverse, given the understanding of retention and protention as genuine absence inhabiting the present. Instead of retention and protention taking their meaning from a form that is always the same, retention and protention force the reconceptualization of form as the product of repetition. Form itself, and not the signs that represent it, is an effect of repetition. Form, which was first conceived within this framework as something fundamentally distinguished from signs, as the prerequisite of signs, now seems to have a sign structure. About retention and protention Derrida writes:

> One then sees quickly that the presence of the perceived present can appear as such only inasmuch as it is *continuously compounded* with a nonpresence and nonperception, with primary memory and expectation (retention and protention). These nonperceptions are neither added to, nor do they *occasionally* accompany, the actually perceived now; they are essentially and indispensably involved in its possibility. Husserl admittedly says that retention is still a perception. But this is the absolutely unique case—Husserl never recognized any other—of a perceiving in which the perceived is not a present but a past existing as a modification of the present. (Derrida 1973:64, italics in original)

In this passage Derrida is insisting that Husserl's own insights regarding the horizons of retention and protention in the "now" will undermine Husserl's general view of originary experience and the way in which signs then represent originary experiences.[9] He continues:

---

[9] It is interesting that highly objectivistic explorations of the nature of consciousness lead to similar conclusions but fail to apply their conclusions to their own mode of analysis. In *Bright Air, Brilliant Fire* (1992), Gerald M. Edelman calls upon his several decades of experience as a neuroscientist to develop what is basically an objectivist theory of mind, even though he claims explicitly that his theory is not objectivist. He distinguishes between "primary consciousness"—consciousness that is unmediated by structures of time, of anticipation, and of retention—from "higher order consciousness" in which time and self-consciousness play a constitutive role. Once the latter has evolved it is impossible to reach the former, impossible to experience primary consciousness again although its nature is taken up, transformed, and implicitly referenced within higher order consciousness. Thus Edelman uses the term "remembered present" to refer to consciousness through an insight that parallels those of Derrida and the phenomenologists.

> As soon as we admit this continuity of the now and the not-now, perception and nonperception, in the zone of primordiality common to primordial impression and primordial retention, we admit the other into the self-identity of the *Augenblick* [the blink of an eye, the "now"]; nonpresence and nonevidence are admitted into the *blink of the instant*. There is a duration to the blink, and it closes the eye. This alterity is in fact the condition for presence, presentation, and thus for *Vorstellung* [representation] in general; it precedes all the dissociations that could be produced in presence, in *Vorstellung*. ... Once again, this relation to nonpresence neither befalls, surrounds, nor conceals the presence of the primordial impression; rather it makes possible its ever renewed upsurge and virginity. However, it radically destroys any possibility of a simple self-identity. And this holds in depth for the constituting flux itself. (Derrida 1973:65-6, italics in original)

The Trace as a (Non)concept

"Presence" is conditioned by repetition, sign-like repetitions, and not the reverse. The reverse case, I remind the reader, was the view that originary experiences of objects in a present "now" are the condition for an indefinite repetition of signs, each of which stands for the "same" object. Derrida reversed the conclusion by arguing that retention and protention refer to actual absence within any "now," altering our idea of an object of experience so that it becomes like a sign, a symbol of what is no longer. Thus, phenomenological efforts to explain form as the result of originary experiences in which a genuine present reveals an object to us without mediation produce a logic that undermines itself. Such originary objects turn out to be "traces" of something already past. Something like "the trace" would have to replace primordial presence as an originary concept.

But concepts themselves are framed against this belief in uncorrupted "nows," are themselves a product of the metaphysics of presence. Concepts are constructed against "thingness" which is itself rooted in a scene of primordial presence. Thus Derrida tells us not to substitute "trace" or any of his other core terms ("differance," "arche-writing") for traditional Western concepts that are used to represent a ground for knowledge. In *Of Grammatology* he writes:

Four Scenes 161

> The trace is not only the disappearance of origin—within the discourse that we sustain and according to the path that we follow it means that the origin did not even disappear, that it was never constituted except reciprocally by a nonorigin, the trace, which thus becomes the origin of the origin. From then on, to wrench the concept of the trace from the classical scheme, which would derive it from a presence or from an originary nontrace and which would make of it an empirical mark, one must indeed speak of an originary trace or arche-trace. Yet we know that that concept destroys its name and that, if all begins with the trace, there is above all no originary trace. (Derrida 1974:61)

This is to say, minimally, that the essential idea carried by Derrida's use of "trace" erases or cancels out any explication of what it is in words. Closer examination of Husserl's term "retention" gave us the representation of an "actual absence" instead of a past "taken up" within the present. The representation of this actual absence is the trace of what is already gone. But these new concepts, absence and trace, appear only within Husserl's original forestructures and they implode those forestructures as soon as they appear. To assert that there is a trace is finally to proclaim an arche-trace; a concept that erases its name(s).

Then What Does It Mean to Feel That One Has Understood Derrida?

The notion of an idea whose expression in words must erase itself, of a concept that "destroys its name," dovetails with some of the points made in the previous section on meaningful action phenomenologically considered. I shall try to show this through a list of items:

1) When we feel confident that we "understand" what Derrida is doing with his term "trace," we feel we have mastered a repeatable project. Derrida usually calls this project "deconstruction." But Derrida also tells us that this project will always erase any name given to it. That is to say, our understanding of "trace" symbolizes an *implicitly* understood project that can be employed to undermine any name given to it as well as employed for other

purposes. It is rather like the knowledge we have of walking. We feel confident that we can walk—we have walked frequently in the past and we are confident that we can repeat the project of walking indefinitely in the future—but it is futile to try to explain precisely how we do it. We lift one foot, set it down and then lift the other. But how do we lift our feet? Knowing-how cannot always be perfectly translated into symbolic knowledge. Knowing-how is often only demonstrable. The best way to explain walking is to demonstrate walking.

Deconstruction is a form of knowing-how. It cannot be perfectly translated into symbolic knowledge. It can only be demonstrated. Moreover it is a special kind of know-how that immediately destroys any sign fashioned to represent it. As soon as we refer to "it" in any way we also indicate our ability to undermine any representation of it, including prelinguistic but conceptual representations. "It" cannot really be "an it." Deconstruction, trace, differance, arche-writing, absence, are all self-destroying concepts we could call "(non)concepts." Since a nonconcept is unavoidably a concept, the immediate self-contradiction is captured with this logism. Derrida often drew lines through words to produce the same effect. The trace is that ~~concept~~ that destroys ~~its name~~.

To understand Derrida is to have certain action impeti on hand. I use the terms "project" and "direction of activity" instead of "impetus" because this understanding is that of a series of activities whose sequential relationships are holistically, implicitly grasped. An understanding of this particular sense of "trace" is a sort of grand impetus. To understand "trace," "arche-writing," "differance" is to have an implicit and holistic understanding of how to write or talk in certain (implicitly understood) contexts toward certain (implicitly understood) ends. It is a matter of being able to act rather than a matter of correctly representing something with theory.

2) Since this is an implicit, holistic understanding, it is not something "present" to us with certainty; it is rather a symbol that points ahead toward activity that would have to be acted out to

increase any certainty associated with it. It is a sort of confidence that we could respond to the formulations of others, or to our own formulations, in a certain (deconstructive) manner without understanding beforehand just precisely how each response would take shape.

3) Although only a few words are used by Derrida to indicate this understanding (trace, differance, arche-writing, deconstruction), these words "stand for" their own inability to stand for the understanding. Similarly, in terms of meaningful action impeti generally, once an impetus has been objectified to the slightest extent, say as an image of barest form, its origin has already vanished. "It" has been occulted by its objectification. By the time we get to a word, from the evolution of an impetus, we have simply built up a series of symbols of symbols. Before the word are preobjective (evolving-objective) marks which have interpreted or have taken the impetus in just one of many possible directions. "Understanding" an impetus to act includes the difference between the understanding and the impetus, the latter being an unreachable vanishing point. "Understanding" the term arche-trace, and so forth, is much the same.

4) As stated already, the implicit, holistic understanding is not a form of certain knowledge. It points ahead. It waits to be acted out. Our understanding of "trace," "differance," and so on, is like an anticipation of activity and its consequences. But what it points toward is a vanishing point. Like all impeti to act, "doing" deconstruction does not leave one with a sense of certainty. At best, doing deconstruction or doing the arche-trace gives us a brief period in which an idea has been demonstrated, but all one is left with is the feeling that one could do "it," or something like it, yet again.

5) So the notion of a point ahead, and this point ahead being a vanishing point, is intrinsic to Derrida's idea of the "trace." My phenomenological analysis of meaningful action seems to have stumbled upon insights that parallel those of Derrida, though my

investigations are far less penetrating and far less subtle than are those of this great thinker. The parallels, however, are important for they offer the possibility of bringing some of the power of Derrida's thought to an area of interest that differs from those he has chosen to explore. Deconstruction has something to offer the phenomenology of meaningful action.

6) To remain with this effort to display parallels between Derrida's deconstruction of "form and the flux" and my own phenomenological sketch of meaningful action, let us ask what the "point behind" might be when the impetus to act is termed "arche-trace." Here the special feature of Derrida's core terms come to light for us. In the case of "trace," "arche-trace," "arche-writing" and so on, the point behind is *the same* as the point ahead. Derrida has demonstrated the trace through the general project of following any form backward phenomenologically. The "trace" is what we always come to, with any experience of an object, with any impetus to act, when we subject such forms of experience to phenomenological investigation. But Derrida's core terms have the special property of being about (i.e., pointing ahead toward) the very process of acting and representing (pointing back toward). The "trace" is our understanding of a vanishing point behind and a vanishing point ahead unified. One could thus substitute "self-reference" for "trace" in many contexts of discussion, and could throw much light on the difficulties of self-reference in doing so.

Juxtaposing the Phenomenology of Action and Its Deconstruction

This discussion of scene one, the scene of form and the flux, plays *for and against* the earlier phenomenological sketch in the following ways.

First, it illuminates the strategy used in the phenomenological sketch. This strategy could be called "stretching" the phenomenology of action against the limits of scene one as much as possible. Instead of examining objects present to consciousness, I discussed "preobjects"; feeling configurations. These were described, furthermore, not as objects in immediate relation to consciousness but rather as symbols of symbols. Scene one is thus qualified and stretched by my phenomenological investigation of meaningful acts in important ways. But after the above discussion of form and the flux we can see that the core concepts employed, the primary imagery, are of the scene one variety just the same.

Second, Derrida's work alters our mode of awareness of the points made in the phenomenological sketch. These can now be understood as self-referring. When I write about the "symbol of the symbol" and about the "feeling configuration" I am writing about experiences and understandings that include their own deconstruction as written, as acted out. That is, the entire phenomenological sketch of meaningful acts can now be taken as a way to introduce certain iterable but implicit understandings to the reader. The entire sketch could be taken to be something like "indirect teaching" (Kierkegaard 1941) that always runs the risk of becoming reified. It is only a mode of awareness that can save us from the reification and by placing this discussion of scene one next to the phenomenological sketch, an alteration in awareness is sought.

Third, the phenomenology of meaningful acts juxtaposed with its deconstruction expand the terms used by Derrida from specialized, third person style terms useful for philosophers and literary critics who must concern themselves with the impulse of great authors and thinkers to totalize knowledge. These terms expand to include a popularized context into which all people enter with every act. Another way to say this is to say that the phenomenology of meaningful action, considered alongside its deconstruction, introduces one to an ontology of social life. This is an ontology of social life that must be implicitly understood. It must be an ontology from which to act rather than an ontology that describes in objective form the fundamental structures of being. Yet another way to say this is to say that these two discussions juxtaposed provide insights into the nature of body feeling and desire that connect these to an ontology of existence. This is an ontology of existence that must be implicitly grasped as an iterable understanding. Scene two, in fact, will be an effort to demonstrate this last formulation.

Repetition versus Recollection

Another angle on this problematic has been developed by John Caputo, who exploits Kierkegaard's contrast between "recollection" and "repetition" (Caputo 1987). Caputo demonstrates the way in which the concept of "repetition" first arises in a postmodernist manner with Kierkegaard, who criticized Western modes of knowledge as being efforts to effect a grand recollection of what has already passed. Such efforts lead the philosopher, argued Kierkegaard, to "forget himself [sic]" and attempt to escape existence in an identification with the abstract formulations of his or her philosophy.

Choosing to exist, instead of trying to escape existence, requires an acceptance of repetition as opposed to an effort to fix existence objectively in a recollection. In repetition we "act again" in light of our "infinite interest" in existence and the knowledge that we have no formulated grounds for claiming our existence in each act. Each act is an existential risk.

Recollection attempts to avoid the risks and the suspicion of a lack of ground that existing necessarily involves. Recollection tries to objectify what cannot be objectified: ongoing, uncertain existence.

For phenomenologists, recollection has a primordial and non-reflective form in the structure of retention that accompanies every "now." Husserl believed, as indicated in a quotation from Derrida above, that recollection as retention is a unique form of perception.

But Derrida denies this manner of conceiving it: recollection is simply impossible if it is conceived to be a re-presentation or conceived in any way that makes something genuinely past part of a purely given present. Recollections are simply a particular mode of repetition that correspond to a particular cluster of desires and fears. Recollecting is thus partly constructing anew. It is impossible to glance backward in a pure sense; one always moves ahead. We will encounter the distinction between repetition and recollection again in scenes two and three.

ORIGINARY SCENE TWO: THE FEELING-BODY

The remarks made about proprioceptive configurations in the phenomenological sketch of meaningful action suggest the scene of the feeling-body. Proprioceptive configurations are discovered when one considers the impetus to act as it appears within the awareness of the first person: the actor. However, this scene of the feeling-body could also have been suggested had I spent more time on modes through which one receives impressions of meaning when in the second or third person position. The posture of a body, a gesture, tensed facial muscles all convey meaning. Some ethnographies that make use of the concept of embodied meaning work primarily with this second/third person perspective on the feeling-body.[10] However, for our purposes the scene of the feeling-body is best opened as a scene of proprioception and therefore as a first person scene.

Before proceeding with an extensive investigation of the feeling-body let me note that one could in principle frame one's considerations of it through the problem of perception. Careful investigation of perception reveals its constructed nature: its dependence on repeated mental acts in order to maintain the suggestion of a form present to the senses in time. If I turn my head to gaze at what is to my side I first experience a visual field that is not in focus. I must "look again" to bring focus, which is a mental act. Looking again, however, will not in itself bring out a visual object with duration; it will bring out an impetus to act once more in relation to a foregrounded portion of the visual field. The "object" in this foregrounded position is one portion of a new impetus to act: its "object pole." The impetus to act yet again could be one in which words for the object pole are brought into consciousness, an internalized discursive articulation of what is there. Or it could be a project for moving the eyes about other

---

[10] See *Schooling as a Ritual Performance* by Peter McLaren (1993), in which body postures are noted as representative of normative "states." That is, patterns of posturing and gesturing are indicative of distinctive, routinely established, normative realms within which particular types of social action are displayed. McLaren has perceptively spotted the holistic, implicit modes of meaning within both static and active positions of the body.

portions of the visual field, following some of its lines and surfaces in a patterned manner without bringing words to mind. Either way the object has duration in experience only as a portion of a series of action impeti.

Instead of bringing out the object as one portion of a related set of action impeti, one could notice that body feelings are associated with the foregrounded portion of the visual field. "Sharp" objects may bring (and do for me) certain sensations to the eye region. Smooth objects may be associated with smooth sensations in the hands, face, or trunk of the body. Any project associated with the object pole, a project of bringing a series of words to mind that describe its features for an imaginary audience or a project of moving one's attention about the visual field, will be associated with alterations in body sensations.

Thus, without mental movement there is no form in time, and such movement is associated with body-feelings. Because "mental movement" consists of action impeti and because such impeti occur in holistic figurations felt within the body, one could even explore the idea that perception is "grounded" in body sensations. What is "primordial" in perception is the coordination of activities that differentiate an object pole rather than the object pole itself, and such coordinated projects of activity take holistic forms in body sensation.

So movement and feeling seem to go together and both are important for a prolonged perception. Feeling is rooted in the body, always correlated with a localized proprioceptive configuration. I could consider the proprioceptive configuration, rather than the image, the central differentiation that brings out the foregrounded visual object and thus arrive at a scene of the feeling-body instead of the scene of form and flux. Body feeling, rather than form, could be taken as the frame for the meaning problematic as given through prioritizing perception.

An approach like this, moreover, could begin with primary texts in phenomenology and expand on certain insights found there. Husserl, in *The Crisis of European Sciences and Transcendental Phenomenology*, wrote that all perception of objects correlates to kinesthetic sensations in the "living body" (1970:106-7). One could exploit his limited focus on kinesthetic, as opposed to proprioceptive, body sensation and his limited conception of action as goal-rational action, excluding its normative and dramaturgical forms. From here, the phenomenology of perception could be brought around, in its own terms, toward the feeling-body.

However, because of the complex relationship between proprioceptions (body feelings) and the I-feeling, I find a second road to scene two more fruitful. This road begins with proprioception itself, rather than perception.

Approaching the Body-Feeling from Proprioception

We shall need an exercise that works directly with proprioception: body awareness.

The Exercise

Imagine lying on your back in a very relaxed state. You relax out of a mode of conceptual thinking to become aware of your body, how it feels. You notice that certain muscles are rather tight. You have been carrying some tension without fully realizing it. You relax the tense areas, which is rather like "letting go" of the tension. Visual imagery may accompany this: tightness (proprioception) and opacity (visual imagery) together arise as the forms that represent an area of tension. Letting it go is first felt. Then it is represented by a spreading of opacity occurring "on its own," merging with areas nearby so that more and more homogeneity is felt in the body. The image of the abstract "field," "energy field," emerges to represent this: a field with different degrees of opacity that become more even in density and sensation as you relax more and more. The body is a field of sensation that becomes more and more homogeneous as you relax.

Now you run your awareness gently from your toes up through your whole body, slowly, until you reach the top of your head, "letting go" every place you discover tension. Then back down. Temptations to think will arise but you must let these go and remember to stay with your body-feeling, over and over again. Moving awareness about the body is the way to stay with it. You are approaching homogeneity, a *single* sensation that encompasses the entire body. This is entirely possible and is experienced by those who practice deep relaxation and/or meditation.

A single body sensation. It feels very good. It is a form of pleasure. But the mind has to keep moving to remain with proprioception, rather than wander off with thoughts, and you decide to keep the mental movement with what you represented as "letting go," and "opening." You must let go of pleasure to stay with proprioception. Temptations to think keep arising but you let them go. Temptations to barely note the pleasurable feelings arise and you let them go. They, you understand, would soon lead to thinking.

The single sensation seems to be associated with a single process. Actively undifferentiating, letting go, keeps what normally differentiates as "subjectivity" very close to the object: body-feeling.

Single Sensation as the "I-Feeling"

A new series of tempting thoughts begin to present themselves: thoughts *about* what is happening. You have the thought, for example, that you *are* the feeling-body that you have actively undifferentiated. This thought arises because there does seem to be an I-feeling that fuses with the body feeling when you are letting go instead of thinking. Your thought, actually, is that you *could* be the single homogeneous body sensation if only you could "get there"; if you could only remain undifferentiated as a subjectivity, a totally implicit "I," a single sensation of I-ness and body together. But this thought is based on a differentiation. Even when you are able to "let go" of such temptations before they delineate into actual thought, your awareness of this possibility, that you are the feeling-body and would know it if only you could "get there," let go "enough," is always ahead of itself. It is based on a distinction between experience and awareness of experience that is your movement in time or that perhaps makes time.

You continue this movement for a while: a single sensation that feels good and feels as if it is "you"; awareness that that is what just *was*, that you were in that state but could only have some cognizance of it through difference, through being aware of it as object, and then returning to single sensation by letting go. The primordial rhythm, the primordial repetition, is suggested as: sensation inclusive of "I-feeling," awareness of this, letting go, repeated awareness of sensation as inclusive of "I-feeling," and so on. The rhythm has three primordial moments.

Representation as Desire

Now another very tempting thought arises. You are not the single sensation of body awareness from which you seem to come and toward which you seem to go, but you are a single *process* of letting go. Or you are both, or are the play between the two. You are aware of yourself as a single sensation without differentiation, except that there is always the differentiation of awareness from sensation. Yet this differentiation of awareness from sensation is always responded to by a "letting go" that is like "opening." Over and over. It occurs to you that part of the process is learning to respond in *one* way, in the same way, to your own representation of it, again and again. The process is a single thing, like a single way of responding to "your self." But you have to remember this one response, and yet you cannot hold on to the memory of it because you cannot maintain the differentiation required to retain a memory. You cannot formulate it, or otherwise represent it, without breaking out of the rhythm. So it is not exactly *you* who always responds in the same way, it is rather a way of being open to having something *given* to you over and over again. And it is like "finding yourself," more than constructing yourself or being yourself, over and over again.

Several things stand out that may be formulated as a list:

1) It makes sense to think of "responding to your self," or responding to the representation of yourself, as an "I-feeling" that arises. (This insight will occur again against a new scene, scene three, and have expanded significance there.)

2) "Remembering" is important. The response to the representation "single embodied sensation" must be "the same" each

time and it must be a "letting go" or "opening." Because you cannot hold on to a formulation of this same way of responding to yourself, "remembering" simply must occur over and over again. It must come to be part of the awareness-of that comes and goes.

3) "Finding," "being given," "letting happen" all also make sense. The experience is given, not willed or constructed, when you remember to be open, or to let go. It makes sense to describe part of it as having its own agency, which you simply allow to take place.

4) Your experience of thinking as temptation takes on added significance. The representation "single sensation" is tempting because it is not a neutral representation of something conceived to be an object, but is a *desire*, and a forestructure. The single sensation is the representation and a feeling at the same time. In particular, it feels good, it is a pleasure. But in addition, this pleasure points beyond itself: on the one hand toward greater pleasure, toward its indefinite intensification, an intensification of the sensation via letting go again;[11] on the other hand toward a lot of exciting thoughts, if you do not let go but rather try to draw some conclusions from your experience. To yield to either desire is to forget to let go. Thinking is indeed a temptation for it leads away from the experience and from the goal toward which the experience points. It is a way of acting from a forestructure. Becoming excited about more intense pleasure turns into a lack of genuine "letting go," for it amounts to an effort at retaining pleasure or at retaining a conception (forestructure) of what is ahead; both of which must go.

5) So desire appears here in a primordial, undifferentiated form as representation. Representation is an impetus to act; here to "act in thought." As soon as you have a representation of the sensation you have an impetus to hold on to pleasure, or to think about the

---

[11] This experience of pleasure and the promise of an indefinite extension of pleasure is well known to yogis and meditators. It is described in Ajaya 1978.

Four Scenes 173

experience which offers its own pleasures. The representation is totally prefocal; it is structured by a bare differentiation between passive sensation and responding impetus.

6) Desire seems to give birth to time. It differentiates from what just was and it points toward what could be. But desire seems to simply come; it is not willed or chosen. You learned how to stay open and not act, and this led to a rhythm: sensation, desire, sensation; which is also, sensation, representation of sensation, sensation; which is also sensation, awareness of sensation, sensation.

7) Desire is contradictory. The rhythm "sensation, desire, sensation" always seems to result in an intensification of "sensation" in its third phase. And this points toward a grand experience of pleasure: of total sensation, or total merger in sensation to come. It is as if the forestructures of desire are accumulating each time you let one go. If you can just stay with it all and keep letting go,[12] the grand experience may come. But desire appears as the second phase. A sort of choice is there: one can either let go or surrender to an action impetus (a thought). When one is cognizant of the teleology of the experience—the pointing toward a grand experience just ahead—one wishes to act *for* this. But one must remember not to act toward this telos if one is to move closer to it. The desire for the end point must be totally given up every time it arises as a second moment in the rhythm, if one is to make any progress toward what the desire promises. And giving up is what makes the third moment a more intense sensation of pleasure, pointing ever more clearly toward a consummate pleasure. Letting go is what allows the forestructures to accumulate; the implicit portions of each anticipation seem to contain more and more possibilities. Thus the situation is

---

[12] Various meditation techniques exist to help the meditator "let go." Mantras are a common technique to this end. Repetition of a mantra requires letting go of desires: letting go of the desire to hold on to a pleasurable feeling as well as letting go of the desire to begin thinking about the experiences one is having.

contradictory. To have what is desired and anticipated one must let go of desire.

8) Letting go results in a repetition. It results in the repetition of (i) sensation, (ii) awareness-of-sensation, (iii) letting-go, (iv) intensified-sensation. It is not a repeated "act" because the only agency involved is the choice not to act, "letting go." This allows an anonymous repetition to act of itself; a sort of vibration that throws one out in the second phase ("awareness of") but waits for one to fall back in.

Intensification of Desire

The single sensation intensifies and it gets harder to keep from thinking, to keep letting go, to keep opening, because the potential thoughts seem increasingly important, increasingly tempting. The pleasure is related to the I-feeling. The I-feeling appears in pleasurable modes of desire, as foreunderstandings of how the I-feeling could be fixed and enhanced by the articulation of its nature. The temptation to think increasingly becomes a temptation to think about the process that is occurring, a promise that doing so would reveal the secret of the "I," that would affirm the self in an infinite and incontestable way. Yet this exercise has taught you that an even greater promise of articulating the "I" will occur, in a pleasurable and intensified way, if you let go rather than articulate the tempting forestructures. The exercise is increasingly becoming something that fundamentally concerns you and your most exciting, promising, existentially basic desires.

You notice that each new temptation, each new impetus to represent and claim the "I" in an articulation, is a recollection of what has just occurred. You think that you are the process of letting go from recollection of the process. Your identity rests between this split between sensation and awareness of sensation that repeats. You have represented this as "process," as "letting go again and again and again," as a rhythm or vibration. As a process it is caught in time but you think that the secret of time is getting close to your understanding. It is a repetition that you must allow to exist. Your only "act" is to relax away from all temptations to act. The movement simply is. Time is close to collapsing because there is just one thing, a process, which, however, keeps making two things and from these two, many possible things. It is an eternal now, just one thing, but it eludes you. By opening, letting go, over and over you feel you are moving toward the total now, the eternal now, the consummation of a primordial desire.

Accumulative Incorporation of Forestructures and Self-Reference

So the intensification of desire is also an intensification of sensation, of pleasure. And this is because desire is a mode of I-feeling, a state that in this case is at once pleasurable and yet a pointing forward toward more. As a state of pointing forward, the I-feeling mode is fused with a forestructure to recollect what just was. But you have learned to let go of recollecting in order to allow the repetition to repeat itself. When it repeats you have an intensified sensation and a new desire to recollect. The new forestructures incorporate older forestructures; assimilate the newly given sensation of I-ness as the result of a letting go of a prior forestructure to recollect. Forestructures seem to accumulate, potentialities seem to assimilate previous potentialities.

The intensification of desire and pleasure, you realize in another indulgent thought, involves the concept of the "limit": the idea of capturing an infinite process in a singular representation that is also the end or goal of the infinite process. The process is infinite. It is an infinite letting go of temptations to think that have increasingly become temptations to think about or recollect the process itself. The goal of the process is felt as a desire; a feeling of pleasure that promises more. The goal is thus not known, the desire not fulfilled, when one is within the state of desire. The goal is yet to come and is felt this way. But since the secret of the experience lies in repetition, would not formulating the rule of the repetition give us the goal in conceptual form?

For example, we might say that what is occurring is something like a mathematical series that goes on forever by repeating the same rule. But by not articulating this foreunderstanding we are applying this very same "rule" (letting go) to itself, to a fore-conception of itself, an implicit representation of itself. And this suggests an infinite series of letting go of the concept of an infinite series. Not an infinite process of letting go of the same foreunderstanding of an infinite series, but a process in which one locates an I-feeling mode within an infinite series of repeated openings ("letting goes"), and then lets go of this articulation to include the prior location of self within an infinite series that is within yet another infinite series of letting go that is orthogonal to the first. This in turn is let go of to result in yet another series inclusive of all prior series and orthogonal to them.

I realize that my spatial imagery might be confusing; the imagery of series along axes orthogonal to each other. Another way to represent this is to think of it as a series of reflections that continuously objectify what was taken for granted and unnoticed in the previous moment. The image of the rhythm is an objectification of what has been happening in time; an objectification suggestive of a linear movement with "letting go" a crucial process for moving from one phase of the linear rhythm to the next. Once conceptualized as a rhythm, a temporal process is encapsulated in one image. The objectification was a recollection that gave an image to represent what had been taking place before. It was an act of recollection, involving forestructures to bring out the form "rhythmic linear process." But then this conceptualization, "the rhythm," may also be "let go." This is the shift from one axis to another that is orthogonal to the first. It is a letting go of the whole process or rhythm. Yet this too can be objectified, or recollected and then let go to produce a new series. The image of the rhythm represents a process that can be applied to itself, much in the way that the movement from point to point along a line can be applied to the line itself, generating movement along a plane.

Through this you (we) keep finding hints of something "that is the same." What is it? It could be the process of letting go, so that we are letting go of letting go of letting go. ... Or it could be the rhythm produced by this letting go, and that includes the moment of letting go within its moments. Then this rhythm begins to be a rhythm of rhythms.

Perhaps what is the same is neither the letting go nor the resulting rhythm but the movement from one dropped forestructure to the next. This movement is understood to be infinite, in that it repeats over and over again, representing itself in forestructures of articulation that each time include prior forestructures.

Oh, but how to really grasp that eternal movement? How to really represent it? It is not the I-feeling mode, for that only appears when one has moved away from an impetus to articulate it as incorporated. It is not the "letting go," for that also depends upon the impetus to recollect, which must be dropped.

Each infinite series amounts to the projecting behind of the impetus to represent, and the projecting ahead of this same impetus, which is more and more like a project from which many impeti would differentiate were one to indulge in thinking. Each infinite series points behind toward a vanishing point and ahead toward a vanishing point. What remains the same is given over and over again outside of any representation, any feeling-configuration, any impetus. It was always "just there" and "just there again." But it cannot be pinned down. It is the movement implicated by the continuous rise of new modes of desire that we understand to be the goal of the movement itself but that seem to never actually "appear" before us, even though the forestructures promise ever more convincingly to possess a grasp of it all. It cannot appear before us and we even understand this, experience forestructures that try to pin it down by promising to explicate (pin down) the impossibility of pinning it down.

At any rate, successful series of letting go do not result in indulgent thoughts like those just articulated above. But they do result in a building of body sensations, a building of the energies in your feeling-body, to an intolerable potential. At some point you have to act, you cannot let go any longer, and you realize that you already are acting by thinking about this experience: recollecting it and representing it and making conclusions from it. In doing so, you have lost it.

Representation as "Flattening"

Your last tempting thought was that you are the single process-of-body-feeling-and-letting-that-go-moving-toward-an-ending-state-which-is-an-understanding-of-the-process-itself. You are the movement that never takes a form. Yet this movement is also given to you just as much as it is you. It is infinitely you, infinitely other than you.

Long ago in the period of this exercise, your representations of singularity hovered about "single embodied sensation." Now this has become "single process-of-body-feeling-and-letting-that-go." This representation, it occurs to you, is sort of like "flattening" process into form. That is, it is a grand recollection, a single idea that seems to fully capture a primordial temporal process plus all forms that implicate it, and thus it is a grand recollection that almost escapes temporal process by grasping it as a singularity. There is just "one thing," and it is eternal, and it is you, and it is all else as well. All possibilities are contained in it but you have recognized all possibilities as temptations or desires, and have returned them to the "one" by letting go over and over again. Because you could "think," "represent," the infinite over-and-over you have finally "grasped it," that is, grasped "It," that is, "made it like a thing." You have flattened an infinite process differentiated through an infinite number of self-reflective moves, each one of which incorporated those previous to it into a single idea.

"Wow!" you think, "I could construct a whole philosophy from this! I could apply the metaphors of (a) always being beyond myself, (b) embodied meaning which always moves outside its embodiment, (c) truth as a single thing that implicitly holds everything within it, (d) meaning as desire, (e) the teleology of meaning-as-desire—its pointing toward a single thing or experience, (f) this single experience ahead being its own movement toward itself! I could apply these metaphors to all sorts of things! Isn't such a flattening, the representation of a process as a single thing that in turn is this very process, rather like what Hegel was doing with *Geist*?" *Geist* is the product of an effort to flatten process into thing. *Geist* is supposed to be the primordial "thing" outside of time that unfolds to create time only so that it might then come back to itself. *Geist* is inclusive of the understanding that formulations like "*Geist*" are not what it is. *Geist* is not really a "thing."

Hegel must have understood this. On the other hand, in trying to write it down he perhaps betrayed a merely partial understanding of it, or perhaps an indulgence. Was not his philosophy just a grandiose identity claim, as Kierkegaard suspected? But then Kierkegaard wrote lots of books too! One can in fact never know whether another has grasped this insight or not, nor to what extent. As Gayatri Spivak writes in her introduction to Derrida's *Of Grammatology*; "Perhaps this entire argument hangs on who *knew* how much of what he was doing. The will to knowledge is not easy to discard" (1974:xxxviii, italics in original). The will to knowledge is a form of the will to exist; it is a primordial structure of motivation constituting all identity claims. The temptation to stop letting go and start thinking is a version of the "will to knowledge." It is the desire to assert one's self into a world of many not-selves.

If we (I and you) could only write all this down, and of course write it down so thoroughly as to ensure that all our readers will understand us, what a grand thing that would be! How immensely valuable and important our work would be! Yet, because of the impossibility of pure presence, because of the "pre-understanding of subjectivity," because of the sign structure of experience, we never could write it down in such a seamless manner, we never could feel certain that we would be understood by others, and thus, we could never be ourselves certain of these formulations. The will to knowledge is fundamentally futile because it is fundamentally in contradiction with itself.

And, correlatively, by now I (you) have left our single body-feeling far behind by differentiating so much! We have indulged. And we never reached the promised goal intrinsic to the single process and the single sensation. Shucks! We have only indulged in partial forestructures and petty identity claims and the full sense of it all still eludes.

Is This a Legitimate Scene? Should We Take It Seriously?

If the above fantasy seems mystical and improbable it may be only because this fantasy is not the sort of scene that has informed Western academic discourse. The themes raised by this scene are no doubt consistent with the writings of various Western mystics. But mystics are generally discredited by academia in the West. Certainly, the themes raised by this scene do have parallels in the work of Hegel, Kierkegaard, Nietzsche, Heidegger, Sartre, Derrida and other Western thinkers, but generally as they are developed against the scene of form and the flux. The scene of the feeling-body has not yet been thoroughly probed in the way that the scene of visual perception has in the West. But this "fantasy" is no more fantastic than is the scene of flux and form. Actually, for me it is much less fantastic and requires less artificiality than considerations of object perception do. One can have an experience like the one described above by practicing meditation and relaxation techniques.

Moreover, scene two is quite commonly implied in Eastern discourses on knowledge and truth. Yogic meditation is nothing but a way to induce a state similar to that described above. It is a "willed" repetition, usually of a sound (a mantra) that is done in order to achieve the experience of repeated opening—"letting go." Sometimes it is attention to the breath, rather than a mantra, that is used. And Eastern philosophy is absolutely insistent that the vanishing point of the feeling-body is the merging of awareness into a single sensation that implicitly "contains" everything. It is a vanishing point because once entered there is nothing to be said. There is no person who is experiencing, there is no object being experienced, there is no time, there is nothing to represent. It is somehow both the singular Idea (*Geist*) and a primordial void. This is because there is no differentiation within this state. In the East the vanishing point is ahead of experience. It is what "just was," true, but more importantly it is what one is moving toward. And it is completely possible to experience with much effort: effort to learn effortlessness, as the yogis would say. Effort as well to increase one's stamina for containing high levels of "energy." When one has this experience one's personal identity is destroyed;

no memory of the experience can be retained, no words can represent it. One remembers going into it and falling back out, nothing else. It is called samadhi in yogic philosophy, nirvana in Buddhist philosophy. It is said to be an ecstatic and self-transforming state, so that one is altered when one comes back from it (Anandamurti 1968, 1978; Vahiduddin 1974).

This scene has been ignored in mainstream Western discourses but it now seems more legitimate, more credible to Western minds, with the popularity of postmodern thought and its own versions of the concept of "repetition" and "embodied meaning."[13] Kierkegaard's "third stage" of repetition, the stage beyond his esthetic and ethical stages, is really a "waiting for" or "allowing," a repetition that repeats itself (Kierkegaard 1983). It is "letting go," is spiritual surrender. It is related to the concept of "grace" in many religions.

Feeling-Body as Flux

I deliberately used the term "vanishing point" in the section above to display some congruence between scene two and scene one. The problem of "representation" was already made explicit in my discussion of both scenes. Other core terms come up in both scenes as well.

The "flux," for example, can be reconceptualized against the scene of the feeling-body. Here, however, it is tied much more closely to what some Eastern writers call the "I-feeling" or the *mahatatva* (Anandamurti 1968). You are the flux, are the ground, but "you" are more than what you usually think you are in that you are not an entity, not a form, and thus nothing that could be recollected.

In the West, conceptual approaches usually work toward the flux by prioritizing the "object," or form, in experience and then working on the presuppositions and the phenomenological features of object perception. This is done by distilling our recollection of perceptual experience, our representations of it,

---

[13] The body is often described as a layer of mind in yogic philosophy.

away from feelings in the body. Visual perception dominates Western notions of form.

For our purposes, several differences between certain Eastern and many Western writings related to the flux, to the point ahead and the point behind, are worth listing.

1) In the twentieth century, the works of authors like Heidegger and Derrida have come close in the West to convergence with Eastern ideas. But most readings of the work of these authors emphasize the groundlessness of the flux, the erosion of all claims to a certain origin of knowledge and meaning. In much of Eastern thought there is indeed the claim that a "ground" of sorts exists; but it is not a conceptual ground, it is rather an ~~experience~~ (to use Derrida's strategy of *sous rature*; crossing out a name to indicate a self-destroying concept) of what is both prior to and ahead of existence.

2) In the West, scene number one is most often at the root of those theories of meaning that take experience seriously. Scene number one emphasizes the object pole of perception and from there introduces considerations of the subject pole. In the post-structuralist literature, this scene deconstructs. In the East, scene number two is often at the root of theories of meaning. Scene number two is concerned with proprioception rather than with perception: states of awareness in which the "object pole" is not quite yet objective, for it consists of feeling states, I-feeling modes, configurations of desire. This does not exactly lead to a deconstruction, because a ground is suggested for existence even while Eastern philosophers also claim the impossibility of a ground for conceptual certainty.

3) Philosophy in the West has often been a massive effort to recollect and fix truth conceptually in a form objective to consciousness. Recent postmodern "philosophy" takes its sense from the previous centuries of Western philosophy when this project of fixing all truth conceptually was taken seriously. The point of much postmodern work is the deconstruction of the

scenes upon which this effort of grand recollection had been erected. "Philosophy" in the East, or at least much of it, has not tried to recollect and objectively state what is the case, but has rather viewed systematic modes of thought to be nothing more than guides for living, some of which will work better than others, for some groups of people. Philosophy has been viewed as ideology in the East, at times helpful for guiding spiritual practice but always a distortion, always an imperfect map of the structures of existence, and always ultimately discardable.

Recollection in Scene Two
A final contrast between these particular strands of thought in much Eastern philosophy and the logocentric tradition of the West, one important for our discussion of meaning, can be made by looking again at the concept of recollection. For many Eastern philosophers, as for Kierkegaard in the West, recollection, representation of what just was as something that is, amounts to:

a) *a condition of existence*, though one can choose not to invest oneself in it, can choose to let its temptations go

b) *a process always motivated*, the product of some form of desire and/or fear

c) *a process resulting in frustration* because once a state of gratification is reached one becomes aware of it and is thereby beyond it

These aspects of recollection apply whether it is conceived against scene one or scene two. Scene two does not give us a conceptual "ground" for meaning. In fact, the way I have treated scene two works against the notion of "ground." My treatment supports the idea that it is not helpful to think in terms of grounds aside from a state such as that of samadhi—a state that cannot be known unless it is experienced, and once experienced cannot be represented or even remembered in explicit form. The aporias (conceptual *cul de sacs*) that theories of representation encounter make states like samadhi and nirvana seem all the more plausible.

Scene two does suggest that desire is essential to meaning and knowing. And it suggests that desire appears in the body, as a feeling. Desire is by its nature teleological: an impetus to act for a gratification. So we do not have literally a "ground" with the feeling-body but we do, perhaps, have a direction. Scene two does not necessarily result in an existential aporia while it clarifies conceptual aporias. Our analysis of the question of meaning against scene two resulted in the possibility of reconceptualizing what I have called the "vanishing point" as a "limit point" toward which desire aims. I am only indicating that this is possible here, but the fact that it *is* possible is important. By sinking back into the feeling-body, desire arises in holistic and implicit forms that would take more shape if acted upon. But letting go of all such desire, not repressing but letting go, builds and intensifies body feeling and results in an anticipation of a single consummate experience. At the same time this single experience would be an experience of unmediated presence; at the same time this single experience would have no differentiation, not even that between subject and object; at the same time it would be the flux; at the same time it would be genuine certainty; at the same time it would be destruction; at the same time it would be the self-affirmation one always seeks.

For social researchers the significance of scene two does not immediately reside in the sort of totalizing considerations made above. It resides in secondary structures that may be derived from what has been said above. In particular, the existence of what I have called the "identity claim" in all acts of meaning takes much of its sense against the findings made from this discussion of scene two. But that point will be more clear after a discussion of scene three.

Additionally, we have yet to understand what "recollection" consists of. Futile or not, it seems that recollection is a structure of existence central to the question of meaning. Scene three will further illuminate the nature of recollection.

ORIGINARY SCENE THREE: THE ORIGIN OF INTERSUBJECTIVITY

Scene three is a fantasy that begins back in time and then moves suggestively toward us. It is a scene that is traditionally developed outside of twentieth-century style phenomenological investigations, and thus is a scene that begins with more unexamined presuppositions than do scenes one and two. This is both its charm and its weakness. By avoiding the sort of beginnings we made in scenes one and two, which foreground the first person perspective, scene three has given hope to some contemporary thinkers who wish to evade the difficulties involved when one consciousness attempts to know itself through reflection. Scene three, however, is dependent on all the substantial presuppositions of science, those presuppositions that phenomenology specifically problematizes. All originary scenes have presuppositions, just different types, and something like scene three is necessary in efforts to give explanations of various phenomena that can be revealed only through phenomenological analysis.

I will discuss scene three first as it appears in the work of George Herbert Mead and then as it appears in the writings of Georg Hegel. I produce a substantial reinterpretation of George Herbert Mead's theory in what follows, devoting the bulk of my discussion in this section to him. I discuss portions of Hegel's philosophy afterwards, primarily for the sake of insights that are absent in Mead's work.

Scene Three in the Legacy of George Herbert Mead

Scene three is perhaps most persuasively formulated in modern discourses in the work of George Herbert Mead (1967) and those contemporary authors like Jürgen Habermas (1987b, ch. v) and Ernst Tugendhat (1986) who have tightened and improved upon Mead's original insights. The main idea in this work is to begin by accepting the existence of a physical world that exhibits the basic laws and processes we find in nature, including species evolution. Then the way in which consciousness and language might have evolved within a species that lives in groups is considered.

Mead and Hegel approached this problem, which is the phylogenesis of consciousness for Mead and the history of consciousness for Hegel, *dialogically*. Self-consciousness originated in interactions and its basic structures evolved from the basic structures of a dialogue. That is the specific feature that distinguishes this scene from other possible "scientific" sorts of scenes one could imagine (such as those employed by evolutionary biologists, cognitive scientists, and neuroscientists). Something like a scene three mode of investigation does arise in the work of currently popular "consciousness theorists" who, like Mead, find the idea of an organism that learns to stimulate itself through various modes of "talking to itself" unavoidable in efforts to explain thought, the conscious monitoring of action, and the existence (actual or virtual) of selves (e.g., see Dennett 1991: ch. 7). Dialogical theories of thought and consciousness can also be framed as ontogenetic problems and studied through developmental psychology or psychoanalytic theory. However, I will only discuss the phylogenesis of the dialogical mind in this essay and I will only work with Mead's initiating version of it.

In this phylogenetic scene, early forms of interaction, characterized by something like stimulus-response patterns between group members, develop toward symbolic interactions through learning processes. At some stage in this evolutionary process, group members begin to internalize the standard first and second person positions associated with routine interactions. Meaning could not exist as such, according to this view, until an entire species developed learned interactive routines which then become progressively internalized.

Imagine an early human or prehuman species living in groups. Members of a group share a repertoire of routine acts and routine responses to acts emitted by fellow members. This shared repertoire of interactive patterns forms the basis for the emergence of early symbols such that the beginning portion of a shared stimulating action comes to implicitly symbolize the full act and its consequences to organisms in the responding position. Through these early implicit symbols—the beginning portions of routine acts—organisms eventually learn to internalize the associated first and second person positions. That is, they learn to conjoin (or otherwise transpose) their experience of emitting the stimulating act with their experience of responding to this same act when another member exhibits it toward them.

The crucial moment is thought to occur when the act in question *means the same thing* to both actor and addressee. The identical meaning is constituted by the position taking of each organism; both actor and addressee can take the position of each other through the symbolic act.

In this way intersubjectivity is born. The transposition of first and second person positions through symbolic action simultaneously establishes the preconditions for developing the capacity for multiple perspective taking and for developing a sense of self or self-consciousness. So, what begins as patterns of shared routine actions and shared routine responses becomes, through several intermediate stages of symbol-dependent internalization, an early form of intersubjectivity.

Internalization, Expectation, and Responding to One's Own Act

The concept of "internalization" is treated by Mead through two crucial terms: "expectation" and "responding to one's own act." Let's pull up a fantasy consistent with this scene to understand these two important terms. Consider one routine action shared by organisms living in a group, that is made by a member toward another member with routinely experienced consequences. Mead liked to use dog behavior to exemplify many of his points, so let's follow him here and take his example of routine canine attacking behavior: one dog attacking another with biting. All dogs in the group exhibit the attacking behavior at times, and all dogs in the group are at times attacked by other dogs.

Now, why should we use dog behavior to illustrate the basic principles of this theory, which after all is meant to apply to prehuman groups or even early human groups? Mead chose the example of dog behavior no doubt because it is convenient. Most of us are familiar with dogs and even interact with dogs routinely. For the sake of armchair speculations, dogs are an advantageous choice. But we must not take "dog" literally. I will continue to write of mythical "dogs" in much of what follows, but the idea is to think of a rather advanced mammal and use your familiarity with real dogs as a way to fill in details so that a *theory sketch* may develop (Dennett 1991:41). A theory sketch is meant to be suggestive in terms of principles and is willing to make errors on the level of details.

For dogs to be useful in building a theory sketch, the limitations of this choice should always be kept in mind. There are several limitations; the fact that dogs are not even in the primate group is only one of them. In addition, Mead's preoccupation with attacking behavior and, by implication, with actions leading toward relationships of dominance and submission that are so prominent among dogs, must be noted as a bias. Hegel displays a similar bias toward competition and domination in his discussion of the origins of intersubjectivity. The evolution of gestures and symbols in groups of mammals could well have originated in two other modes of interaction: mother-infant relations motivated by care, and noncompetitive interactions between adults motivated by the need for help. Very possibly, symbol evolution developed from all three modes of interaction: those motivated by competition, those motivated by care, and those motivated by the need for assistance.

On the other hand, the emphasis on attacking behavior in dogs is certainly suggestive and serves heuristic purposes specifically for speculations about the roles played by act truncation, anticipation, gesture evolution, and symbol formation. In Hegel's case, the emphasis on a competition for dominance also produces insights into the connections between meaningful action and power: the internal role that a will to power (ultimately a will to knowledge) plays in meaning. Thus I will not apologize too much for following Mead and speculating about competitive interactions as illustrated by dogs. Speculations similar to those that follow ought to be developed as well about these same factors (act truncation, anticipation, and power) as they appear in mother-infant interactions and cooperative behaviors between adult organisms.

Returning now to Mead's theory and his use of dog behavior to develop it, expectations enter the plot of this specific story initially from the second person position: the position in which one is attacked. Through learning processes, dogs begin to expect that they will soon be bitten when they perceive the *beginning* of the attacking action exhibited toward them. Thus, they begin to dodge or retreat when they perceive the bared teeth and hear the snarl-like sounds of an attack behavior emitted in their direction. No doubt smells associated with the beginning of an attack are also important.

Once the attack behavior begins, with its sights, sounds, and smells, the animal in second person position gets out of the way—retreats. This is a form of second person expectation that constitutes a new form of action: dodging or retreating before actually being bitten because of an expectation. Of course animals in the second person position could also learn to quickly counterattack before receiving bites, and this would also involve a form of second person expectation. But I will limit the discussion to the consideration of retreating behaviors so that the main ideas about act truncation, expectation, and early symbol formation may be developed. Retreating behavior has the conceptual advantage of evolving into a consequence desired by the first person, as we will soon see. Counterattacking lacks this advantage for our conceptual inquiries.

Second person expectation constitutes a new act. The actual behavior of retreating upon sensing the beginning of an attack could well be identical to a primary act of retreat that was previously committed only when actually coming under attack and receiving bites. When this older act is committed due to an expectation it becomes newly constituted. It is an old act committed under new circumstances.

Implicitly, second person expectation also constitutes the beginning portion of the first person attack behavior as a sort of presymbol. This is the case if we stick to Mead's arguments. The beginning of the attack now implicitly stands for, or represents, the full act of attack and its consequences as it is experienced *from the second person position*. The symbolic value of the beginning of an attack is not experienced as such by the retreating dog. Its status as a symbol is only implicit at this point and is also limited to the perspective of the second person. More developmental steps will have to be completed before symbols become explicit portions of experience.

Second person expectation generates new actions that become shared and thus become part of the group's action repertoire. All dogs, in time, begin to dodge or retreat when they perceive the beginning of an attack addressed toward them. All dogs continue, of course, to attack other dogs at times too. Now conditions are set for forms of first person expectation to be learned in the group.[14] When beginning an attack, dogs frequently find that their object (the dog they wish to bite) dodges or retreats. They learn to expect dodging and retreating behavior when beginning an attack. At a certain point in time, these dogs will come to *desire* to produce a response of dodging or retreating in other dogs and will truncate their attacking action to its beginning portions only. The learned expectation, that the other dog will retreat, makes it possible for a new desire to emerge: that of causing another dog to retreat.

The snarl is born in this way, constituted by the expectation that other dogs will retreat when the start of an attack is exhibited. Mead calls truncated actions like these, constituted by first person expectations and the new desires they make possible "gestures." The snarl is a "gesture." Its constituting first person expectation is that the one snarled at will back off. Its constituting desire is also that the one snarled toward will back off.

Implicitly, our presymbol has evolved to a new level. The beginning of an attacking behavior comes to represent, for the dog

---

[14] Although the development of a snarl from original attacking behaviors in dogs could have begun from second person expectations, there is no reason to assume that all gestures and, eventually, symbolic acts themselves, originated with second person expectation in the antecedent position. First person expectations could have been antecedent in the case of any gesture we choose for speculative purposes. Either way, both first and second person expectations would have to be brought into the picture and the question of which might have been antecedent is not relevant to the insights sought after. This fantasy assumes an antecedent status for second person expectations, but an equally illuminating fantasy could be invented that begins with first person expectations.

in first person position, the movement of a dog in second person position "out of the way." The snarl stands for the response of the dog in second person position *as this response is experienced by the dog in first person position*. All the sensory experiences aroused when another dog retreats from one's truncated attack, plus the experiential components of an ending state (the state experienced when the other dog is driven off) are implicitly represented by the way a snarl feels to the dog in first person position.

The snarl implicitly symbolizes the retreat of the other dog for the dog who snarls. It could only do this, of course, if it also implicitly represented the full act of attack and its consequences to the dog in second person position. The snarl, at this stage of development, has implicit symbolic value for both the first person and the second person: but no organism yet experiences both "meanings" of the snarl simultaneously. Rather, organisms either experience the snarl as first persons to implicitly mean that the one addressed will back off; or as second persons to implicitly mean that the one snarling is about to attack and bite.

The gesture "snarl" is an implicit symbol that roughly means, "Move or be bitten!" to both the dog in first person position and the dog in second person position, but from different and nonexperientially integrated perspectives. The identity of this symbol for *both* dogs is not yet within the experience of either one. The dog in first person position simply desires the other dog to move while the dog in second person position simply desires to move so as not to be attacked. Neither dog has a grasp of the situation from the other's perspective. The dog in second person position does not read any symbolic intentions into the act of the dog in first person position. The dog in first person position does not act in order to communicate an intention to the dog in second person position. For both, learning is occurring only with respect to what objective events may be expected in certain situations.

When gestures like the snarl become distributed throughout the group and routine interaction patterns develop based on them, a sort of culture of gesture-mediated interaction exists. Gesture-mediated interaction depends on an objective association between learned second person expectations and learned first person expectations. This association is objective, at this point, in the sense that it exists outside the experience of the organisms themselves but is clearly visible to outside, sophisticated observers such as ourselves. "Move or be bitten" is, in the jargon of ethologists, the *objective meaning* of the symbol "snarl." More developmental steps must be completed to internalize objective meaning so that it becomes actual meaning—intersubjectively constituted meaning in the experience of all organisms involved.

The third main stage in Mead's theory of the evolution of symbols depends upon established routines of gesture-mediated interaction. This third stage of symbol evolution involves bringing two objectively associated perspectives together within one experience, or experience sequence. The third stage is the internalization of standard first and second person positions associated with routine gestures, through what Mead called "the significant symbol."

Significant symbols were explained by Mead through the idea of responding to one's own act. Using the terminology of currency in his day, Mead tried to explain the significant symbol with the terms "stimulus" and "response." The idea is that organisms in the first person position that direct a gesture toward other group members stimulate the routine response they expect from the other within themselves. Mead placed much emphasis on the auditory portions of gestures in order to explain this. Because an emitted sound will generally be heard by the organism emitting it almost as soon as it is emitted, and because it will be heard in a way similar to the way it is heard by this same organism when others make such a sound toward her, it makes sense to think that this acting organism will respond to her own sound through her learned second person expectations. The acting organism will experience the same routine response, now stimulated by the sounds of her own act, that she has learned when other group members make this same sort of sound toward her. She responds to her own gesture in a way "identical" to the way the fellow group member she addresses will respond to it, because the sound is part of a routine gesture that all group members emit at times and to which all group members respond at times. When she responds to her own gesture identically to the response of the one she addresses, the significant symbol is born. The organism has stimulated the "attitude of the other" within herself. She has acted from the first person position with expectations that the organism in second person position will respond in a certain way, and she has stimulated this response of the second person position within herself.

Of course, by "identical response" Mead did not mean that the organism in first person position responds with identical *behavior*. Our mythical dog does not snarl at another and then retreat herself. Rather, Mead named the response called forth in the actor by her own act an "implicit response." Through something like a neurological delay, the self-stimulated response takes place but is barred from behavioral expression. Something within either the subjective experiences of the two organisms or the neurological states of the two organisms, or both, is identical. The behaviors of the two organisms are distinctive.

Once the significant symbol has evolved, all sorts of important developmental paths are now open for exploration. The significant symbol, in Mead's dialogical theory, becomes a foundation for the development of thought and self-consciousness. Self-consciousness may grow from the experience of significant symbols because they make it possible to experience one's self as others do; to experience one's own acts as others experience them. When internalizations generalize a "me" forms: a general way of understanding one's self across many interactive domains by assuming the position of others to one's self. As the "me" develops, so does an "I": the experience of one's self primarily from the first person position that is now differentiated from the experiences of one's self had by others. The "me" is the self from the second person perspective, the "I" is the self from the first person perspective, and a growing differentiation between these two modes of experiencing the self evolves in time.

Consistent understandings of one's self from the perspective of others develops in conjunction with the formation of "generalized others": another important concept we owe to Mead. Generalized others constitute systems of values and norms, as well as identities and roles, and are thus fundamental to symbolic cultures.

Hence the significant symbol is a crucial concept to Mead's dialogical theory of mind, self, and society. The emergence of significant symbols in evolutionary time gives birth to genuine intersubjectivity that in turn makes possible the development of symbolic communication, thought, reflection, self-consciousness, social identity, values, and norms. Any flaws in Mead's theory of the significant symbol could be lethal to his dialogical, intersubjective model of consciousness and meaning.

Rethinking Mead

There *are* flaws in Mead's basic theory of the significant symbol, but they are not actually lethal to his dialogical theory of meaning and self-consciousness.

Flaws and Remedies
Basic Flaws

First, Mead's arguments shift ambiguously between objectivist modes of explanation and quasi-phenomenological modes of explanation. The stimulus-response vocabulary used by Mead provides us with an objectivist framework. The crucial notion of "taking the attitude of the other" is hard to understand without a framework that acknowledges subjective states. This is quasi-phenomenological because it requires a third person perspective but invites the theorist and her readers into the subjective states of others. It invites them to imagine these subjective states as they would appear to these others from *their* first person perspective. It is therefore not objectivist but quasi-phenomenological.

Many terms used by Mead fall between these two frameworks; in particular, "expectation," "implicit response," and "significant symbol." At bottom is an assumed equation between objective states and subjective states: neurological activations and experience. Thus we are invited to make sense of the concept of "implicit response" through some notion of neurological delay. The brain is supposed to respond just as it does when a behavior is produced but, through a neurological delay, this behavior is not actually produced, which makes the response "implicit." What, then, is the relevance of such a response if no behavior comes forth in relation to it? It must be the subjective experience it gives rise to. But we are not in a position, even with contemporary theories of the brain and mind, to make such a simplistic equation between brain states and experience.

Second, Mead's concept of the significant symbol is inadequate because it depends on the notion of "identical response." Within Mead's phylogenetic story, significant symbols emerge as soon as an act stimulates a response in the actor that is identical to the response it stimulates in the organism addressed. At this point in the story, a gesture acquires a rudimentary meaning that is identical for both organisms. Meaning is equated with response.

Several levels of identity are conflated in this explanation. From a third person perspective, two brain states are supposed to be identical. But these two brain states are in fact only subsets of total brain states that must differ a great deal in terms of their totality. Within the overall brain state of an organism under attack, the retreat response is activated. Within the very different overall brain state of an organism attacking, this same retreat response is activated. This is one level of identity: the physiological.

From a first person perspective, each organism has an experience that is identical; the experience "retreat" that matches the actions of one organism but not the actions of the other organism. This experience of "retreat" could at best be a subset of holistic experiences that differ enormously when considered as totalities. The overall subjective state of one under attack is completely different from the overall subjective state of one who is attacking. This is a second level of identity: the experiential, or subjective.

On a third level, there is supposed to be an identical meaning for both organisms. Together, the identical brain state and the identical subjective experience (both located within entirely different total brain states and subjective experiences) are supposed to give rise to an identical meaning. But for a gesture to mean the same thing to two organisms, for a gesture to be a communicative symbol, it must presuppose, *within the experience of the participants,* identical interpretations for both. It must be experienced as intersubjective. Simply experiencing a gesture in the same way, or having brain states activated by a gesture that are the same, will not deliver an *intersubjective* identity. A significant symbol would have to either deliver the *experience* that the other interprets it as the actor does, or be constituted by an implicit *assumption* that the other interprets it as the actor does. I will have more to say about the difference between these two modes of intersubjectivity later in this essay. Here it need simply be noted that Mead's scheme in no way delivers an intersubjective identity. Actual identities in either brain states or subjective experiences do not automatically generate an experienced or assumed identity of meaning. The concept of "identical meaning" cannot be equated to the concepts of identical brain states or identical experiences. It cannot be equated with "identical responses."

This is why human beings can communicate with chimpanzees. We do not assume that chimpanzees have identical brain states to our own nor do we assume that they have identical experiences. Yet the gestures we use *count* as having the same meaning for each of us in both our experiences. This is also why we can imagine developing communications between ourselves and aliens whose experiential states and physiological states differ entirely from our own. Our symbols in this case need not even be objectively similar (sound from us, perhaps light emissions from them); but they would count as having the same meaning. Though the phylogenesis of significant symbols is not the same sort of situation one is in when developing communication with chimpanzees and aliens (because the phylogenesis of symbolic communication must begin without one or both parties already possessing communicative competence), the end result is still the same. The end product is that of intersubjective identity—identical meanings that in essence require nothing identical on the experiential and physiological levels. All that is required on the subjective level is a correlation in patterns of experience.

Two major flaws, then, exist in Mead's phylogenetic story. One is the confusion of objectivistic and quasi-phenomenological frameworks; the other is the equation of identical meaning with identical response. These two major flaws give rise to many other sorts of flaws if one probes them sufficiently. For example, if identical meaning is supposed to be based on identical responses, then the rise of a significant symbol could occur *for the actor* when her own gesture self-stimulates the same response experienced by the one gestured toward; but it would not be a significant symbol *for the one gestured toward*, because it would not stimulate the first person experience in this second person. To remain within Mead's framework, a "theory patch" would be required to explain the development of significant symbols from the second person position.

Another secondary flaw has already been alluded to. Since the total brain states and the total subjective states of both organisms in Mead's story would be very different, exactly how would identities between subsets in either of them have significance? The flaw in this case is an absence of theory needed to connect subsets of neurological states to intersubjective identity.

One could find other secondary flaws that derive from the two fundamental flaws discussed above. But since these problems stem from the identification of meaning with response and the conflation of objectivistic theory with quasi-phenomenological theory, I will proceed directly to a discussion of how one might avoid these two most fundamental problems.

Basic Remedies

Here are my basic remedies to Mead's story in truncated form. *First*, I recommend discarding all simplistic equations between brain states and subjective experiences. This sort of problematic equation is not unique to Mead; many philosophers from Descartes onward have unknowingly done the same thing (see Chalmers 1997 for a good discussion of this). Let's tell Mead's story primarily from the quasi-phenomenological perspective. The quasi-phenomenological perspective is a third person perspective that nevertheless emphasizes the imagined subjective states of others. As brain theories progress it will no doubt be possible, some day, to retell Mead's story once again from an objectivist perspective, up to the point at which subjective experiences must be considered in their own terms, and then move ahead with the confidence that subjective experiences have some known relationship to neurological activations. At present brain science is not developed enough to attempt something like this.

Second, let's drop the equation between meaning and response. In a quasi-phenomenological perspective there is no need to think of meanings in terms of responses. One of Mead's great insights was to emphasize acts rather than perceptions in his theory of the evolution of meaning. We must continue to emphasize acts, but acts as the actor experiences them, and acts as experienced by those who receive them. An act need not be conceived as a response nor as anything framed within an objectivist framework alone.

Third, let's treat the concept of identical meaning in terms of *assumed intersubjective* identities. Mead was well aware of the need to explain the rise of meaningful symbols in terms of identities established *for* the organisms under consideration, but he based the emergence of such identities on the concept of identical responses. That does not work. The rise of a significant symbol will occur when one organism acts in expectation of a certain sort of response from another organism, and this expectation is constituted by an unconscious assumption that something is the same for both organisms.

Now, what will be unconsciously assumed to be identical by the actor when significant symbols arise? Not necessarily the interpretation of her act: not at first. Rather, this unconscious assumption may well first manifest itself at the level of a typical interactive sequence: something like a social typification. Acts and responses to acts are shared within the cultures of social animals, but so are action sequences like a snarl followed by a snarl-back followed by a feint followed by an attack. Typical interactive sequences, or "social typifications," could have been the first assumed identities in the evolution of significant symbols. One very plausible story for the evolution of significant symbols will place the first emergence of intersubjective identity at the level of wholes (social contexts), rather than parts (specific acts). I will clarify this idea later.

A New Version of Mead's Story

The basic plot of first person expectations, followed by second person expectations, followed by significant symbols can be retold without reducing the concept of meaning to that of an identical response and without conflating objectivist and quasi-phenomenological frameworks. Doing so will give us a plausible dialogical theory of how significant symbols may have evolved.

Caveats

However, this retold story will not be as tight as Mead's. There will not be a single step, as there is in Mead's story, that projects us in a sort of quantum leap from mere expectations to significant symbols. There will rather be several possible ways in which significant symbols could have developed.

The new story will be suggestive but not definitive. Moreover, it will not be final or complete. There will still be many unanswered questions at the end of this revised story. Best, I think, to be clear about these unanswered questions before getting on with the tale. Here is the main one:

Mead's plot depends on symmetrical relationships between the key actors. Competitive behaviors between adults of roughly equal developmental status are emphasized so that a gesture will eventually come to stimulate the same response in the actor as in the one acted toward. The equal developmental status of the participants makes it possible for a self-stimulation of this nature to arise, because the actor who self-stimulates must have had previous experience with the position of the other in the interaction. In the case of attacking and retreating, the one who self-stimulates a retreat response while attacking or snarling must have previously been in the position of having to retreat so that she is able to self-stimulate this learned response.

The new version of the story that I shall tell does not depend on an identical response, but it does depend on a typical interaction characterized by symmetry. The actor who self-stimulates in my story will stimulate a response learned through real experiences with the complementary interactive position. It will not matter, in my story, whether the *actual* organism in the second person position has similar experiences to those of the actor or not, because the identical meaning need only be assumed, not actual. But it will matter that a typical interaction be in place that allows for the organism in question to play both roles. The interaction will be symmetrical.

What if significant symbols first developed between mothers and infants rather than between adults at similar developmental stages? An infant will have had no previous experience with the complementary position of the mother. My retold story will not explain the evolution of significant symbols in the case of asymmetrical interactions like these.

It is therefore possible that my new story is far off the mark with respect to the actual emergence of significant symbols. It is also possible that significant symbols first evolved in a way consistent with this story, and then, once evolved, symbolic behavior became learned by infants through other mechanisms, given a symbolically competent mother. I am in no position to argue for one possibility over another.

What, then, is the value of the following theory sketch? I believe that no matter how close or far it is from the actual evolution of significant symbols, it will do much to reveal structures of meaningful action from this scene three perspective. Various ideas presented in this story could well have a place in alternative stories. That is its value. Its results correlate well with purely phenomenological investigations of meaningful action. The new story could stimulate further speculations about significant symbol evolution in asymmetrical relationships. It could stimulate empirical research about learning in human infants and animals. It is worth setting to paper for these reasons.

In the next major section, then, I will rework Mead's story in an effort to avoid the flaws in his original work. At the end of the story I will summarize what it suggests about the evolution of intersubjectivity. Some readers might want to skim through my new version of the story and concentrate on the ending summary.

All readers must bear the limitations of this theory sketch in mind as they read through it.

Action Impeti and Expectations

Now I am going to retell Mead's story with more attention to its subjective, phenomenological side. This will bring the concept of the action impetus, introduced much earlier in this essay, into scene number three.

The notion of action impeti was introduced in my section on the phenomenology of meaningful action. From the first person perspective of a fully socialized adult human being, an action impetus can be phenomenologically identified and analytically separated into proprioceptive and prekinesthetic configurations, implicit I-feeling modes, desires, and expectations that include preunderstood perspectives on the act as others would experience it. Phenomenologically, an impetus has a singular quality, yet these diverse components may be identified through further phenomenological recollections.

The concept of an action impetus happens to fit very well with the third person, objectifying perspective of brain and mind theory. A stimulated brain consists of simultaneous parallel processes that "interpret" a given situation in multiple, often competing ways. A mind organizes some of the neurological interpretations into composites and chains. Though the brain and mind together generally produce a number of competing interpretations, each capable of informing diverse behavioral responses, one such interpretation wins the ensuing contest for dominance and gains expression in action. Other interpretations may be employed to form memories and still others simply die out without effect. This view of the brain and the mind is consistent with Daniel Dennett's "multiple drafts" model of consciousness and is supported by a variety of experimental evidence (Dennett 1991).

The phenomenological experience that we adult humans can have of sensing an action impetus but not allowing it to express itself in order to favor another action correlates well enough with this objective model of the brain and mind. There is no need to assume a direct relationship between subjective experiences and brain/mind processes to find this correlation suggestive. The competition between neurological interpretations, such that one wins out, does indeed correlate with phenomenological experiences, and one can safely assume that this correlation is significant in some as yet unknown way. The multiple drafts model of consciousness correlates with the common subjective experience of having more than one action impetus at hand during a short period of time.

Within experience human beings are capable of noticing action impeti as phenomena before they erupt into action or thought. I can experience an impulse, while writing, to go to the kitchen. I can subjectively notice this impulse but not act on it, bringing my concentration back to writing. My impulse to go to the kitchen lost in the competition with an impulse to resume writing. Such impulses are "impeti." The impetus to go to the kitchen is organized as a complex project with many subprojects and acts, but it is experienced in a singular fashion. I notice it but I do not act on it. It loses in the competition with other action impeti that I also notice phenomenologically in holistic, singular ways.

I can similarly experience an impulse to stop writing in order to think about something different and unrelated to my writing project. I am in a room with a fire burning to keep me warm. The fire reminds me of a time in this room I spent with my son, playing a game. I notice a desire to think about that time, for it would be pleasurable, but I do not; I return to writing. To think about that time would be to allow quasi-linguistic modes of thought to be expressed, which I first sense in holistic form. Thoughts also arise as impeti, organized into projects and subprojects.

Other organisms could be expected to have a similar capability, especially those with brains of complex design, and particularly with respect to actions rather than thoughts. In the speculations that follow, I begin with very rudimentary assumptions about the first person experiences of organisms who will soon develop significant symbols. I will retell Mead's story by alternating between the first person phenomenological perspective and various objective considerations. I will take Mead's fantasy of mythical dogs and start where he starts, with the formation of second person expectations. Readers should recall the basic plot of this story: dogs attacked by other dogs learn to retreat when they experience the beginning portions of a routine attack behavior made toward themselves.

Second Person Expectation

So let's again take the case of an organism, a neurologically complex mammal, that has been repeatedly attacked by other organisms of its own kind. It learns to expect the results of an attack upon its body when experiencing the beginning portions of the attack. By acquiring this expectation, it becomes capable of avoiding consequences by retreating before the attacker can reach it.

For heuristic purposes only we can divide this sequence of events into three parts: the beginning of an attack, the point at which the attack produces pain for the one attacked, and the retreat of the one attacked so as to remove itself from pain. Many neurological events would be taking place simultaneously within the animal attacked during all three segments of this sequence. The brain would be processing smells, sights, tactile sensations, kinesthetic sensations, and proprioceptive sensations continuously. Multiple neurological interpretations[15] derived from integrations of these sensations would arise in a continuous manner as well. Multiple neurological processes would accompany each segment of this sequence.

Let's assume that pain sensations, which are added to the sequence during segment number two, quite automatically produce a "flight" response on the level of behavior. As soon as there is pain, flight follows. Segment two produces segment three. The neurological activities associated with this sort of pain and

---

[15] Whenever I write of "neurological interpretations" I do not mean reflective or even experienced interpretations. Contemporary philosophers interested in the mind and the brain consider an interpretation of this sort to be a physiological response to the brain state (Dennett 1991). The response may not be experienced by the organism. I use the expression "neurological interpretations" in this sense.

the neurological activities associated with flight are linked: the first brings about the second. The subjective experience of pain is linked to the subjective experience of flight. The neurological activities stimulated by the beginning of the attack are not initially linked to the neurological activities associated with pain and those associated with flight. The subjective experiences produced by the beginning of the attack (hearing, seeing, smelling the first moves of the other dog's attack) are not initially linked to the subjective experience of pain nor to the subjective experiences of flight.

Acquisition of the expectation would amount to the forging of a new link. In the brain, some of the neurological processes that the beginning of the attack stimulate within the organism assaulted now call forth the flight behavior. A sequence that originally consisted of three roughly hewn segments now becomes a two-segment sequence; the original middle term has seemingly been removed.

A new link would also have been forged phenomenologically through this expectation, but not exactly through the removal of the middle term. Before I discuss what may take place within the experience of the organism, I will introduce the concept of "compression" with respect to the objective features of this learning process.

Objective Compression

Objectively, a sort of compression has occurred when a second person expectation is acquired. On the level of observable interactions that take routine sequences, one sequence has been compressed by removing a middle term. Originally the beginning of an attack was followed by an actual assault upon the body of the one attacked, and this was followed by flight. Now the beginning of an attack is simply followed by the flight of the dog addressed. The sequence has compressed.

On the level of brain and mind, neurological processes have received a new "interpretation" by calling forth an action that had not been previously associated with them. These neurological processes, those associated with sensory information that arise from the beginning of an attack made toward one prior to the time at which one is usually bitten and scratched, once had a sort of accidental connection with the flight response; a connection that did not exist within the brain or mind of the organism but one that an observer could have noted as part of a routine temporal sequence. With the new interpretation, the temporal compression is achieved and a noncontingent relationship is formed between neurological processes aroused by the beginning of another's attack and neurological processes corresponding to the flight behavior. This temporal compression is also a neurological internalization. The objectively observable connection between the beginning of an attack and the consequences of the attack (including both the effects on the one attacked and the retreat response) now have a neurological representation.

Subjective, or Somatic, Compression

Within the experience of the organism a new link is also forged by the acquisition of an expectation, but not necessarily through the full removal of a middle term. A compression has occurred subjectively as well, but with a reduced form of the middle term compressed within the impetus for flight. Let me explain in more detail what I have in mind.

When I was in elementary school I often played football informally with my friends. My position on our informal teams was usually that of the end, because I wasn't bad at catching passes. On one occasion I found myself running with my head turned toward the quarterback to be ready for a pass. On this particular day I caught the pass, turned my head forward to keep running for the goal line, and discovered a tree smack in my path, inches away from my face. I could not halt my drive forward and smashed my face painfully into the tree. From that day until the present I still "feel" a diminished version of the pain caused by the collision whenever I discover myself moving quickly with my head turned away from what is in front of me. This "pain" I call *pre-pain* because it is not literally painful but bears a resemblance to the original pain I felt and warns me that precisely those areas of my body in which the sensations are located may indeed register actual pain within moments.

The pre-pain I now routinely feel when in this situation causes me to stop in an automatic nonreflective way and turn my head to see what is there. When I smashed into that tree the pain I experienced in the face immediately followed the turning of my head. The nearly automatic response I learned from that experience is to stop first and then turn my head carefully because I feel a pre-pain sensation in my face. I also sort of cringe from the neck up.

There are many similar experiences in my own phenomenological life that I suspect are common enough for other people. Some such experiences are totally analogous to the beginning of an attack described by Mead. I was once hit in the face by a baseball and I still feel a pre-pain sensation and cringing response anytime I see someone raising their arm as if to throw a ball toward me within a certain maximum distance. The beginning portions of ball throws beyond that distance will not cause me to cringe and feel pre-pain. But the beginning of a ball throw within that distance will cause the sensations. I must overcome an impetus to duck and hold my hands in front of my face whenever I am in such situations if I want to actually catch a ball.

Another accident I had when young was to clip one of my fingers with a shears. Whenever I see a similar pair of shears I feel quasi-painful sensations in my fingers and experience an impetus, which I usually block, to pull my fingers together and put my hands behind my back. The exact place on the exact finger that was clipped almost throbs when I see such shears.

This is the subjective side of compressions related to the acquisition of an expectation. Roughly speaking, we again have three temporal segments. The three segments are differentiated in my phenomenological world in terms of subjective states. Let me concentrate for the moment on my experience of smashing my face into a tree. The three segments are as follows: 1) there are sensations corresponding to the first segment that are mainly kinesthetic and proprioceptive produced by running with my head turned backwards, 2) there is the experience of having my face hurt, 3) there are experiences that correspond to my response to the pain: cringing and pulling my face back.

Once the lesson was learned, the subjective experiences that correspond to the first temporal segment quickly elicit a somatic memory of what it was like to experience the second temporal segment (pre-pain) and also to quickly bring about behavioral responses to the pre-pain (cringing, pulling the face in, and an impetus to stop running).

This is very rudimentary learning, and the subjective components of it are primarily somatic sensations of various sorts. Three phenomenological temporal periods are compressed into two; the middle term is literally compressed into the third. The sensations associated with the first temporal period now quickly give rise to reduced sensations of the middle period which are simultaneously experienced with an impulse to respond (cringe, pull the face in). The middle phenomenological term in this sequence is not removed to produce the compression, it rather arises in reduced form as pre-pain and is experienced as compressed within the next moment and as a part of it. Thus I call the subjective side of learning experiences like these "somatic compression."

Couldn't a dog or another mammal experience something similar when learning that the sensations associated with the beginning of an attack made toward her will quickly be followed by pain and the impulse to retreat? Dogs, Mead's favorite example, often act as if they have learned through a somatic compression. Some dogs cringe and cry out whenever they simply see a stick in a human's hand. They also back off. Obviously, they must have been beaten with sticks in the past. They have learned that seeing the stick in a human's hand precedes the pain caused by a stick striking their bodies. They have learned this through the temporal compression of three "moments." They don't *think* they will be hit with the stick, when they see it in the human's hand, they act as if they *feel* a somatic memory of what it is like to be hit and simultaneously back off. It is reasonable to assume that they feel pre-pain, just as I do when someone raises an arm as if to throw a ball to me.

The learning process is much like that undergone by Pavlov's dogs. The body of a dog trained in this way responds with salivation to events repeatedly experienced prior to being fed (the ringing bell). The body of the dog who has repeatedly been attacked responds with pre-pain sensations and then cringes and/or runs away. The pre-pain is compressed into the impetus to retreat.

Expectations as Somatic Compressions

An expectation of the sort Mead was concerned with would have a somatic compression as its subjective side. In a presymbolic but neurologically complex organism, "to expect" is not to have a certain kind of "thought," in the sense of a reflection or a deduction. It is rather to experience a state much like those I experience with shears and baseballs. The term "expectation" is logically tied to temporal progression: one segment of time becomes associated with a moment still to come. The second moment is expected. Before thought, reflection, and deduction can evolve, the way that the second moment is expected subjectively is to experience a somatic memory like pre-pain.

Use of the term "compression" in relation to the objective perspective on learning processes may have little value, though it is logically consistent and metaphorically sound (enough) to employ the term that way. Use of the term "compression" in relation to the subjective perspective, by contrast, provides us with a very useful construct. An expectation is experienced when three somatic states that were originally separated in time come to be experienced all at once, or during a short temporal duration. Seeing/hearing/smelling the beginning of an attack gives rise to pre-pain/cringing sensations and the impulse (felt kinesthetically and proprioceptively) to run. The second two terms are experientially compressed. The subjective side of rudimentary expectations involve somatic compressions.

The Presymbol as a Somatic Compression

Now we can better capture the subjective side of a presymbol. Somatic compression, the pre-pain and cringing sensations closely associated with the impetus to retreat, provides the organism with a somatic state that implicitly stands for the full experience of being attacked and the full experience of fleeing. A symbol is something that stands for something else. In the case of rudimentary expectations, the sensations experienced stand for something else because the subjective portions of this "something else" are compressed into one temporal segment. The truncated attack of one dog toward another stimulates sensations of pre-pain and the impetus to flee, compressed together. This is an *implicit* symbol because for the organism it is simply an experience. The relation of this experience to other experiences and events is not explicitly "grasped."

Within Mead's original framework, second person expectation implicitly constructs the beginning portions of the act addressed toward one as a presymbol. That is, Mead considered the beginning of the attack to be a presymbol that implicitly represents the full act and its consequences.

But what are the beginning portions of the act for the organism in second person position? The beginning of the attack would not be as we, adult and fully socialized human beings, conceive of it. It would not be the sights and sounds of a snarl abstracted from the smells and visceral responses felt by an organism actually about to be assaulted. It would rather be the subjective side of a dominant neurological interpretation, probably made objectively through "software" processes of a mind, felt subjectively as somatic sensations and an impetus to flee. The presymbol would be the pre-pain sensations and the cringing response, compressed toward a felt impetus to flee. This roughly organized complex of sensation would be the implicit symbol.

Therefore, to call the beginning portions of the attack the presymbol is not incorrect. But it is through the expectation as *felt* by the organism in second person position that the beginning of the attack takes on symbolic value. Indeed, for the organism about to be attacked, the beginning of the attack is nothing other than the way this organism experiences it. The evolution of this presymbol toward an actual symbol, for an organism that is capable of experiencing pre-pain and other sorts of somatic memories, would occur on the side of the subjective sensations.

First Person Expectation

First person expectation considered within the limited confines of this paradigmatic fantasy takes place after second person expectations have been learned and widely distributed among members of the group. A dog who attacks will then frequently have the experience of an opponent who retreats. This will result in a learning process: beginning an attack ought to produce a response of retreat. In time, the beginning of an attack can be committed as an act in itself, constituted by the expectation of driving another dog off.

What would acquisition of a first person expectation be like phenomenologically, from the perspective of the organism acquiring it? Once again, three temporal segments would become compressed. In the case of certain types of first person learning experiences, many of the arguments I used in my speculations about second person expectations would directly apply. A dog who learns that jumping through a hoop will result in receiving food might begin to salivate as well as jump when seeing the hoop, anticipating the reward that will come after acting in the required way. The temporal segments of seeing the hoop, jumping through the hoop, and receiving food are not compressed, in this case, but are rather linked together for the first time. Objectively no compression has occurred.

But subjectively, presentations of the final term in the sequence are compressed to the impulse for jumping. The presentations of having food become aroused by the experience of a hoop, and the middle term, jumping through, quickly follows. A phenomenological link has been forged between three distinct experiences, and somatic memories of the final state are compressed to an impulse for acting out the middle segment. Somatic compression has occurred, but a somatic memory of the last segment in the sequence is now aroused by the first segment and is compressed with the impetus to act out the middle term. First person expectations are distinguishable from second person expectations through this directly teleological component: the act is produced in order to attain a desired state, rather than to avoid undesirable consequences.

Four Scenes

When a learning process has taken place, such that the desired state is anticipated to be attained through an action that is not "hardwired" to the desire, then somatic compression would explain the subjective side of the learning process. Presensations of the desired state arise, compressed with the act that will produce the full sensations. Expectation is once again a somatic presensation compressed with an impetus to act.

So much for hoops and food; what about attacks? Learning to truncate an attack so as to drive off another dog would plausibly involve similar sorts of compressions. But the situation in this case is a little more complicated because the organisms under consideration would have to first learn that it is desirable to drive off another dog without actually attacking it. This is a restriction of the fantasy as here composed, for we are introducing first person expectations as a development subsequent to second person expectations. The primal acts of this story are attacking and fleeing. Second person expectation produces fleeing before an attack can be completed. Dogs who attack must go through a learning period in which they have the experience of their attacks failing, frequently, because their opponent has run off before they could reach her. They must learn that the state of having simply driven a dog off is desirable before they will start to truncate their attacks in expectation of it.

So let us simply assume that this has occurred. The ending state experienced after another dog has retreated must feel good in some way. If attacks are the result of a sense of threat that is felt when another is too close, then the state of driving off the offender would indeed feel good. The sense of threat would be dispelled with the departure of the offending animal.

Probably some steps would be involved in learning the full first person expectation. First, there is discovery that having a dog run off is desirable. Second, the somatic memory of this desirable state repeatedly arises during a full attack when seeing the other dog begin its retreat. In this step it is the beginning motions of the other dog's retreat that bring about the somatic memory, just as in second person expectation. Next, the attacking dog might halt its attack as soon as it sees the other dog begin a retreat because of the somatic memory arising within. Lastly, this somatic memory is compressed within the impetus to attack itself, such that the attack behavior becomes truncated by the expectation of a desired ending state. At the end of this series of steps, compression has constituted a new act, the snarl.

First Person Expectation as a Presymbol

The somatic anticipation that constitutes the impetus to snarl would represent the retreat of the other dog as it is routinely experienced by the snarling dog. So the presymbol constituted by first person expectation is the felt impetus to snarl, derived from several stages of somatic compression. Such an anticipation would be experienced somatically as the presentations of greater social distance and the lessening of a sense of threat produced by close proximity. The presymbol is thus teleological in nature, considered from the first person perspective. The action impetus would involve presentations of the state to be arrived at when a full snarl is acted out that causes the addressee to move away.

The snarl impetus, if it could be stopped in time and phenomenologically analyzed, would include proprioceptive configurations associated with the threat posed by a dog in proximity, prekinesthetic sensations of the snarl (formed as a truncation of the kinesthetics of full attack), and somatically represented expectations of greater social distance after acting. The telos of the snarl would have a somatic representation in the constitution of the impetus; presentations of what it is like to have the other dog move away, compressed into the moment the impetus arises. The gesture is partially constituted by its telos. It is an early form of goal-rational action in social contexts, and it has a "premonitored" component. Within the impetus to gesture itself are sensations that anticipate a subjective state to come that is to result from the response of the other organism to the gesture.

Simultaneous Impeti

Because the same basic "stimuli" would activate both the attack impetus and the snarl impetus, experiences of having two action impeti emerge within one's self, but consequent movement that

Four Scenes   213

corresponds to only one of them, are now possible. In other words, because first person expectation constitutes a new act through the truncation of a more primal act, the experience could occur of having two possible acts, two impeti to act, arising simultaneously with one more dominant than the other. Such experiences of simultaneous impeti would establish conditions for subjectively noting the difference between an action impetus and the action it would lead to. The impetus not acted out, because another impetus was somehow dominant, would be implicitly experienced in distinction from its corresponding behaviors since these were not expressed. Something analogous could occur with second person responses too, but for different reasons: the organism attacked might experience both an impetus to flee and an impetus to attack back.

Simultaneous action impeti ought to be a fairly common event for organisms of this complexity on the level of the brain and mind. Multiple, parallel, and continuous interpretations integrated neurologically would be common in many diverse contexts of stimulation and action. The point of noting simultaneous impeti here is to arbitrarily mark off a point in time when competing responses are *subjectively experienced*. I believe that this development in the subjectivity of organisms will be important for understanding the development of significant symbols.

Further Developments Prior to the Significant Symbol

So now I have speculated about the development of second and first person expectations from a quasi-phenomenological perspective. The next stage in Mead's theory is the emergence of a significant symbol. But I do not feel ready for this next big step. For reasons clarified a little later on, I believe that other developments must be considered before a credible tale may be constructed about significant symbols.

Elaboration of Action Repertoire

Let us imagine gesture-mediated interactions of the snarl variety to be routinely exhibited within a group of organisms belonging to one species. Somatic compression has occurred in relation to routine acts as they are experienced from both the first and second person positions, that lead up to the emergence of gestures. Snarls routinely produce retreating behaviors. All organisms learn to snarl as well as retreat.

Over time second person expectations would further evolve such that a snarl would no longer produce the expectation of being bitten while it would continue to elicit retreating behaviors. A "snarl" evolves to the status of an implicit symbol for submission: moving out of the way, or retreating partially, without an intense expectation of being attacked.

A new form of "retreat" would in this way be added to the action repertoire of the group. There would be "real retreats" exhibited when real attacks are expected, and "figurative retreats" exhibited in expectation that an attack will not take place.

Gesture-mediated interactions would evolve, in this way, through stages that produce a variety of routine "conversations of gestures" as Mead called it. Somatic compression would continue to be the primary process that evolves more complex forms of gesture and gesture conversation. Somatic configurations would modify and diversify as the gesture and response repertoire elaborates.

Impetus Clusters

Through processes like these, the experience of having several competing action impeti arise within one's self would become more and more common in both the second and first person positions. For the second person position, retreat or snarl back or attack back are examples of simultaneous response impeti. Full dodges and feints would evolve through steps like these, characterized by multiple action impeti. When competing impeti are stimulated by a gesture, some of them will have to be ignored in order to favor one. Or, perhaps more accurately, one will have experiential dominance over the others. Producing a snarl back instead of a retreat could stimulate competing response impeti in the organism that snarled first, and the experience of one dominant impetus differentiated from other simultaneous impeti would occur in this case as well.

The experience of "going with" one action impetus as opposed to others that were stimulated would establish an important condition for internalizing gesture-mediated interactions. For one thing, it would greatly elaborate the action repertoire of the organisms and complexify patterns of "gesture conversation." For another, it would gradually make the differentiation between an impetus and the action it would produce increasingly separate experiences. Finally, it would introduce experientially differentiated impeti within clusters.

Experientially differentiated impeti could well be preconditions for identifying acts communicatively. Given one impetus cluster as *context*, a single possible act could be identified or even indicated through its contrasts to other possible acts in the cluster. The identification or indication of specific acts, of course, could only occur much later in the developmental process. But the impetus cluster may well be an important precondition.

Readiness Positions

Another development during the phase of the elaboration of gesture-mediated interactions would be learning processes associated with the ambiguity of responses to a gesture. A snarl could produce a retreat, a symbolic retreat, a snarl back, or an attack back. Regular use of snarls would produce repeated experiences with all of these responses. Somatic anticipations that constitute the snarl impetus could well become shaded in intensity and inclusive of several possible ending states. Gesture-mediated interactions, over time, would objectively link gestures to clustered responses instead of to single responses. Gestures themselves would become complexly constituted through anticipations of several possible responses.

A gesture could be made and then followed with a stance of readiness: a posture that facilitates several possible second acts that would depend on the response of the addressee. Dogs often adopt readiness positions. If I crouch within the gaze of my dog Ginger she will crouch back and stare at me intently. She is in a readiness position. In fact, my crouch is also taking a readiness position, to which she responds with her own position of readiness. Ginger is in a state of readiness for a bounded set of possible acts I may commit next.

The readiness position is not simply an act but is rather the adoption of a *state* composed of multiple somatic anticipations compressed together. The readiness position is something like a role. Within the state of readiness taken on by a dog there are several action impeti ready to erupt into action depending upon what the other does next. Any of the possible acts that could be committed from a readiness position would be consistent with the "role" adopted.

Gesture Chains

The formation of gesture conversations could be expected to develop into routine patterns of gesture/countergesture/new gesture. I call these "gesture chains." Dog behavior remains a good example of this. A snarl is responded to by a snarl back followed by a figurative attack followed by a jump toward a more easily defended position followed by a figurative retreat and so on. Dogs and other mammals exhibit such gesture chains frequently. The sequence of events in any actual gesture conversation would not be fixed. Rather, the chain would be a loosely sequenced set of impetus clusters making possible many variations in real chains of gesture and response. The variations would be bounded: snarls stimulate only retreats, figurative retreats, submissive postures, counterattacks, countersnarls: they do not stimulate anything else.

By gesture chain, then, I mean the routine experience of entering into a series of interactions characterized by the same impetus clusters. Though specific gestures and responses vary, and though the number of actual interactions that take place before the organisms go on to something else also vary, these variations occur within bounds. An organism receiving an initiating gesture would anticipate a forthcoming period of interaction that is familiar to it in its basic form.

The readiness positions adopted as punctuations within the flow of interaction would most accurately represent the gesture chain, with its empirically variable but bounded acts. Other chain-dependent action impeti could also represent the gesture chain, I do not mean to overemphasize readiness positions here. The readiness position is, however, particularly useful to illustrate the way in which an impetus cluster may become a presymbol for an entire gesture chain.

Notice that first and second person positions in a gesture chain are rapidly shifted between the two organisms. Each organism occupies many first person positions and each occupies many second person positions during the course of a single chain. All members of the group would have regular experiences with both types of responses in such chains, and thus all members of the group would experience the rapid alternation between first and second person positions. The presymbols constituted would come to implicitly represent chained interactions inclusive of clustered gesture and response possibilities.

Objective Social Typifications

Presymbols of chained interactions, inclusive of clustered response possibilities, would tacitly represent the interactive situation as a whole, rather than single acts, consequences, and responses. Through somatic compressions, each moment of a gesture chain would anticipate, and thus implicitly stand for, several additional moves down the chain. Because of the ambiguity built into the situation that produces anticipations of response clusters rather than single responses, readiness positions along the chain would be particularly appropriate presymbols to represent the chain as a whole, though not the only impetus clusters capable of such representation.

Readiness positions and other chain-dependent impetus clusters, in other words, would implicitly represent objective social typifications: entire situations in which routine gesture chains are exhibited. I call the gesture chain, viewed in terms of its potential for symbolic representation and internalization, an objective social typification in analogy to the term "objective meaning" used by ethologists. Routine gesture chains are objectively perceivable as typical social situations: typifications. But their existence would not be a conscious feature of the experience of the organisms. They are, accordingly, *objective* social typifications.

The rapid alternation between first and second person positions for each participant in a gesture chain would correspond to early role behavior. The subjective experience of taking on a "role" here would involve the somatics of readiness positions and other chain-dependent acts that anticipate several moves to come.

Elaborated Gesture-Mediated Interaction: A Summary

In summary, the stage of elaborated gesture-mediated interaction would introduce the following as common experiences to all members of the group:

* the experience of an impetus cluster, in which several impeti to act are experienced at once but only one such impetus becomes behaviorally expressed

* the experience of differentiations between action impeti arising within a cluster

* the experience of ambiguity, of anticipating several possible responses after gesturing rather than just one

* the experience of gesture chains in which both organisms rapidly shift between first and second person positions with respect to each other

* the development of readiness positions in a gesture chain, experienced as special sorts of somatic configurations, and from which a bounded number of possible acts could be displayed

* the development of early "roles" that are characterized by one's position in a typical chain rather than by a specific gesture or a specific response: several possible acts can be expected from one role

* the development of objective social typifications

* the development of presymbols for objective social typifications that would be the somatic state of a readiness position or of other chain-dependent impetus clusters

The Significant Symbol
Significant Gestures

I will now examine more carefully how this developmental stage, the stage of elaborated gesture-mediated interaction, could lead to the development of significant symbols.

Let's say that our group of organisms regularly interact through gesture chains that are basically objective social typifications. Let's take one such gesture chain, a competitive one similar to that of two dogs who snarl, attack, retreat, feint, and pause in readiness positions within the typification. Most impeti that arise within this chain are now constituted by multiple somatic compressions. A single impetus anticipates both:

* a self-stimulated state to come that corresponds to the sensations that routinely occur when in the complementary position of the chain, and

* a state to come next that the organism will adopt just after acting.

Many times during the actual flow of interaction within this typical situation impetus clusters rather than single impeti will characterize the state of each participant. This is particularly evident when readiness positions are adopted, but this would occur at many other moments during the interaction as well. The future state that will be self-stimulated as well as the future state that will arise when the other responds to one's act will often be characterized by several action impeti on-hand, not just one.

"Selection processes" of some sort must operate so that one impetus from a cluster will be expressed rather than its competitors. Each impetus in a cluster will be constituted by multiple somatic compressions. What would the selection process be like, considered from the first person perspective of the organism? It is of course difficult to say. One impetus will simply have more experiential weight than the others in its cluster; its selection will immediately follow the experience of its greater weight.

The next step that I imagine introduces an assumed identity. I call this step the development of a *significant gesture*. I retain "significant" from "significant symbol" because an identity is assumed when this arises, but I substitute "gesture" for symbol because no communicative intentions are yet involved. A significant gesture would arise at a time when one impetus is selected over others because of the anticipated self-stimulation. Perhaps a selection of this nature would occur when a somatic anticipation of the second variety—the state to adopt just after acting—feels best to the actor. It is through the anticipated self-stimulation compressed to this impetus that this most desirable outcome is felt. The new phenomenological link that gives rise to a significant gesture would involve anticipations of self-stimulation, associated with the complementary position within the chain and the subjective state that will follow one's act.

As soon as something like this occurs, the actor has put an unconscious assumption in place: that the actual other organism shares the same typification with the actor. Given the ambiguity of responses to acts, and yet the bounded nature of this ambiguity; and given that the nature of responses will be those of impetus clusters rather than single acts; the assumption of identity would occur at the level of the typification rather than at the level of the single act.

The implicit logic of a selection of this nature would have its fully explicated form as follows: "I could act out A, B, or C but I will act out B because then the other will probably respond with cluster Z and I will be ready for that. I think the other will respond with cluster Z because I would do so if I were in her position." In fact, the implicit logic of the particular impetus selection that constitutes significant gestures would be layered as follows:

1) "Impetus B feels best, better than impeti A and C."

2) "Impetus B will bring about anticipated state 2, which feels better than anticipated states 1 or 3 that would result from impeti A and C."

3) "I know that impetus B will bring about state 2 because it will self-stimulate state ii that I feel in connection with state 2."

4) "If I act out B, the other will probably respond with cluster Z which will give me the feeling 2. I expect the other to respond with Z if I act out B because I would do so (via state ii) if I were in her position."

Notice that this process does not require identical responses or even identical experiences. It is the organism's own states that have been compressed and that connect complementary positions. The two organisms involved need not experience anything identical on any level considered. The core objective condition required is that of routine interactions that generate complementary positions which both organisms have routinely occupied. In principle, responses and experiences could be totally different for each organism. However, given the fact that the gesture chains that we are considering developed within a group of the same species, a pattern of similar experiences would no doubt have arisen for all members. But identical responses and identical experiences are neither necessary nor sufficient conditions for this process to occur. This same basic process could in principle take place between organisms of entirely different physiological structure.

For the actor, however, an assumption has unconsciously been set in place that both organisms share the same typification: that the roles in which the other is located are the same as the roles the actor has occupied in the past. This unconscious nonreflective assumption makes the gesture a "significant gesture," one that assumes an intersubjective identity at the level of the typification.

And this unconscious assumption sets in place the implicit logic worked out above. That implicit logic would be instantiated at the moment this sort of selection occurs.

The logic is to be regarded as entirely implicit, of course. Its mark in experience is simply on the level of feeling states and experiential weights. But once it is set in place, the ground for a long process of differentiation and explication is established for the first time. This will be a process that will lead to subject-subject frames in experience and, eventually, a fully evolved symbolic system.

Significant Symbols

With this scenario in mind further developments may be imagined that would refine early significant gestures toward significant symbols. I am roughly defining significant symbol here to mean a significant gesture that also possesses communicative intent. Remember that I have defined a significant gesture as one constituted by an (unconsciously made) assumption of inter-subjective identity. The assumption that has unknowingly been made by our mythical organisms is that both participants in a gesture chain share an identical "definition of the situation," to use the terminology of symbolic interactionists. This assumption was developed through somatic compressions that linked together portions of each organism's own experiences, compressing them into singular action impeti. Therefore, the two organisms in question need not actually share a common situation definition at all. Moreover, they need not have identical or even similar experiences. And finally, they need not have identical or even similar brain states.

The significant symbol also requires nothing identical in the actual experiences or brain responses of the participating organisms. It is a significant gesture accompanied by communicative intentions. It could have developed in several ways, and perhaps did so simultaneously such that the lines of development eventually converged.

The processes involved are not as important as the structures required. The rise of significant gestures would produce, over

Four Scenes 223

time, a sort of trust in the experiential weight of certain anticipated self-stimulations to select one impetus over another. Many variations in impetus selection might develop from this. Here are a few possibilities:

> * Learning, perhaps from "too quick" responses, that anticipated self-stimulations that were initially associated with less experiential weight produce more highly desired results; thus the weight of these anticipations increased over time. This would invoke experiential differentiations between impeti in a cluster and also would encourage experiential differentiations between the moment of anticipated self-stimulation and the moment of the anticipated next state felt within a single impetus.
>
> * Learning to repeat an act when the next state produced by the response of the other organism is not what was anticipated. Learning that repeating acts will encourage the other organism to try a different impetus from within the same complementary cluster. In this case the anticipated self-stimulation would be sort of subjectively insisted upon, via act repetition, and differentiated from other features of the impetus.
>
> * Learning that a grunt of disappointment encourages the other to try another act from within an impetus cluster when the acting organism has been disappointed.

One can think of many other possibilities. In each case, however, communicative intentions emerge from the structures of significant gestures, from the unconscious assumption that a social typification is shared identically. From within this assumed identical typification, differentiations are learned between impeti in a single cluster. Differentiations are also learned between the moment of anticipated self-stimulation (of sensations corresponding to the complementary state) and the moment of anticipated next states (sensations produced by the actual response of the other organism). The anticipated self-stimulation that an act will provide is employed more and more frequently in the selection processes that must handle competing action impeti.

Communicative intentions evolve slowly, then, as an effect of experiential differentiations. Again, what become differentiated are the experiential sides of action impeti, with an emphasis on the anticipated self-stimulations that are associated with the complementary position. In place at all times is the assumption of a shared typification.

As these processes advance, organisms begin to select acts with an implicit communicative logic. The other organism is "told," implicitly: "not *that* act, but *this* one." Significant symbols would depend on the assumption of a shared array of possible acts, that in turn depend on the assumption of a shared situation definition, such that one act can be indicated as opposed to others.

Within the framework of my story, then, significant symbols depend already on an assumed *shared structure of differences*. It is this assumption of shared impetus arrays that makes it possible to indicate one impetus. The significant symbol advances over the significant gesture by assuming an identical meaning to a single gesture, rather than by assuming only an identical situation definition. But the assumption of an identical situation definition had to come first. The assumed identity of meaning associated with a significant symbol first arises in the form of an indication of one impetus in opposition to others, all of which are assumed to be shared within a typification.

Norms

Jürgen Habermas has reworked Mead's theory by claiming that three modes of "taking the attitude of the other" must evolve sequentially. Here is how Habermas theorizes the situation:

> With the first taking of the attitude of the other, participants learn to internalize a segment of the objective meaning structure to such an extent that the interpretations they connect with the same symbol are in agreement, in the sense that each of them implicitly or explicitly responds to it in the same way. With the second taking of the attitude of the other, they learn what it means to employ a gesture with

communicative intent and to enter into a reciprocal relationship between speaker and hearer. Now the participants can differentiate between the social object in the role of speaker or hearer and the other as an object of external influence, between communicative acts addressed to one's counterpart and consequence-oriented actions that bring something about. And this is in turn the presupposition for a *third* way of taking the attitude of the other, which is constitutive for participants ascribing to the same gesture an *identical* meaning rather than merely undertaking interpretations that are objectively in agreement. (1987b:14, italics in original)

My revised story is in good agreement with Habermas's views. The first taking of the position of the other, in my version of the theory, is really the significant gesture: the moment when an identically shared social typification is assumed. Obviously, I do not think that identical responses are the mechanism for this first mode of position taking. But I am in agreement with Habermas that this first mode is essentially noncommunicative.

The second way of taking the position of the other, according to Habermas, brings about communicative intentions without the norming of identical meanings. Once again we find a close match with my own story. The significant symbol arises, after the significant gesture is in place, as a way to specify one impetus in opposition to others. My story, however, adds an important feature: the dependence of significant symbols (which I define, again, as significant gestures with communicative intentions) on a structure of assumed shared differences.

Habermas's third taking of the attitude of the other involves the norming of meanings. I do not find it obvious that this third mode of position taking would come after, rather than alongside, the second mode. Communicative intentions could have developed first through acts of repetition to mend a disappointed outcome, or through learning processes that begin with the selection of an experientially weaker impetus (by impulse, timing, accident) with the surprising result of a favorable outcome and then end with more experientially differentiated impeti such that selection becomes closer to rudimentary considerations of the other's position. Or communicative intentions could have *begun* with norming, as would be the case when an organism learns that a snarl or grunt of disappointment will produce a second try on the part of the other. In this case the grunt of disappointment becomes a way of saying "no" to one impetus so as to indicate another. Very possibly all of these processes and others as well developed significant symbols during the same rough period of time.

Habermas's point is, of course, essential to understanding the evolution of intersubjectivity. Norming had to enter the picture at some point. The significance of norming is that an identical meaning can only be communicatively indicated simultaneously with a norm: the other organism *should* understand one's gesture in a particular way, to indicate one impetus rather than others. Norming requires two previously established structures—the assumption of a shared social typification and the assumption of a shared structure of differences. The second structure is nothing more than the explication of one feature of the shared social typification; the existence of impetus clusters in which each composite impetus is the result of multiple somatic compressions.

We are now ready to explore some of the basic structures of significant symbols, each of which depends on the nature of social typifications. Before discussing these basic structures, however, I wish to remind the reader of the caveats with which I began this revised theory of George Herbert Mead.

The Problem of Asymmetrical Interactions: Communicative Intentions and the Self

Central to the caveats about my revision of Mead's tale is the dependence of this story on a symmetrical interactive chain with roles that can be occupied by all participants. A symmetrical interactive chain rules out typical interactions between mothers and infants. It makes it difficult as well to explain how something close to significant symbols can develop between humans and other animals.

My dog Ginger, for example, acts toward me very much as if she has communicative intentions and as if she regards me as a subject rather than an object. Ginger expects a walk every evening. When it is evening she often places herself near me and waits until I begin the first steps toward getting us both ready for a walk. If I wait too long, Ginger starts to whine or even bark while she stares directly at me. She appears to be trying to remind me what time it is. Barking at me and whining at me while she stares at me are acts difficult to interpret without assuming that Ginger takes me to be a subject rather than an object.

When I begin the usual preparatory steps for taking Ginger on a walk her activities seem to become even more communicative. I start putting on my shoes or a coat, and Ginger begins to dance about in excitement. As I then walk toward the place where her leash is kept she becomes even more animated and yelps excitedly. Once the leash is in my hand she often cries out and jumps up on me. Now, if I put on my shoes and then start toward the location of the leash but halt on the way, Ginger will do things that seem designed to persuade. She will bark and then wait for me to continue. If I do not, she will repeat the bark. Though these acts on Ginger's part could be explained without reference to any communicative intentions it is very difficult to drop this interpretation. She uses expressions of anger, as if I *should* continue toward the leash. She also uses repetition, as if she is trying to get me to perform "A" rather than "B."

It is possible that communicative intentions and some distinction between subject-to-object and subject-to-subject inter-actions could have evolved without self-stimulating sensations that have been learned from the complementary position in an interactive sequence. Certainly Ginger's behavior toward me during walk time appears communicative without any past experiences, on Ginger's part, of being in the complementary position. Ginger's various acts could not stimulate within herself the sensations of what it is like to be in my position.

What, then, of the acquisition of a sense of self in Ginger? Mead's theory, as is well known, would posit a sense of self dependent on the self-stimulation of acts, in the way that meaningful acts arouse experiences associated with the complementary position. A sense of self begins with the internalized response of others to one's own acts. Nothing in my movement toward the leash and Ginger's responses to it would give Ginger an experience of how I experience her. Does Ginger then lack a sense of self? Well, if I praise Ginger she behaves as if she relishes my praise and feels, well, "good about herself." And if I scold Ginger she acts ashamed, as if she really feels bad about herself. She seems to want my positive regard and yet we cannot theorize her grasp of either a positive or a negative regard through the self-stimulation of gestures.

We all know about anthropomorphism. To interpret Ginger's actions as displaying communicative intentions and to interpret her responses to praise and scolding in terms of her sense of a self probably is anthropomorphic in everyday life. But reflecting upon the situation in an effort to avoid anthropomorphism will not give us a certain counterinterpretation. I am certainly not willing to say that Ginger has no communicative intentions or any sense of self just because I cannot easily come up with a theory capable of explaining these things.

If some of Hegel's insights were correct, then all creatures could possess a nascent sense of self that emerges most prominently through symbolically mediated position taking. Many Eastern models of the mind also insist on this. In one such model (Anandamurti 1968) the self is conceived of in terms of three stages: the "I have done" (or *citta*), the "I do" (or *aham*), and the "I am" (or *mahat*). This model links the self to action much as Mead's theory does. But only the stage of "I have done," or *citta*, would require full communicative position taking. The "I do" is a sense of self felt as one acts that disappears just afterward. The "I am" is both the totally implicit self that exists prior to maturing through developmental stages, and the totally real self, found in the experience of *samadhi*. If this model is at all in tune, Ginger might "feel her self" in prereflective ways; she might experience a nascent version of the "I-feeling."

At any rate, one of the most appealing features of Mead's story is that it assumes the worst in order to deliver a desired result. It assumes that the mythical organisms discussed begin with no communicative intentions at all and no subject-object distinction in their experience and no nascent sense of self. My reworked version of Mead's story does the same thing, while being open to alternatives. The development of symbolic consciousness in the growth of human infants into children is not well explained by these stories. Nor are a large variety of interactions between humans and other animals, such as dogs. These Meadian stories are not final or complete, but by "assuming the worst" these stories are very helpful in our quest to understand the basic structures of intersubjectivity.

The Evolved Structures of Meaningful Acts
Importance of the typification

By the time the significant symbol arises, an umbrella structure, the social typification, exists as a precondition to the first mode of position taking. Position taking that evolves beyond this stage, as in the movement from significant gestures to significant symbols, occurs "within" this umbrella structure.

The existence of this umbrella structure is itself claimed, and thereby instantiated, with each meaningful act that is dependent on it. Its existence is virtual, not actual. This theory of the typification, then, is completely consistent with Anthony Giddens' notion of structure: the medium and the outcome of action (1979).

Thus typifications are constituents of meaningful acts, of action impeti in fact. This would explain why action impeti contain preunderstood audiences and, at least implicitly, both the second and third person perspectives on the act. The second person position is rooted in the anticipation of self-stimulation compressed to the impetus. The third person position is rooted in the assumption of a shared typification with its array of impeti. The third person position is a *possible* perspective, whereby both organisms could in principle objectify their assumptions of a shared situation definition in order to discuss the applicability of a norm or the array of acts that are available to each participant.

Within the significant symbol in its full, normed form are the implicitly distinguishable categories of objectivity, subjectivity, and the normative realm. As Habermas has famously argued, differentiations between these realms will become necessary under adaptation pressures to communicate more precisely and to mend misunderstandings. The first significant symbols, via the typifications that constitute them, simultaneously imply objective, subjective, and normative claims. Adaptation pressures will begin to specialize the symbol system so that an objective, normative, and subjective vocabulary evolves, as well as grammatical distinctions between first, second, and third person.

While the symbol systems that evolve in relation to objectivity unfold within expectations characterized by shared access and perception, the symbol systems evolving in relation to subjectivity require mappings between a privileged realm and a shared realm via root symbols that are constituted in analogies and metaphors. In order to communicate an experience that is differentiated as one of the privileged variety, analogies to experiences of the shared variety are important. If I say "I have a deep longing for moral purity" I am referring to subjective experiences and states but use metaphors from the world of shared access. "Longing," "deep," and "purity" are metaphorically structured concepts when used in this way. Subjectivity, the world of privileged access, is frequently represented with analogies from the world of multiple access.

Acting to Clarify Meanings

Mead's theory offers an explanation of the fact, long noted by expressivists (Taylor 1979), that acts clarify their meanings as they are acted out. Meaningful acts are constituted by processes of compression that anticipate full experiences to be brought forth by the acts themselves. Thus we are able to phenomenologically examine action impeti to obtain a vague and uncertain sense of what they will fully mean to ourselves if we act them out.

The I-Feeling Mode

There are two ways in which the concept of the I-feeling mode might be incorporated within Mead's theory. The first way is the weakest. Mead's theory of the self is that it develops only after position taking has developed. The self then becomes an emergent structure, an internalized and generalized response to one's own act that is dependent on the typical ways that others respond to one. Most social acts will accordingly provide some sense of the self for the actor through the responses of others. Such responses to one's acts will not only internalize so that a *reflective* concept of self becomes available, they will also compress to action impeti so that a vague *feeling of self* will feature in the impeti of meaningful acts. This is not a necessary conclusion from either Mead's theory or my revision of it, but it is certainly a possible conclusion if the theory of subjective compression that I have advocated is valid.

The second way in which an I-feeling mode might be incorporated within a Meadian framework is stronger and cannot be derived from Mead's theory. I personally favor this interpretation and find it congruent with both Hegel's theory of self-consciousness (outlined a little later on) and Eastern theories like the one intimated earlier: the composition of self by various moments linked to action—the *citta* (I have done), the *aham* (I do), and the *mahat* (I am). In both of these theories a sense of self is believed to be nascent within all forms of consciousness. Not only is it nascent, it is infused with desire. It is nascent as the desire for recognition in Hegel's theory and as the desire to experience one's self as infinite in many Eastern philosophies. The desire to experience one's self as infinite and unlimited is actually a feature shared by Hegel and many Eastern philosophers.

Mead's theory is not inconsistent with this second, stronger, theory of the I-feeling mode. Full incorporation of this idea within the Meadian framework would be achieved, however, only if the drive for recognition were to be demonstrated as a crucial motivation complex that emerges when certain developmental stages are reached. Such developmental stages would require, at minimum, the prior development of significant symbols. Mead's theory could be linked to a revised theory of praxis in this way.

Recollection and Reflection as Evolutionary Products

This dialogical theory of meaning and consciousness relegates the mental acts of recollection and reflection to the status of internalized interaction patterns. When one is able to recollect what has just passed in experience, and thus to reflect on one's experience, one is basically taking a second or third person perspective on what was initially a first person phenomena. The ability to take second and third person perspectives within an umbrella of first person privileged access is an evolutionary product: the result of internalizing interaction patterns via the significant symbol. One understands one's own impeti to act only by "responding to one's self" from the position of another. But this means that one understands one's self only through application of analogies and metaphors.

Juxtaposing the Phenomenological Sketch with Mead's Scene Three

When we say that an act is "meaningful" we are referring to the possibility of understanding the act from diverse social positions structured by the three formal positions of first, second, and third person. Meaning has everything to do with position taking, with intersubjectivity. Scene three employs the presuppositions of realism to make possible explorations of the origin of intersubjectivity. In this section I will review the conclusions at which we arrived in the discussion of scene three to emphasize their correlation with the phenomenology of meaningful acts.

The ability to take first, second, and third person positions in relation to the same act is structured through a preunderstanding of subjectivity. That is to say, the differentiation between first and second or third person positions is dependent on an understanding that actors have privileged access to portions of every impetus to act and have shared access to portions of every act. Therefore, the meaning of an act, if it is mapped on to as explicit a semantic field as possible (i.e., if articulated through conventional communication structures like language), must make reference to Habermas's three formal ontological realms:

> a) the subjective realm, in which signs are used to reference portions of experience to which actors have privileged access

> b) the objective realm, in which signs are used to reference portions of experience to which actors share access

> c) the normative realm, in which signs are used to reference horizon structures that formerly were not part of explicit

experience but apperceived and assumed to be shared in all communicative processes. The horizon structures originate in the internalized social typification.

The contrast between experiences characterized by privileged access and experiences characterized by shared access assigns the status of *claim* to all references made to each of the three realms (the subjective, objective, and normative realms). This is another point emphasized by Habermas. An actor implicitly makes a series of claims concerning her subjectivity, concerning entities and relations in the objective realm, and concerning normative rules governing comprehensible and appropriate modes of activity (the normative realm). The concept of claims here is ontologically grounded in the necessity of monitoring an action in order for it to be meaningful to one's self. Taking a second or third person position with respect to an act requires the placement of one's self in a position with respect to the act that renders portions of the impetus inaccessible. Another way of saying this is to say that one's subjective states are never a certain affair, even to one's self, for subjectivity itself is differentiated in experience only when one is able to take the imagined positions of others with respect to one's own acts. The references made by an act are therefore claims dependent on the possibility that others will recognize or acknowledge them. No perceived act of acknowledgment, however, will make a claim a matter of certainty. This is also due to the contrast between privileged access and shared access. When another affirms a claim there necessarily remains the possibility that the privileged access the other has with respect to her impression of the act does not correspond to the privileged access of the actor. Those who seem to affirm may not really affirm within their privileged realms, or, if they really affirm they may misunderstand and affirm for the wrong reasons. It is impossible to ever be certain with respect to claims.

Explication of the subjective realm will frequently be a matter of applying analogies, similes, and metaphors to indicate I-feeling modes, feelings, intentions, and holistic understandings that are preobjective or nonobjective. From a scene three analysis we arrive at something like Derrida's "trace," because signs have meaning in this scene by virtue of the fact that they transpose first, second, and third person positions alongside the fact that such transpositions must presuppose the distinction between privileged and shared access. An impetus to act is both the point of the act and a "trace," or "vanishing point," because of its dependence on the recognition of another, and because of the impossibility of ever achieving unambiguous recognition. Dependence on the recognition of another is explained with scene three, for scene three suggests that all signs (linguistic, imagery, even proprioceptive configurations) are evolutionary products—internalizations of expectations arising from social interaction. Thus:

a) When a mental object "stands for" something else one can move between first, second, and third person positions with respect to it.

b) Reflection and recollection involve the movement between first, second, and third person positions.

c) This movement is plagued by uncertainty because of the distinction between privileged and shared access.

d) Signs that stand for subjectivity and normative claims will generally do so as analogies because such signs basically consist of a mapping from the realm of privileged access to the realm of shared access.

e) Such mapping is also a "flattening," because an implicit, holistic understanding must be explicated temporally and for the sake of others.

Among all the claims carried by a meaningful act is the identity claim: the claim that the actor exists with certain (implicitly understood) subjective capacities and traits that may be judged according to normative standards. The identity claim thus works with claims that bridge the subjective and normative realms. The identity claim too, can never be unambiguously affirmed. Hegel's insights come into the model at this point. The desire to be understood will be associated with the desire to be recognizable in all acts, though it may not play a thematized role in most meaningful acts. The desire to be recognized is related to being-as-desire which was explored from a different perspective in the section on scene two.

A little more can be said about recollection and reflection as they appear within scene three. As stated above, they are associated with position taking. Scene one rendered pure recollection an impossibility and described it instead as a special form of repetition: a new meaningful act. The reason for its impossibility was given through an analysis of perception and problems associated with the concept of "now." With scene three, however, perception is simply one kind of action; internalized though it may be. It is a series of impeti oriented toward the explication of an object of experience for another; a project in articulation. Recollection in scene three appears as a form of representation, of taking the stance of another with respect to an experience. It is impossible in pure form not so much because of time and temporality but because of the distinction between privileged and shared access.

Mead's Scene Three and Deconstruction

The "trace" appears within Mead's version of scene three as the result of the distinction between privileged and shared access rather than as the result of temporality. Indeed, temporality appears in scene three only as a secondary effect of intersubjectivity. So subjectivity is never known with certainty because objectifying it is like "presenting" it, and thus constitutes it against the distinction between privileged and shared access, even when this is done for "one's self." One's self is constructed by such internalized "presentations" and is not knowable as such. One's self, and particularly its moment within an impetus as an I-feeling mode, is always already past in time because of the distinction between shared and privileged access, the shift from a first to a second person position. The shift from a first to a second person position is what constructs "first" and "second" person positions: privileged access exists primordially as such only when it has already gone by in time. However, "privileged access" is always a preunderstanding: when one contemplates the always already goneness of primordial first person experience one does so with the understanding that this act of contemplation occurs within the privileged access of the thinker. It is a preunderstanding that layers itself whenever one attempts to capture it.

Thus one could argue that scenes one and three are simply different beginning places for posing the question of meaning. We could start with scene one to explain intersubjectivity as a secondary phenomena that is derived from primordial experiences of the privileged sort. But doing this deconstructs when one encounters the temporality problematic. On the other hand, we could start with scene three to explain experiences within the privileged realm (reflecting, perceiving) as derived from internalized interaction patterns and the significant symbol. But this deconstructs when one encounters the mutual dependence of first, second, and third person positions. The distinction between privileged access and shared access, carefully considered, is impossible to pin down because in fact there is no purely privileged access and there is no certain shared access.

Hegel's Construction of a Scene Three

Hegel's treatment of scene three has the disadvantage of being a *complete* fantasy. It is not grounded in a modern theory of evolution nor is it informed by the work of ethologists who have contributed greatly, since Hegel's time, to our knowledge of animal interactions. But Hegel's treatment of the scene, fantastic though it is, possesses insights into the nature of desire and the I-feeling that are absent in the work of Mead and Habermas.

Dialectic of Passive Consciousness: From Certainty Toward Truth

Hegel's *Phenomenology of Spirit* (1967) is a preHusserl sort of phenomenology that works with presuppositions of a type

Husserl would have disallowed. The first part of the book, following the famous preface, consists of a "scene one" sort of discussion. It begins with a passive consciousness who feels certain of its knowledge of sense objects. This is called "sense certainty." Objects seem to be given directly to consciousness through the senses. There is a feeling of certainty that the objects are there, exist there, and the truth of this certainty appears to reside in the immediacy of sense experience.

Hegel then produces a sort of deconstruction of this scene by playing off certainty against truth. The certainty of immediate knowledge permeates the experience of viewing an object, but all efforts to *indicate the truth* of this certainty fail. In fact, all such efforts lead us dialectically past sense-certainty into what Hegel calls "perception." But then perception also results in dialectical movement into what he calls "force." The gist of the whole dialectical argument is that the truth of sense certainty at first appears on the objective side of the situation. The object before us is self-evidently there; it supplies its own truth. By the time we get to "force," however, the truth of sense certainty is found to lie on the subjective side. This is because efforts to articulate the truth of sense certainty have led to an understanding of the object as an "activity" Hegel associated with "thought"—a set of negations that bring the object out in its particularity.

A bowl has shape, color, size, and so forth, each of which can be understood only through a set of negations (circular is such by not being angular, blue is such through negations of other colors on the spectrum, all qualities have their identity through a structure of contrasts). When we understand that our perception of an object depends on an implicit set of negations we have grasped what Hegelian scholars call "first negation." First negations are related to the concept of "difference" in twentieth century structuralist theories of meaning. But Hegel argues that our efforts to get to the truth of the situation may go further and result in a grasp of "second negation": the object *is* the unified activity of negations that bring it about. Such activity, Hegel argues, is "thought." The object "is" thought in that its identity is the activity of negating what it is not. Second negation brings out objectivity as a process of self-construction through negation: it is one insight into Hegel's famous formulation: "substance is subject."

In the third stage of part one of the *Phenomenology*, the stage called "force," abstract entities like fields, forces, energy, and so on, are posited by consciousness to explain the truth of the object, and these are clearly features of "thought" for Hegel, because they are totally posited and in no way experienced with the illusion of immediacy. "Force" is analogous to twentieth century constructs like quarks, neutrinos, and mesons, which are not perceivable but are posited in order to explain perceivable phenomena. A better term than "force" might therefore be "model," as it is used in science. Scientific models are metaphors that originate in sense experience (the idea of a force abstracted from experiences of pushing and pulling, of an atom initially abstracted from experiences with small bounded objects, etc.). But once the abstraction has been applied we end up with a concept whose identity depends upon structures of difference (as in first negation) and whose existence is thought to be beyond objective appearances (as in second negation). The full second negation is grasped when we think of the forces and entities posited by science as generative activities. The first appearance of objectivity is structured by the difference between the self and the world that is not-self. By the end of this dialectic this difference structures the distinction between appearance and reality. Reality is not the object pole within experience, the object pole within experience is rather appearance, which implicates nonperceivable forces that, for Hegel, are aspects of thought or subjectivity.

Thus, Hegel ends the first part of the *Phenomenology* by claiming that passive consciousness grasps the truth of its certainty of sense objects as *itself*. The truth of the object is the subject, in that the principle that originally distinguished the subjective side of sense certainty (negation as activity) turns out to be fundamental in the domain of the objective side.

At the end of the stage "force," passive consciousness finds itself (subjectivity) to be the truth of all possible objectivity. Passive consciousness has found itself to be an infinite principle that underlies all possible objective forms. And when this occurs it finds itself in disquiet, desire, and "life." Passive consciousness transmutes into active consciousness that begins its own process of dialectical development.

Dialectic of Active Consciousness: Implicit Truth as Desire

The second part of the *Phenomenology of Spirit* leads us to Hegel's scene three: the origins of intersubjectivity. This part begins with the "discovery" that the truth of sense certainty is subjectivity, a discovery that has moved us from a passive consciousness to an active one. Passive consciousness found itself to be the truth of sense certainty and objectivity generally. Passive consciousness found some form of identity between those core differentiations that characterize subjectivity in opposition to objectivity and the nature of objectivity when it is carefully explored. This is an abstract identity, however, suggested by thought, and is not experienced with the certainty that one initially feels in sense-certainty. The truth that objectivity is rooted in subjectivity, that substance is subject, is not certain.

Now active consciousness will attempt to (1) become certain of this truth, and (2) consequently, become certain of what it, itself, is. Active consciousness does not begin, as passive consciousness did, with a feeling of certainty (in "sense certainty") but with a feeling of *desire*.

Desire as a Play Between Implicit Truth and Certainty

Hegel thus frames the concept of "desire" around the distinction between certainty and truth. To fully understand the beginning of the scene described in part two, the reader must understand a point repeatedly made by Hyppolite in his rigorous commentary on the *Phenomenology of Spirit*: each new major section of the *Phenomenology* begins as if consciousness has "forgotten" the previous stages and the results of their dialectical movement (Hyppolite 1974). So active consciousness does not begin with full conceptual thought. Active consciousness cannot recall discovering that the truth of sense certainty is itself. Rather, this "result" is an implicit feature of desire. Active consciousness begins as desire, which is rather like an urge to make an implicitly known truth explicit.

So the desire characteristic of reflective consciousness, of human consciousness, is ontologically rooted in an implicit truth and oriented toward an experience of certainty about this truth. Active consciousness begins as the desire to be certain of a preunderstanding it possesses with respect to itself: that it is the truth of all form and therefore that it is the unlimited possibility of all form.

Consciousness as Nothingness Striving for Being

Yet active consciousness begins in "life" and experiences itself as limited. It has a body, it is distinguished from other objects, it is a sort of object itself. It is a finite subject. But the finite subject is not limited in the way that an object is because a subject is aware of its limits and continually seeks to transgress them. That is the mode in which the identity of the subject first becomes present to itself: as desire to strive beyond limits, desire for certainty of its unlimited nature. The "being" of active consciousness is not a "being-in-itself" determined by delimitable form, but rather a "being-for-itself" determined by its efforts to feel certain of its unlimited nature. Effort and desire are its modes of being, not qualities attached externally to that being.

At first active consciousness seeks certainty of this preunderstood truth, that it is unlimited, infinite, through the way it experiences objects. The identity of the subject is not form but is first given through experience as the negation of form. The subject is the "not-this" within the experience of the "this." In Eastern philosophy the same idea is expressed as *neti, neti*: "[I am] not this, not that." In "pure life," says Hegel, "nothing as such does not exist ... but we are the nothingness" (Hegel quoted in Hyppolite 1974:155). One of Sartre's major philosophical texts is entitled with the same scene in mind: *Being and Nothingness*. Consciousness is "nothingness" that tends toward being (form), but that is plagued by the contradiction that it is beyond all form; that it is unlimited.

The experience of being "not this" comes through actively negating a "this," an external form, by eating it, or moving it, or otherwise exercising power over it. Objects are negated in developmentally early modes of desire. New objects appear within experience and they, too, are "consumed" or altered through some action undertaken by the subject. An endless process of desiring objects outside the self and negating them through acting upon them gives a repeated feeling of certainty that the truth of the subject is negation of form (and thus a bare feeling/touch upon the truth that the unlimited subject is the substance of all objects). This process of negating objects, however, does not satisfy for long. For Hegel, a slight feeling of certainty with respect to the truth of the self as unlimited is provided with every act of consumption (every act of object-negation) but active consciousness desires genuine, full, lasting certainty of its infinite nature. Endless consumption will not satisfy this desire.

Thus the subject "tends toward the infinite, the unconditioned," but "this infinite is not an object; it is a task, the accomplishment of which is forever deferred" (Hyppolite 1974:145). In Hegelian language, desire is the *form* of the infinite seeking to overcome the limits of the subject, the limits of form. Continual consumption provides a vague and temporary feeling of certainty, a "promise" that the subject is unlimited, infinite, but one that defers full gratification with every act. To become fully certain of itself as unlimited, consciousness must raise the implicit truth in desire to an explicit truth. Hegel plays beautifully with the terms "certainty" and "truth" and provides us with important insights, in this way, as to the nature of desire.

The Contradiction in Desire

Now, "truth" for Hegel is conceptual truth, which amounts to having a "grasp" on something. To have a grasp on something is to be detached from it so as to recognize its boundaries, or "determinations." My certainty of the existence of this bowl in all its particularities requires the delineation and full representation of its features to become a truth. My desire for certainty of the truth of myself amounts to a desire to take an implicit truth and make it explicit in a similar way. This will also require delineation and representation of features.

But how could my unlimited, infinite nature be grasped in this way? How could I delimit what is unlimited? In the case of an active consciousness that becomes bored with continual consumption this problem appears in a specific way. If I try to grasp the truth of myself I must have myself before me. Having one's self before one is objectifying one's self in some way. But how is it possible to objectify one's self when one is unlimited, when one is that which always transgresses all limits? In Hegel's words, consciousness "never is what it is and always is what it is not" (see Hyppolite 1974:150).

Hegel begins with an active consciousness that does not yet reflect and conceptualize. The active consciousness gains an implicit sense of itself through action. It feels itself as the "not" of all active experiences, as that which is beyond the objects of action. Consciousness is not a form to itself but a preconceptual I-feeling that is gained fleetingly through continuously negating forms in various ways. It is a feeling that by its nature escapes the boundaries necessary for it to become an explicit truth, an object of knowledge. Consciousness suspects but does not know its infinite nature.

The Desire for Recognition

This prereflective consciousness comes to seek certainty of itself through the eyes of another active consciousness. It cannot be an object for itself but perhaps it can be an object in the eyes of another. If this other is an unlimited subjectivity, and if it then recognizes the implicit truth of active consciousness as unlimited and infinite, then a full feeling of certainty may arise. Preconceptually, desire becomes desire for the recognition of another consciousness. The implicit truth that consciousness is unlimited and infinite constitutes a desire of infinite promise and anticipation: the desire for recognition. The way to explicate the implicit truth seems to rest on the possibility of the totally affirming gaze of another.

The next scene in Hegel's story is famous and is his version of our scene three. Two active consciousnesses engage in a life-and-death struggle with each other, each desiring the recognition of the other. Recognition can only be one-way in this setting: it amounts to one consciousness consenting to limit itself as an affirmation of the limitlessness of the other. It is a scene rather like that of two schoolchildren fighting. Each one will be satisfied if the other gives in by indicating in words or otherwise that the winner is "the best," that the winner is beyond the one defeated and is not limited by the loser. It does not matter to the children whether or not the other is "objectively beaten" (the limit case being the other's death). Rather, the point of the fight is to have the defeated *agree* or recognize that she or he is defeated, which is the ultimate way to affirm or recognize the victory of the other.

Desire and Fear

This is a life-and-death struggle in Hegel's scene because it is a scene of only two consciousnesses, both of whom pin everything on the outcome. "Pinning everything on the outcome" is to be taken in a very strong sense, because Hegel describes this struggle as the *origin* of self-consciousness. The fear involved is not simply a matter of "losing face," it is a matter of not existing at all, it is fear of the void. Losing is an affirmation of the absolute nothingness experienced in desire. Losing locates the implicit truth that consciousness is infinite solely in the victor. When the fight begins, each participant must cope with this total fear, this total uncertainty, this terror that one might be nothing. The loser bends to fear, chooses "life" (biological life), and acknowledges herself or himself as nothingness. The winner does not bend to fear, risks life absolutely, and thereby feels infinitely affirmed through the recognition of the other. Winning is an ultimate fear rendered baseless and impotent. Losing is an ultimate fear come true. The desire for recognition is intimately linked to a primordial form of fear.

Self Consciousness and Intersubjectivity

With the completion of this struggle, *self*-consciousness has evolved. The victor is self-conscious by virtue of the affirmative gaze of the defeated. The defeated is only implicitly self-conscious, for it finds its truth in the victor and sees itself as nothing through the victor's eyes.

Self-consciousness begins, then, with a social relationship: the relationship of the master to the slave. The social relationship is now internalized in two distinctive ways. The master struts about feeling infinitely affirmed, but only for a brief period. The slave begins to work for the master and internalizes the master's attitude toward herself or himself by disciplining herself or himself to perform work.

Hegel goes on from here to show the dialectics inherent in the situation. The master requires the slave to perform work, but the recognition won by the master turns out to be a dead-end. The slave is no longer a full subject whose recognition could really "count," whose withdrawal of recognition is infinitely feared. Repeated affirmations from the slave do not satisfy the continuously arising desire for self-certainty. It is rather like the author of a bestseller who begins to suspect that people who "really matter" do not appreciate the book, that those who applaud the book's brilliance do not really understand it. The slave has become a sort of "object" in the master's eyes, and recognition can count only if it comes from another unlimited subject who symbolizes the possibility of being nothing as well as the possibility of being all. Since this sort of recognition turns out to be impossible after every single act to win it, fear of the void is not vanquished, only dulled, with each victory.

The slave, meanwhile, internalizes its relationship to the master through work. While working, the truth of the slave's own nature is discovered through the internalization of the relationship: the slave's ability to take both positions, master and slave, within herself or himself. And this truth takes an objective form in the products of her or his work. The unlimited nature of consciousness is felt once again within the consciousness of the slave, each time her or his creativity and self-discipline produce another product. Yet this too turns out to be unsatisfactory. Slave consciousness evolves into the stoical attitude in which nothing external is allowed to limit the nature of consciousness. Consciousness is unlimited thought, now possible because a social relationship has been internalized and because internal reflection between self and implicit other may take place. But this also turns out to be limited: the stoic finds it necessary to act toward an external world once again in a continuously negating way in order to experience the fleeting sense of being beyond all form. This time, however, "form" is the intellectual products of others, all of which carry some claim of unconditionality, of infinitely being-beyond with respect to the authors' identity. The stoic has become the skeptic, displaying her or his own limitlessness through the negation of others' claims to limitlessness. And so on: the dialectic keeps going, from stoicism to skepticism to unhappy consciousness ... eventually to "absolute knowledge."

Insights

Remember that it is the insights Hegel provides us, rather than his specific arguments, that must capture our interest. In this section I will specify nine insights from Hegel's *Phenomenology* that illuminate scene three in important ways.

The idea that an ontologically fundamental desire constitutes consciousness.

This fundamental desire is the desire to overcome limits as well as the desire to attain certain knowledge about the real nature of the self. In contrast to various desires that consciousness may have from time to time, this desire is part of what consciousness is. Less-fundamental desires that seem to come and to go, such as desires for food and for sex, appear rather like vehicles for this ever-present mode of desire within Hegel's dialectic of active consciousness. Most modern theories of evolution would consider the emergence of self-consciousness from consciousness to be merely the product of adaptation and survival needs. For Hegel, self-consciousness emerges as the product of a primordial desire for certain self-knowledge. Once self-consciousness has emerged this fundamental desire is still unfulfilled; it remains to drive further developments in consciousness.

The idea that desire may be related to the concept of "implicit truth."

The desire for certainty that Hegel wrote about begins as a preunderstanding that seeks to make itself explicit and therefore certain. Self-consciousness is originally constituted by desire as the anticipation of a grand and fundamental self-validation. Consciousness is teleological, directed toward the realization of a truth about itself that it has always suspected to be true.

The relationship between desire and the fear of being nothing.

The fear of being nothing is a prominent feature of human motivation. The desire to become certain of one's self seems to be primordially linked to an existential fear of being groundless or of not being at all. Weaker versions of this fear include the dread of being worthless.

The experience of a preunderstanding of one's true nature as a fleeting feeling of certainty: rather like the I-feeling mode discussed earlier in scene two.

The preunderstanding of what Hegel regarded as the implicit truth of the self is a desire that receives partial satisfaction through continuous action. Prior to the internalization of social relationships, this satisfaction comes just after each act (of negation, in Hegel's scheme) but then quickly fades away into new desire.

The orientation of desire toward another consciousness; desire as desire for recognition.

After social relationships are internalized so as to produce self-consciousness, the preunderstanding of the self develops into a preunderstanding of the stances others take toward one's self. Eventually this preunderstanding takes its various forms against generalized, internalized others, in accordance with Mead's views.

The origin of self-consciousness in social relationships that centrally involve power.

Hegel gave central roles to power and domination at the very beginnings of self-consciousness. Many humans seem to pin their sense of having a valid identity on being powerful, and only through further development, should this occur, learn to maintain valid identities in equal social relationships. Historically, women have often been the dominated others for men and yet have developed and maintained identities within this structure of inequality. Though power may not be a necessary structure for the emergence of self-consciousness, it frequently does play a crucial role. Feminist theories, postcolonial theories, all theories that concern domination and oppression can benefit from Hegel's insights into the relationship between power, desire, and the self.

The desire for recognition arises out of a problematic similar to those raised in our scenes one and two.

Recognition is a sort of "recollection"; a second "seeing" of one's self which requires the "eyes" of another. It is one's own actions that one is able to gain a second seeing of through the eyes of another; one's actions (the "me") rather than the origin of these actions (the "I") and always just after these actions have taken place. Superimposed onto the question "who am I and how may I know it?," recollection appears as the contradiction of trying to represent what is not form (the "I") as a form (the "me"). Thus desire for recognition informs our understanding of recollection, and our analysis of recollection informs our understanding of the desire for recognition.

The understanding that recollection, which appears as a sort of given subjective process or capacity in our previous two scenes, appears here as constituted by intersubjectivity, or position taking.

This insight is of course totally in line with Mead's theory. Recollection is the metaphorical viewing of something that just occurred (an act or performance from a first person perspective) from different perspectives that are socially given (second and third person positions). Recollection amounts to the effort to capture and fix the meaning of a performative act from the positions of others who observed the performance.

Thus, recollection depends on experiences of having others respond to one's acts and performances.

Recollection is motivated by a desire for an affirmative response to one's acts—"yes" as opposed to "no." And responses of others to any of one's acts may always have implications with respect to the self of the actor. The desired affirmative responses, moreover, are not going to permanently satisfy the desire for recognition.

The Self and Presence

Mead's handling of scene three misses many insights that one can find in the Hegelian fantasy. A particularly important contribution from Hegel is the desire for recognition. The desire for recognition, in turn, is rooted in a teleological view of the self; the self as desire to know itself for certain to be eternal, limitless being. This insight is missing from Mead, but it seems congruent with some of the discussion presented on scenes one and two, and it adds significantly to our understanding of recollection. It can be reformulated in nonHegelian terminology and in nonHegelian contexts. It is clearly related to what Derrida calls "the longing for presence" (1974). In Gayatri Spivak's discussion of Derrida's work, she says the self is constituted by its "never-fully-to-be-recognized-ness" (1974:xliv). The longing for presence is also a longing for recognition. Total recognition, however, is as impossible to experience as pure presence, and for the same ontological reasons. Impossible, that is, unless the Eastern theories discussed within the section on the feeling-body bear truth. If they do, pure presence and total recognition are indeed possible but only with the mutual collapse of world and self into a state that can never be represented for either communication or memory. In many Eastern philosophies it is said that one can never remember the state of enlightenment, only the moments just before and the moments just after.

Scene Three, the I-Feeling, and the Trace

An I-feeling mode can be recollected as an experience that comes close to containing its own self-erasure. We need fewer conceptual steps to realize that the I-feeling mode is going-gone as soon as we reflect upon it than we need in the case of perceived "objects." In fact, it is the almost immediacy of the fading away of an I-feeling mode that seems to suggest the less immediately understood fading away of any object of experience; the "trace" as Derrida first introduced it in his deconstruction of Husserl.

The I-feeling mode accompanies all perception because perception, in my view, is a set of acts, a group of impeti that are organized by a project. An object is first a preobject in experience that is only differentiated from the impetus within which it first appears through a special sort of internalized action: perception. The problem that time poses for "presence" is something felt, is a feature of experience, before it becomes a concept like the "trace" when impeti to act are the units of phenomenological study.

Thus the I-feeling mode is prior to the trace. The claim I am making here is subtle and could be missed. As a *concept*, the I-feeling mode is just a different iteration of "trace" and must be regarded as the result of a framework of reflection that has been pushed to its self-destructing limits. As a concept alone, nothing more could be theoretically built upon the "I-feeling mode" than could be built upon the "trace." And Derrida's use of "trace" is purely deconstructive.

But my claim is that *within experience* there is a sensation always present that is felt to be ungraspable, unrepresentable. The I-feeling-as-fading-away is experienced though not exactly perceived and thus not experienced in quite the same way that Husserl claimed to perceive retentions. To make this claim I must use a certain understanding of "presence." I must write as if this experience is somehow "the same" each time it occurs and I must write as if there were an intersubjectively recognizable identity between this experience as I repeatedly have it and this experience as you repeatedly have it. Yet the nature of this experience is that it slips away, that it is both always the same and yet always differently embodied in that there is always a different "mode" of

I-ness. So I am describing an experience that, though a "sensation," is also a type of understanding that this sensation cannot be represented in thought or language. One might question whether or not such a claim on my part is coherent, an issue that I will now address.

Scene two, and portions of my discussion of Hegel, serve us by illuminating the possible coherence of this claim. Hegel's idea of an implicit understanding that tries to become certain of itself is completely congruent with my description of the I-feeling mode. An implicit understanding, argues Hegel, accompanies all acts of consumption (object negation) that partially and temporarily satisfy a desire for certainty about one's true nature. Desire is related to an implicit understanding, argues Hegel, that the self is unlimited. Because desire is a form of anticipation, it prefigures the nature of its gratification. The desire and the pre-understanding (the implicit truth) are conjoined within a single sensation.

Hegel simply *tells* us that part of this anticipation involves the implicit understanding that the self is unlimited. He feels justified in asserting this because of his dialectic of passive consciousness, which supposedly leads from a feeling of certainty that sense objects exist as independent objects toward the conceptual understanding that subjectivity is the truth of all objectivity. This is the conclusion of the first book of *The Phenomenology of Spirit*. Hegel does not give us a full phenomenological treatment of the nature of desire as an implicit understanding that the self is unlimited.

In my phenomenological investigation of proprioception (scene two), on the other hand, I found an I-feeling mode to be part of every impetus to act or think, and I found this I-feeling mode to be a form of desire. The gratification Hegel writes of is experienced on the level of sensation and feeling: an enhanced I-feeling that follows a successful act. In my analysis there is also an implicit understanding associated with an I-feeling mode. As the symbol pointing forward, the understanding is that the I-feeling will be enhanced through action. As the symbol pointing backward, however, the understanding is that the nature of the I-feeling might be grasped through reflection. Associated with this is a new mode of the I-feeling itself, the mode correlated with the desire to reflect upon the I-feeling mode. This sort of self-reference brings about a movement in which the implicit understanding senses its certainty in the object already fading away (the I-feeling mode as that which just was: as intended object of reflection) and projects the gratification of the promise of implicit certainty ahead as the explification of the I-feeling mode (I-feeling modes are always embedded within action impeti).

In Hegelian terminology, the subject is in possession of the implicit truth that the object is itself and seeks certainty of this implicit truth through an explication of it; through acquiring a rational grasp of it. In other words, the subject is seeking self-knowledge, seeking to explicate the truth that its object is itself. But this process encounters the problematic of presence, which is one reason why Hegel's dialectic leads next to the encounter with another consciousness. The desire to explicate the preunderstanding evolves into a desire for recognition.

A MODEL OF MEANING

In this essay I have described meaningful action through a phenomenological sketch and then considered the question of meaning against three originary scenes. We might now experience a temptation to bring things together and draw some conclusions. However, given the complexities of this subject, "bringing things together" is not a straightforward affair. The meaning of meaning has been an implicit understanding of mine as I wrote each section of this essay. Each major section, each scene, has been something like an explication of implicit understandings, which, plowed back into the soils of tacit understandings, has enriched what must remain implicit. Perhaps the more this state of affairs is accepted, by sort of "letting go" on a conceptual level, the more our forestructures will accumulate toward something like wisdom rather than philosophy. Perhaps all this effort to explicate implicit hunches and yearnings ought to be left in a movement rather like that described in scene two, but within the alternative register that writing and thinking employ.

Nevertheless, I regularly use some of the formulations that emerged from the various exercises that compose this essay. I have already formulated and published a model of meaning based on much of what is contained in the previous pages. I have described it, drawn diagrams of it, taught it to students, and used it in my own qualitative research. This model can be found explained and illustrated in my book on critical ethnography (Carspecken 1996). I find it highly effective for hermeneutic, reconstructive analyses of culture and in-depth self-exploratory interviews. I do not regard it as finished. I am sure I will continue to fill in its various regions and alter it in other ways as my work continues.

But we know that even a more complete version of the model would be necessarily limited, for it was composed with the understanding that formulations of meaning amount to acts directed toward vanishing points. The model can be used to undermine itself, if one wishes to do so, and that is something I rather like about it. It can also be used in an unlimited number of creative ways: each use will be different, will be a guided work of creativity. Each use can change and enrich the guiding model. I like that about it too.

Since the model itself has been explained in another publication, I choose a weak ending to this particular essay. I will not present the full model here. I will not try to synthesize all that has been said in earlier sections in order to produce a neat and tidied ending. All that I will do is outline the essential components of the model. Here are the components:

An Expressivist Model of Action

A meaningful act can be viewed as the explication of an implicit, holistic meaning. The act manifests an impetus into a temporal sequence of behaviors. The meaning of the act is dependent on its embodiment in the act itself. A meaningful act interprets and clarifies its point.

The implicit and holistic moment is a form of desire that points toward its own expression as a promise or anticipation. For an act to be meaningful, the desire entering into its constitution must be inclusive of the clarification of the point, either directly (as in acts oriented toward reaching an understanding) or indirectly (as in acts oriented toward producing certain responses from others, who must understand the act in order to *do* what is desired).

The articulated, embodied, moment clarifies the implicit meaning constituting the impetus but only through the process of "monitoring"—the process by which an actor takes second and third person perspectives on her act, during and just after the act's manifestation. By "act" I mean to include thought. Thought is the "internal evolution" of impeti through internalized forms of expressive action and monitoring.

All monitoring, however, results in an impression of meaning that is also holistic and implicit. Understanding the act of another also occurs through acquiring such impressions. An impression of meaning is a set of impeti to act again, and this may be accomplished in three modes corresponding to first, second, and third person positions.

Thus a meaningful act involves complex part-whole relationships that are related to its constitution through monitoring and, in many cases, its premonitored nature. Meaning is constituted through taking first, second, and third person positions with respect to an act. Meaning is intersubjectively constituted.

This initial frame within which to sketch my model of meaning is similar to the expressivist theory of human existence that Charles Taylor traces to the philosophy of Herder (Taylor 1979). However, the frame introduced here adds the concept of monitoring and includes the experience of receiving an impression of meaning. The first person position emphasized in expressivism is here conjoined to second and third person positions. The transposition of positions within the constitution of a meaningful act will be considered next.

Moment-Totality Relations along Horizontal and Vertical Dimensions

We can analyze the meaning horizon of an act along two dimensions. Let us use a spatial metaphor to call these dimensions the horizontal and the vertical.

Horizontally, meaningful acts are constituted within the holistic, implicit, impetus through tacit assumptions and claims about the subjective state of the actor, about the nature of the objective world shared between actors, and about standards for judging the well-formedness of the act (what is comprehensible, what is "proper") and its moral and ethical implications (what is good, bad, right, wrong). This is basically Habermas's theory of communicative action conjoined with an expressivist model. The researcher must reconstruct these tacit claims to approach an articulation of the meaning of an act. But such reconstructions will always be partial. Horizon disclosure cannot totally exhaust the implicit and holistic impetus that constitutes both the act and the impressions produced by the act in those addressed by it or otherwise experiencing it. As Habermas says:

> [The horizon] contains parareflective certainties of a holistic nature which can't be exhausted by a finite specification of conditions. (Habermas 1987a:195).

Vertically, all such reconstructed claims can be layered from claims most immediate to the meaning of an act to those most remote. Again, Habermas is helpful for understanding this aspect of the horizon or forestructure of an act:

> Inasmuch as communicative agents reciprocally raise validity claims with their speech acts, they are relying on the potential of assailable grounds. Hence, a moment of unconditionality is built into factual processes of mutual understanding—the validity laid claim to is

distinguished from the social currency of a de facto established practice and yet serves it as the foundation of an existing consensus. The validity claimed for propositions and norms transcends spaces and times, "blots out" space and time; but the claim is always raised here and now, in specific contexts, and is either accepted or rejected with factual consequences for action. (Habermas 1987a:322-323)

The reconstruction of a horizon, when inferring meaning from social action, must note levels of unconditionality. Immediate claims within any of the three horizontal categories will depend on less immediate claims which will in turn implicate more remote claims. Often, the more remote a claim is within a meaning horizon, the stronger is its particular claim to unconditional status. This is because remote claims are usually least noticed and most assumed. But the moment of unconditionality applies to all claims within a meaning horizon. More of this is discussed and illustrated in the last essay within this collection: "Five Third Person Positions."

A meaning horizon is therefore rather like an entire world that is tacitly claimed into existence with every meaningful act. The qualitative researcher can reconstruct the presuppositions of such worlds, beginning with those most particular to the act and then moving outwards toward what is most universal and unconditional. The further outward one goes, the more data one requires to substantiate the reconstruction.

Use of the Text Metaphor

Relations between the reconstructed claims of a meaning horizon may be examined. The world claimed by every act structures its various elements in diverse ways. Sets of structured semantic and pragmatic terms are implicated in every meaningful act. Relations of homology and binary opposition are often found (e.g.: masculine is to feminine as street knowledge is to school knowledge), as well as relations of logical inclusion and implication (e.g.: unreasonable requests need not be obeyed, asking one to take a test when it is too hard is unreasonable, tests can be ranked from "hard" to "easy"). For examples of the use of the text metaphor, see Carspecken and Apple 1992, Carspecken and Cordeiro 1995, Carspecken 1996.

The Idea of Embodied Meaning

Qualitative researchers can gain much by describing the gestures and postures accompanying an act in order to gain more immediate insights on the nature of the impetus. This sort of analysis has been well exemplified in *Schooling as a Ritual Performance* by Peter McLaren (1993). This model of meaning allows perceptions of the body position of another to help the researcher reconstruct portions of the horizon constituting an act. Body posture and gesture not only indicate subjective states, however, they also reveal much of the normative and identity references involved.

The Desire for Recognition

Lastly, the concept of the horizon takes on added depth when viewed next to our analysis of scenes two and three together. All meaningful acts will have an existential, ontological dimension to them. Sometimes this dimension, which occupies the identity claim most immediately, is foregrounded and sometimes it is not. However, the qualitative researcher needs to understand that it is always there. People claim their valid being across the abyss of scene one with every act. Meaningful acts express something like the "will to power" and the "will to knowledge" (see my essay "Power, Truth, and Method" in this collection). Tacit levels of awareness supply a level of ontological suspicion that one may in fact be nothing and this suspicion is layered over by secondary suspicions that one may be limitable, objectifiable, and thus less than one desires to be. Meaningful acts are expressed against such ontological suspicions, at varying levels of risk depending upon purposes and contexts.

When reconstructing a horizon in terms of its normative and objective world claims, the qualitative researcher must be attuned to the fact that actors ultimately stake their existence on their activity. Challenges to the validity of a claim about the world or a claim about what is right and what is wrong could be experienced as challenges to one's ontological security. The full implications of the connection between horizon structures and existential claims has been exploited in another publication that may be consulted as an illustration of this point (Carspecken 1992).

SUMMARY

These, then, are components of a model of meaning, congruent with my phenomenological analysis of meaningful acts followed by the discussion of three originary scenes. Meaningful acts can be reconstructed by employing the horizon model with its horizontal and vertical dimensions and by paying attention to the identity claim that accompanies every meaningful act. Moments and components of meaning constituting acts can be analyzed via the text metaphor to reveal structural relations typical of a culture or a personality.

The model as described above is a set of images from which many specific strategies for inferring meaning may be derived. I have only provided the barest of frameworks in this essay and I have discussed many things in this essay that have not been explicitly addressed by the model.

The various discussions conducted within this essay should make it clear that this model is not meant to be a definitive statement on the nature of meaning. Rather, the impossibility of making any such definitive statement is part of the meaning of this model. The model is self-consciously a grand act of recollection, an assertion of the will-to-knowledge. It is intended to be at once useful and deconstructable.

I promised to provide a very weak ending to this essay and now I have done so. The various discussions conducted within the various sections of this paper are meant to be intrinsically interesting explorations of meaning. They were not conducted mainly for the purpose of ending in a model of meaning useful for qualitative researchers. The sketch of a model I have presented at the end is nevertheless consistent with major themes that emerged and it was formulated with the previous explorations in mind.

Essay Four

FIVE THIRD PERSON POSITIONS AND THEIR RELEVANCE TO REFLECTION, VALIDITY, AND SYSTEMS ANALYSIS

INTRODUCTION

In 1997 I coauthored a paper with Laurie MacGillivray designed to address the issue of reflection in fieldwork.[1] One of my contributions to this article was a longish section that was deleted before publication. The book editors believed our article too long and found this particular section especially dense and unsupported. I was sorry to see it go and am most happy to have it published in this book of essays.

Many students have asked me about the third person position and whether or not there is more than one third person position involved in understanding and constructing meaning. There is indeed more than one third person position, and variations between third person positions follow both an analytic and an empirical continuum. I present five such positions in these notes. I also relate the constitution of third person positions to the concepts of validity and reflection. At the end of these notes, I discuss how the third person position comes into play with systems analysis.

VALIDITY CLAIMS AND THE THREE FORMAL SPEECH POSITIONS

Validity claims are related to the three formal speech positions: the first, second, and third person positions. Subjective validity claims are associated with the first person position; normative-evaluative validity claims with the second person as well as the first person plural positions; and objective validity claims with the third person position. It is from the first person position taken

---

[1] The full reference is P. Carspecken and L. MacGillivray, "Raising Consciousness about Reflection, Validity, and Meaning." In *Being Reflexive in Critical Educational and Social Research*, edited by G. Shacklock and J. Symth (London: Falmer Press, 1998).

most primordially that we have such subjective claims as "I intend," "I feel," "I am aware of." It is with respect to the second person position that we experience the impositions of imperatives on us or impose them on others: "You should," "You ought." We also impose imperatives on others inclusive of ourselves through the first person plural position: "We do things this way," "This is not appropriate for us." Finally, it is with respect to the third person position that we assert: "This is here now," "This took place," "This has these sensual qualities," and "When such-and-such occurs, such-and-such occurs next."

The constitution of an act also implicitly involves structures of reflection. Reflection involves a relation of perspectives that constitute acts and responses to acts. Reflections usually just seem to happen in experience, but higher order reflections can be deliberately induced as a special sort of project; as when a researcher decides to "get reflective" and deliberately thinks over her field experiences.

Reflection is structured in relation to the formal speech positions, as the following discussion will illustrate.

REFLECTION AND POSITION-TAKING

Reflection is inherent to intersubjectivity. Reflecting is basically an internal shift of position, so that a former state could in principle be *talked about* with others. The former state I am referring to could be any subjective or communicative state. If communicative it would be structured by a typification: a culturally shared understanding of a meaningful situation in which agents interact. When a reflection occurs the former state becomes an objectification framed within a new typification for communicating with others. The former state was something to be and act through; after reflection it becomes something to talk about. A former state can be talked about when one occupies a new state in which to be and act through: a new typification. One must take a new position in order to represent an older position to an audience. Reflection is therefore internalized position-taking. One either talks about the former state with others or thinks about it in relation to an internalized audience. The sorts of internalized position-taking that can bring about a reflection may be specified as various points along a continuum.

Primordial forms of reflection show up in basic action monitoring. Higher order forms of reflection occur when communicating with others explicitly about past interactions, and when thinking about one's own thoughts. Many in-between points could be arbitrarily marked on the reflection continuum. In all cases, reflection means occupying some kind of third person position with respect to one's own (previous) activities, situation, and thinking.

What is this third person position? It is the position that any anonymous member of a specific cultural grouping could take, and it is thus itself a culturally constituted position. Using the metaphor of stepping outside of something in order to better examine it, the third person position can be described as always in some sense *outside* a typification: either right at the typification's *edge*, as when one monitors an act to be sure it conforms to the typification in play; or firmly within a second typification, as when a group of people talk together about the interactions of others. The third person position always has this empirical and contingent dimension to it: it is "outside" one typification specific to a cultural group but "inside" another.

Yet this third person position has an idealized moment to it, a moment that feels like a God's-eye, noncontingent view. At first reflection, one feels as if one occupies a universal outsider's position from which all else can be seen clearly.

Then, as soon as we notice that our perspective on a prior interaction, or on an interaction performed by others, is *also* culturally constructed, we have reflected once again. We have moved into another, more universal third person position. Of course this position also has its empirical and contingent dimension, even though it first feels like a God's-eye view. But as we reflect again and again, the typifications we progressively enter, typifications that subsume many other typifications as objects to be discussed, the empirical side takes broader and broader cultural groupings into account. It claims to fuse more cultural horizons toward a limit case of a position that any sentient being could occupy.

The "empirical side" of the idealized moment of the third person position comes from the understanding that any actual position occupied could be reflected from, objectified, and shown to be culturally constituted. From the third person we can claim that such-and-such happened in an interaction and that its range of possible meanings to the participants include such-and-such. And we make such claims with the implication that any sentient being who shares our third person position would agree. From the perspective of the empirical side, the perspective that acknowledges cultural contingencies to all points of view, such claims can always be tested simply by inviting members of various cultural groupings to examine one's claims and discuss them. If they agree with the claims, the universality of the position gains some contingent (always fallible) support. If they disagree and successfully explain why to us, then our third person position shifts yet again to include their cultural horizon.

There is also an analytic, noncontingent side to the universalizing moment of the third person position. This comes from the fact that third person claims carry an assertion that all others *ought* to agree despite actual contingencies associated with the claim. The basis of this universalizing claim is its dependence on a claimed universal third person audience.

Let's take a hypothetical example that has a normative-evaluative claim in the foreground. Because a normative-evaluative claim is in the foreground, the universalizing third person position carried by the claim pertains to the audience: the abstract and universalized group implied by the claim that would assent to the validity of the claim.

Here is the hypothetical example: Imagine that I said to you, "Torture is bad in most situations, so let's donate money to Amnesty International." You agree, and we all pool money together to send off to Amnesty International. My claim won your support and helped to coordinate our subsequent activities. But my principal validity claim, and your agreement to it, was based on more than all of the contingencies that influenced your assent. I meant that "in most situations, torture is really bad and all others really should agree." You assented. But empirical contingencies always help to structure validity claims and the assent or rejection of others. They would have been involved in your assent in this hypothetical case. Contingencies in this case could include the fact that we all had enough money to consider donating some, that maybe we wanted to be seen as "good people," that some of us are just plain afraid of being tortured and superstitiously suspect that helping others under torture might ensure that we are never put in that horrible situation. But my initial claim could not include these contingencies, if it was made sincerely rather than as a mask for other claims. And your assent had to be for the validity of that claim, on its own, aside from influences, if your assent was made sincerely. Whether we were *really* sincere or not—whether sincerity in a case like this must anyway be only an approximation—is not relevant to the point. The point is that the distinction between contingent factors that influence both claims and their reception, and a universalizing moment to these claims must structure validity claims. This distinction between the universal and the contingent must be present as constituting structures in all validity claims.

So even if I were trying to trick you into giving money, this distinction had to be in play for the trick to work: to *be* a trick. Even if you really cared only about how you looked to others, the distinction had to be there for your dramaturgy to *be* dramaturgy.

Now, the claim to universality here is the claim that torture really is bad and all others really ought to agree. An audience is presupposed: one that I claim to identify with and one that I claim you *ought* to identify with. This audience is implied to be fully universal, all sentient beings ought to belong to it.

If my claim were to be relativized and its universality challenged, then a reflection would occur moving us from one foregrounded audience to another, more universal, audience. The reflection would move us from the audience that is implied by the original claim to a more universal audience that is implied by the act of challenge. That is, the audience claimed as universal would be shown up as in fact culturally contingent and particular. But the objectification of the original audience implies yet another audience claimed with universal status.

The audience first claimed as something like a universal subject now becomes objectified to the status of a contingent historical-cultural grouping. If one said, "Well, many people think that torture is really and always bad; but in some cases it is not," one then introduces a new universal audience and subject. This new universal audience could spot the contingencies of the initial claim.

The third person position recedes along a continuum of reflection after reflection *because* of the analytic, noncontingent, universalizing moment of all validity claims. Interactions with people from other cultures, who use typifications other than those we are familiar with, press upon the universalizing moment to reveal empirical constituents of the assertion. The contingency of other cultural groupings, other typifications, will generate horizon fusions or broader typifications that include more and yet more members of the human race. Each time such a fusion occurs empirically, a new audience is constructed and claimed to be universal.

The metaphor of stepping outside something in order to see it better helps to capture, in imagery, the movement called reflection. Each step-out-of is a step-in-to the perspective of another grouping. Yet, from within this process, stepping-out-of generates the experience and the associated claim of having reached a universal and noncontingent position.

If a process of reflection stays true to the universalizing moments of the original validity claims, a process of horizon fusion is brought about. Original validity claims are understood from broader perspectives and thus are relativized from those broader perspectives even as they are still understood. The effort to "still understand," as opposed to the effort to negate and replace, requires a fusion of horizons and a broadening of the universal position.

So the metaphor of stepping outside to see better must be supplemented with the metaphor of unfolding what was *always inside*. And "unfolding" involves self-reference. It is a process of unfolding implicit structures and frameworks to produce larger structures and frameworks that can include the former as objectifications about which to talk and think. The contingency of multiple cultural groupings forces the unfolding and allows for empirical tests of claims meant to win universal consent. All one need do to test such claims is to invite representatives from various cultures to examine one's claims and discuss them. Of course, language differences and many other things make empirical tests like these, tests that "member checks" and "peer debriefing" represent, very problematical in practice. But understanding the principles provides us with the regulating rules and the limit cases needed to approximate validation procedures in practice.

THE UNIVERSAL AND THE PARTICULAR

Many currently fashionable discourses used by academics in cultural studies argue against the idea that there is anything universal in validity claims. The idea that there are only cultural pluralities incommensurable with each other is quite popular in some circles. The relationship between the concepts of universal and particular, however, appears to be unavoidably at play in all validity claims. The idea that all cultures have their own validity claims which are incommensurable with the validity claims of other cultures is itself a claim with clearly universalizing intentions.

A careful analysis of reflection and its relationship with validity suggests a solution to the classical philosophical dichotomy between universalism and relativism. The solution is to regard the dichotomy as a false one. No validity claims are truly universal because a cultural and contingent side can always be found with respect to each and every claim. But no validity claims are purely relative to culture and circumstances because all such claims include the claim to universality.

The universal and the particular are moments constituting all specific validity claims. These moments are dialectically related. The dialectical relationship between the universal and the particular drive the internal mode of reflection that is analytic and necessary.

The dialectic between the universal and the particular takes a different embodiment within the three different types of validity claim. Reflections use the third person position differently in the case of each type of claim. How the third person position is employed for objective claims is quite obvious. If we make a claim about the temperature outside and use the centigrade scale we have broadened a claim we might make just for each other, within our culturally specific typifications, that it is "cold." Recast in a refined objective language, we have a claim about the rise of mercury along the centigrade scale. The assertion about the temperature is open to multiple access within a typification claimed to be universal to all human beings. All we need do is make sure that any actual occupant of the third person position understands the centigrade scale.

But if we make either a subjective or a normative-evaluative claim, then use of the third person position occurs in a more complicated way. In the case of normative-evaluative claims the most universal norms/values that can be asserted will involve procedures and pragmatic infrastructures simultaneously asserted to be in place and acknowledged by members of the very audience that constitutes the broadest conceivable typification. That is, the normative-evaluative claims explicated as *content* must simultaneously be assumed as interactive *infrastructure*. Thus the most universal normative-evaluative claims should be pictured at the edge of the universal audience rather than within it, and a discussion of them should involve a refined practice of reflection.

The ultimate ground that can be appealed to in support of normative-evaluative validity claims pertains to the pragmatic infrastructures that all communicative acts require. To imagine a discussion of explicitly universalizing normative-evaluative validity claims is therefore to imagine a discussion *about* claims which requires these very claims to be in place for the discussion to occur. The most universal normative-evaluative claims will be claims about how members of the most universal community should reach understandings with each other and these claims would both be under discussion and required for discussion.

EMPIRICAL AND ANALYTIC CONTINUUMS FOR THE THIRD PERSON POSITION

The key points made in my arguments above are helpful to research methodologies in that they (1) can specify different types of third person position and thus aid researchers in understanding the significance for data analysis of various researcher roles and processes involved in understanding meanings, (2) suggest a way to handle the issue of "ideologically distorted consciousness" as it affects research. I begin with the first of these.

The third person position is not "a" position, but a relation that suggests a continuum. There is an empirical continuum and an analytic continuum. I find it helpful to distinguish five third person positions, two of them analytic and necessary and three of them contingent and empirical. More distinctions could easily be made. The metaphor of the continuum is appropriate here and positions along it are rather arbitrary. Here they are:

1) The Third Person-Performative Position (analytic and necessary)

This position has to do with the third person position associated with a typification that one actively claims and draws upon when one acts toward others, and when one expects ranges of responses from these others. When we act toward others in serious, joking, bantering, or sarcastic modes we do so via a performative third person position conjoined to our first person position as actor. We make our serious statement, or our joke, or begin our banter, as an innovative act within the bounds of a typification we simultaneously offer to the other. The typification *always* involves a third person position; that is, a way of understanding the activity as banter, or joking, or complaining, or arguing, etc. This means that the actor and the one addressed possess some prediscursive grasp of the *form* through which they act: a tacitly objectified view of the interaction that (we would claim, if we articulated this pre-discursive grasp) any anonymous member of some cultural group could occupy. It is through this holistic grasp of the interactive form that one can take both the first and second person performative positions. It is at the metaphorical edge of this constituting third person position that acts and responses are monitored. This third person position is implicit to all typifications and it is "used" regularly during interactions. Hence the name third person-*performative*. And hence its status, analytic and necessary. No empirical contingencies determine whether or not this position is in play: it is always in play.

2) The Third Person Internal-Included Position (empirical and contingent)

When we watch two friends talk seriously, or banter, or joke, and watch them from the position of passive but acknowledged members of an interactive group, we are in a third person internal-included position. We are not acting, we are listening and observing. But we assume that our friends assume that we are listening and are cognizant of the typifications involved. We assume that we *could* join in if we feel moved to do so, and that those performing assume that we could join in. We understand that our presence helps to constitute the actions. This is a third person, nonperformative, but included position: a position that helps to constitute the interactive situation because all parties know we are observing, because all parties assume we could enter in, because all parties assume we understand the typifications employed, and because all of the above helps to constitute the typification. The typifications employed not only are understandable to us, they include us as well. The meanings of the acts include the assumption that we observe and understand.

In participant-observer studies, the researcher is often in this position: especially if the researcher frequently shifts roles (observer, friend, peer, advisor, etc.). If this is the case, the researcher will have become a kind of "generalized insider" but will be expected to simply observe interactions at times.

3) The Third Person Internal-Excluded Position (empirical and contingent)

A qualitative researcher is also often in this position: the position of a third person, internal but excluded, observer. In this position our presence is noted and helps to constitute the typifications used by those observed. But it is not assumed that we share an understanding of these typifications or that we could in principle take part in the interactions. We are noted, but "othered." Our presence enters into the typifications as an "other" who does not (fully) understand. This position is not unique to researcher roles. If we enter a meeting late and see a dispute or a joke going on that is incomprehensible to us at first, and the actors look toward us but immediately continue without addressing us; then we are in this same position. The third person internal-excluded position is one from which we observe interactions without necessarily possessing an understanding of the typifications employed. It is one from which the typifications employed are understood by all actors not to include us as insiders, though they may refer to our presence as to the presence of an outsider who could not in principle join in.

4) The Third Person External-Absent Position (empirical and contingent)

If you hid a video camera in a room and then retired to another room to watch what took place, unnoticed and unknown to the actors you observed, you would be in a third person external-absent position. Since your observing activities are unknown to the actors, their typifications do not include you in any way. This position is usually barred from qualitative researchers for ethical reasons. Sometimes one can find oneself in this position by accident; hearing a conversation through a door or from around a corner are examples. One can learn new things from this position but there are always large moral and ethical questions involved.

5) The Third Person Internal-Universal Position (analytic and necessary)

I have already discussed this position. It resides in the universalizing moment of all validity claims. At low levels of reflection, it is fused with the third person-performative position. Actors assume, when reflection is low, that their various claims are of universal status. As reflection heightens, a distinction between the third person-performative and third person internal-universal is introduced. Actors are able to relativize the claims they make against their understanding that the validity claims they *foreground* to others are really relativized to contingencies in the situation. This means that more abstract, backgrounded, validity claims are implied in their foregrounds and help to constitute the foregrounded claims. One does not step "out" of one contingent typification into another contingent typification to find the internal-universal position. One rather steps "up" the constituting structures to more universal claims. A more universal audience is implied in these claims, but one inclusive of the audience constituting the contingent typification.

I will use an example from my coauthored paper with Laurie MacGillivray (Carspecken and MacGillivray, 1998). Laurie captured an interesting dispute between two elementary students during one of her field projects. One student complained that the other had stuck his tongue out at her. The accused student first argued that he had not stuck out his tongue, then shifted his argument to say that he had not stuck it out at *her*. He defended himself first by disputing an objective claim made by the other student, then by disputing a subjective claim made by her. The objective claim was that his tongue had been thrust out. The subjective claim was that he had *intended* to stick out his tongue *at her*.

During this dispute, neither student challenged an underlying normative claim: "sticking your tongue out at another person is bad." Both students agreed, implicitly, that intentionally sticking out one's tongue at another is rude.

There is a universalizing moment to the claim that intentionally sticking out a tongue at someone else is rude, and this universalizing moment structured the argument between these students in important ways. What if the universal moment of this claim had been challenged: "In some cultures, sticking out one's tongue at another is very polite." The two students in dispute would probably have understood this challenge and agreed that sticking out one's tongue is only rude in some situations. But they would still have held to a claim that was backgrounded and constitutive of the first claim at all times: "Being rude is bad."

These two students might have expected people from all cultures to agree with the broader claim that being rude is bad. This broader claim corresponds to a broadened third person position.

What if we now bring these two students into the present with us and tell them that kings were expected to act rudely to subordinates in order to "be kingly." Many responses to this would be possible, most of which would modify the universalizing claim in some way. But one response could be, "Well, that was a bad system because all people should show respect to each other regardless of social status." This produces a yet more abstract principle, significantly broadening the audience that constitutes its third person position. The audience has broadened, because people from a different era, the era of kings, have been invited as virtual participants in a moral argument. The claim has been broadened such that examples of being rude but not disrespectful might be brought in at this point. Of course, if such examples entered the discussion then the new universalizing claim would become: "People should not be disrespectful to each other."

This is how the third person internal-universal position works. It is a constituting principle. It plays a part in structuring all validity claims. It is a very important principle to understand when considering the concept of "ideologically distorted consciousness."

SYSTEMS ANALYSIS AND IDEOLOGICALLY DISTORTED CONSCIOUSNESS

For my doctoral dissertation I conducted an ethnographic study of a school in Liverpool, England, that was taken over by a working class community after the city government closed it down (Carspecken 1991). The community's name was Croxteth and the school, Croxteth Comprehensive. Militant working class residents occupied the school buildings, changed the locks, barricaded the windows and doors, and kept a twenty-four hour picket on the premises for an entire school year. During this time volunteer teachers taught the secondary school-age children of Croxteth while the residents' Action Committee fought to have the school officially reopened.

In my book I include arguments based on systems analysis and the concept of ideologically distorted consciousness. Though the campaign to save the school was eventually successful and Croxteth Comprehensive was reestablished as a state-funded school, little was changed in the domains of pedagogy and curriculum.

The pedagogy and curriculum traditional to this school did little to promote social mobility or social activism. Core goals of most volunteer teachers during the occupation were to both provide greater mobility options for individual students and to increase the social-political awareness of all students. By the end of the year of occupation, pedagogy and curriculum did seem on the verge of important changes, but, ironically, success in the political battle to restore a state-funded school in Croxteth curtailed progress at the level of school experience. More time would have been needed for changes in schooling practice to really develop.

Volunteer teachers from predominantly middle class backgrounds sought to change teacher-student relations from the very beginning of the school year. Course curriculum was also experimented with. The idea was to provide an educational experience that empowered working-class youth. But subtle forces were at play to ensure a largely reproductive educational experience, and some of these forces roughly fit within the category of ideologically distorted consciousness.

The realm of teacher-student relationships is probably most illustrative. Students were accustomed to being treated as subordinates in unquestionable authority relations. A theme in the culture of this school prior to its occupation was "Do what the teacher says, because she is the teacher."

When middle-class volunteers sought to democratize relationships and allow more power to the students in making classroom decisions, students disrupted and resisted to the point of reducing many classes to mere shouting sessions. Parents in the school regularly intervened to restore order but did so by reaffirming traditional authority relations between teacher and pupil. They reaffirmed traditional authority relations by employing forms of authority organic to Croxteth. I often heard parents tell students: "Do what your teacher tells you to do or I will box your ears."

Parents upheld a system of authority relations isomorphic to those in work settings: the boss-worker relationship transposed into the teacher-student domain via the parent-child domain. Teachers did not help matters. They embraced the national system of examinations in their teaching and presented students with work they did not want to do and could not identify with just to get them ready for these tests. The goal of social mobility was in conflict with the goal of social-political empowerment.

A cultural system that reproduced class relationships was thus upheld through a set of ideological themes long prominent in Croxteth culture. The themes were supported by largely taken-for-granted values and norms, and associated implicit theories (e.g., "Children have impulses toward disobedience, disorder, criminal activity, and laziness that must be suppressed if they are to develop internal controls as they grow into adulthood").

Thus many, but not all, of the outcomes in Croxteth were ironic: a militant Action Committee critical of capitalism and devoted to bettering the position of the working class unwittingly helped to reproduce attitudes and orientations in their children that are historically key cultural supports of the capitalist system. This is an example of ideologically distorted consciousness—people acting without awareness of the full consequences of their actions; without awareness of the functions those unseen consequences have for upholding a system unfair to themselves. Teachers also displayed ideologically distorted consciousness: advocating "progressive" pedagogies while upholding national examinations.

The problem of ideologically distorted consciousness will often arise in field work. Reconstructive analysis, the articulation of commonly used typifications and validity claims, provides the qualitative researcher with an in-depth description of cultural themes. But then the researcher can ask about the *function* those themes play within a system that is largely opaque to the subjects studied. When those themes embody a misperception of the systems of action they help to produce, ideological distortions are in play that have functional significance.

Reconstructive analysis can be validated through procedures that support the researcher's claim of attaining an insider's position. Member checks, prolonged engagement, use of multiple researcher roles, collection of many interviews and many field notes all help to support that claim (see Carspecken 1996).

But what is going on when the researcher asks about the functional significance of her reconstructions and develops a theory that subjects do not readily recognize? What could validate this sort of analysis; systems analysis? Validation becomes even more problematic when the analyst thinks that her subjects misperceive their own interests and would act otherwise if they could perceive these interests more accurately.

I will not worry too much about procedures for validating systems analysis here (see Carspecken 1996: chs. 12-3). I will instead attempt to raise consciousness about the general issue. Systems analysis employs both the third person-universal and the third person external-absent perspectives. It is the product of two sorts of reflection:

> a) Objectifying reconstructed themes to frame them from perspectives largely outside the typifications of the group studied

> b) Reconstructing highly backgrounded but constitutive validity claims common to the culture that are tacitly prominent

within the group's typifications in order to test their claim to universality.

Both types of reflection are involved in my claim that Croxteth residents, as part of their militant campaign to win back a school, ensured the presence of reproductive social relationships within that school. I viewed these social relationships from a sociological perspective that was unfamiliar to Croxteth residents. I used terms to express my theory that were foreign for most residents. The social relationships within the school *functioned* to make Croxteth youth accustomed to being subordinates in institutions whose purposes are outside their control. These relationships were *isomorphic* to relationships in the home (parent-child) and relationships within work settings that parents were used to (boss-worker). The social relationships within the school *reproduced* class relationships.

Locating the cultural reconstructions within a theory of social reproduction was the act of an external-absent outsider; one who examined portions of Croxteth culture in totally objectified forms. Analysis undertaken from a position like this risks becoming an act of arbitrary power: objectifying the culture of "others" and using it to support a theory that corresponds more to the interests of an academic community, one's community of colleagues, than to the interests and concerns of the people studied. That is, the risk involved can be understood as an act of writing about and interpreting the culture of others from a position and in a manner that itself is ideologically distorted.

However, in the case of Croxteth and in the case of many other studies, it is not particularly difficult to invite people who participate in the study to discuss theoretical constructions like social reproduction theory. Croxteth activists had no trouble learning sociological terms I shared with them. They could examine my theory about their own culture and discuss it with me, disagreeing with some of my initial conclusions for good reasons that I, in turn, could understand. This process of sharing sociological terminology with Croxteth residents so that we could all discuss theories about their school occupation began toward the end of the occupation but did not have time to flourish. The political campaign was successful and Croxteth residents were ironically forced out of the school to make room for hired teachers. The general principle here, however, is that member checks can be done on third person systems-theoretic analysis as long as the researcher is willing to discuss the theory and explain the relevant concepts openly and fully.

When this is not possible, when the people studied are not willing or able to understand one's systems analysis and make contributions to it, then one must use peers to challenge one's own analysis. Other qualitative researchers who represent a range in ethnicity, class, and gender should be invited to read and challenge one's writings.

The second sort of reflection involved in systems analysis emphasizes the backgrounded and tacit portions of typifications commonly used by the people under study. In this example from Croxteth, parents and youth alike were very convinced that youth needed coercive treatment in order to "learn discipline." In my dissertation and book, I relativized this belief as an ideology. I also reconstructed validity claims implicit to this belief: that youth will turn out "bad" if they are not disciplined, that learning cannot take place without a teacher in unquestioned authority, that one of the very purposes of education was that of "discipline and control." I theorized this as a form of ideological distortion. With this distortion in place, the *function* of these taught social relationships could make its mark and class relations could be reproduced.

Rather than solely occupy a third person external-absent position when exploring ideological distortions we must also take the reconstructed cultural themes given from an insider's perspective and follow their own logic backward into articulations of the more tacit, more backgrounded assumptions that constituted them. The Croxteth residents believed that students should obey their teachers without question. This reconstructed validity claim can be unpacked into a theory about human development, into a belief about impulses and human nature, into underlying assumptions about what learning is. Once these are articulated their claim to universality can be examined and, if ideological distortions are involved, they will show up here. There are, of course, alternative theories of human nature, of human development, and about the nature of learning. Participants in a study may be invited to discuss, with the researcher, the tacit assumptions underlying their ways of life to determine whether any distortions are present or not.

Hence, there is an *internal standard* that can be followed when exploring ideological distortions. This internal standard involves the moment of universality that operates within every validity claim. This moment of universality must be tested by:

> a) examining consistencies and inconsistencies within a culture and inviting participants to reflect upon the inconsistencies;
>
> b) comparing beliefs with subjective states experienced by those who hold to the beliefs (in Croxteth, for example, many women held the belief that "women want to be led," but they did not feel good, always, when this belief subordinated them to male leadership);
>
> c) opening dialog between typifications of the culture studied and typifications from other cultures (for example, discussing theories of human development and the purposes of an education with Croxteth residents).

The more these activities take place as exercises in mutual consciousness raising between researcher and the subjects of study, the more valid the conclusions will be and the more ethical the study will be.

The second method to be employed in systems analysis, then, momentarily ignores the functional interconnection of action consequences in order to open tacit claims to universality for general debate.

SUMMARY

In these notes I explored the relationship between validity and reflection with attention to the third person position. Reflection was described as internalized position-taking that moves consciousness from one typification into another. Internalized position-taking of this sort is structured by a dialectical relationship between a universal moment and a particular moment that can be found in all validity claims. It is also structured by the nature of typifications, all of which contain an internal-performative third person position in their constitution. A total of five third person positions marked along a continuum were discussed. Two of these were analytic and necessary and three were empirical and contingent. I illustrated the relevance of these five third person positions for understanding various researcher roles. Lastly, I discussed the significance of my findings for systems analysis and the study of ideologically distorted consciousness.

REFERENCES

Ajaya, S. 1978. *Yoga Pyschology.* Pennsylvania: Himalayan Institute.

Althusser, L. 1969. *For Marx.* London: Allen Lane.

Althusser, L. and E. Balibar. 1970. *Reading Capital.* London: New Left Books.

Anandamurti, S. 1968. *Ananda Sutrum.* Calcutta, India: Ananda Printers.

———. 1978. *Idea and Ideology.* Calcutta, India: Ananda Press.

———. 1987. *Ananda Vacanamrtam.* Calcutta, India: Ananda Press.

Anderson, G. 1989. Critical ethnography in education: Origins, current status, and new directions. *Review of Educational Research* 59(3): 249-70.

Anderson, P. 1976. *Considerations of Western Marxism.* London: New Left Books.

———. 1980. *Arguments with English Marxism.* London: Verso Press.

Apple, M. 1979. *Ideology and Curriculum.* London: Routledge and Kegan Paul.

———. 1983. *Education and Power.* London: Routledge and Kegan Paul.

———. 1993. *Official Knowledge: Democratic Education in a Conservative Age.* New York and London: Routledge.

———. 1986. *Teachers and Texts: A Political Economy of Class and Gender Relations in Education.* New York and London: Routledge.

Benhabib, S. 1992. *Situating the Self: Gender, Community and Postmodernism in Contemporary Ethics*. New York: Routledge.

Benhabib, S. and F. Dallmayr, eds. 1991. *The Communicative Ethics Controversy*. Cambridge, MA: MIT Press.

Bernstein, R. 1971. *Praxis and Action*. Philadelphia: University of Pennsylvania Press.

———. 1976. *The Restructuring of Social and Political Theory*. Philadelphia: University of Pennsylvania Press.

———. 1983. *Beyond Objectivism and Relativism: Science, Hermeneutics, and Praxis*. Philadelphia: University of Pennsylvania Press.

Caputo, J. 1987. *Radical Hermeneutics: Repetition, Deconstruction, and the Hermeneutic Project*. Bloomington: Indiana University Press.

Carspecken, P. 1991. *Community Schooling and the Nature of Power,The battle for Croxteth Comprehensive*. London and New York: Routledge.

———. Pragmatic Binary Oppositions and Intersubjectivity in an Illegally Occupied School. *International Journal of Qualitative Research in Education*, 5(1) (January-March).

———. 1996. *Critical Ethnography in Educational Research: A Theoretical and Practical Guide*. New York and London: Routledge.

Carspecken, P. and M. Apple. 1992. Critical qualitative research, theory, method, and practice. In *Handbook of Qualitative Research in Education*. Edited by M. LeCompte, W. Millroy, and J. Preissle. Florida: Academic Press.

Carspecken, P. and P. Cordeiro. 1995. Being, doing, and becoming: Textual models of social identity and a case study. *Qualitative Inquiry* 1(1).

Carspecken, P. and L. MacGillivray. 1998. Raising consciousness about reflection, validity and meaning. In *Being Reflexive in Critical Educational and Social Research*. Edited by G. Shacklock and J. Symth. London: Falmer Press.

Castells, M. 1977. *The Urban Question*. London: Edward Arnold.

———. 1978. *City, Class, and Power*. London: Macmillan Press. Chalmers, D. 1997. *The Conscious Mind: In Search of a Fundamental Theory*. New York and Oxford: Oxford University Press.

Cook, T. and D. Campbell. 1979. *Quasi-experimentation: Design and Analysis Issues for Field Settings*. Chicago: Rand McNally.

Dale, R. 1982. Education and the capitalist state: Contributions and contradictions. In *Cultural and Economic Reproduction in Education*. Edited by M. Apple. London: Routledge and Kegan Paul.

Dennett, D. 1991. *Consciousness Explained*. Boston: Little, Brown, and Co.

Derrida, J. 1962. *Edmund Husserl's Origin of Geometry: An Introduction*. Translated by John Leavey Jr. Lincoln, NE and London: University of Nebraska Press.

———. 1973. *Speech and Phenomena: And Other Essays on Husserl's Theory of Signs*. Translated by David Allison. Evanston: Northwestern University Press.

———. 1974. *Of Grammatology*. Translated by Gayatri Chakravorty Spivak. Baltimore: Johns Hopkins University Press.

Dreyfus, H. and P. Rabinow. 1983. *Michel Foucault, Beyond Structuralism and Hermeneutics.* Chicago: University of Chicago Press.

Dunayevskaya, R. 1989a. *Marxism and Freedom: From 1776 Until Today.* New York: Columbia University Press.

———. 1989b. *Philosophy and Revolution: From Hegel to Sartre, and from Marx to Mao.* 3d ed. New York: Columbia University Press.

———. 1992. *The Marxist-Humanist Theory of State Capitalism.* Detroit: News and Letters Committee Press.

Edelman, G. 1992. *Bright Air, Brilliant Fire: On the Matter of the Mind.* Basic Books.

Everhart, R. 1983. *Reading, Writing, and Resistance: Adolescence and Labor in a Junior High School.* London: Routledge and Kegan Paul.

Flew, A. 1979. *A Dictionary of Philosophy.* 2d ed. New York: St. Martin's Press.

Foucault, M. 1970. *The Order of Things: An Archaeology of the Human Sciences.* New York: Vintage Books.

———. 1979. *Discipline and Punish: The Birth of the Prison.* Translated by Alan Sheridan. New York: Vintage/Random House.

———. 1980. *The History of Sexuality. Volume I: An Introduction.* Translated by Robert Hurley. New York: Vintage/Random House.

Giddens, A. 1979. *Central Problems in Social Theory.* London: Macmillan.

——. 1984. *The Constitution of Society*. Cambridge, UK: Polity Press.

Giroux, H. 1983. *Theory and Resistance in Education: A Pedagogy for the Opposition*. London: Heinemann Educational Books.

Guba, E. 1990. The alternative paradigm dialog". In *The Paradigm Dialog*. Edited by E. Guba. pp. 17-27. Newbury Park: Sage Publications.

——. ed. 1992. *The Paradigm Dialog*. Newbury Park: Sage Publications.

Habermas, J. 1981. *The Theory of Communicative Action. Volume I: Reason and the Rationalization of Society*. Boston: Beacon Press.

——. 1987a. *The Philosophical Discourse of Modernity: Twelve Lectures*. Cambridge, MA: MIT Press.

——. 1987b. *The Theory of Communicative Action. Volume II: Lifeworld and System: A Critique of Functionalist Reason*. Boston: Beacon Press.

——. 1988. *The Logic of the Social Sciences: Methodology Philosophy, and Social Theory*. Cambridge, MA: MIT Press.

Hammersley, M. 1989. *The Dilemma of Qualitative Method: Herbert Blumer and the Chicago Tradition*. London and New York: Routledge.

Hegel, G. 1967. *The Phenomenology of Mind*. Baillie translation. New York: Harper and Row.

Heil, J. 1983. *Perception and Cognition*. Berkeley: University of California Press.

Hofstadter, D. 1979. *Gödel, Escher, Bach: An Eternal Golden Braid.* New York: Vintage Books.

Husserl, E. 1962. *Ideas: General Introduction to Pure Phenomenology.* Translated by Boyce Gibson. New York: Collier Books.

———. 1970. *The Crisis of European Sciences and Transcendental Phenomenology.* Evanston, Illinois: Northwestern University Press.

Hyppolite, J. 1974. *Genesis and Structure of Hegel's Phenomenology of Spirit.* Translated by Samuel Cherniak and John Heckman. Evanston, Illinois: Northwestern University Press.

Ingram, D. 1990. *Critical Theory and Philosophy.* New York: Paragon House.

Johnson, R. 1979. Three problematics: Elements of a theory of working class culture. In *Working Class Culture: Studies in History and Theory.* Edited by J. Clarke, C. Critcher, and R. Johnson. London: Hutchinson and Co.

Kaye, H. 1984. *The British Marxist Historians: An Introductory Analysis.* Cambridge: Polity Press.

Kierkegaard, S. 1941. *Concluding Unscientific Postscript.* Princeton, NJ: Princeton University Press.

———. 1983. *Fear and Trembling. Repetition.* Translated by Howard Hong and Edna Hong. Princeton, NJ: Princeton University Press.

Kuhn, T. 1970. *The Structure of Scientific Revolutions.* 2d ed. Chicago: University of Chicago Press.

Lather, P. 1986. Research as praxis. *Harvard Educational Review* 56(3): 257-77.

———. 1990. Reinscribing otherwise: The play of values in the practices of the human sciences. In *The Paradigm Dialog*. Edited by E. Guba. pp. 315-32. Newbury Park, CA: Sage Publications.

———. 1991. *Getting Smart: Feminist Research and Pedagogy with/in the Postmodern*. New York and London: Routledge.

LeCompte, M. 1990. Emergent paradigms: How new? How necessary? In *The Paradigm Dialog*. Edited by E. Guba. pp. 246-55. Newbury Park, CA: Sage Publications.

Lincoln, Y. and E. Guba. 1985. *Naturalistic Inquiry*. Beverly Hills: Sage Publications.

Markley, O.W. 1976. Changing images of man. *Renaissance Universal Journal* 2(1-3).

Marx, K. 1993. *Grundrisse: Foundations of the Critique of Political Economy*. Translated by Martin Nicolaus Martin. Harmondsworth: Pelican.

———. 1977. *Early Writings*. Harmondsworth: Penguin Books.

Marx, K. and F. Engels. 1976. *Complete Works*. London: Lawrence and Wishart.

McCarthy, T. 1978. *The Critical Theory of Jürgen Habermas*. Cambridge, MA: MIT Press.

McLaren, P. 1992. Collisions with otherness: "Travelling" theory, postcolonial criticism, and the politics of ethnographic practice—the mission of the wounded ethnographer. *The International Journal of Qualitative Studies in Education* 5(1): pp. 77-92.

———. 1993. *Schooling as a Ritual Performance: Towards a Political Economy of Educational Symbols and Gestures.* 2d ed. New York and London: Routledge.

McNeill, D. 1992. *Hand and Mind: What Gestures Reveal about Thought.* Chicago: University of Chicago Press.

McRobbie, A. 1978. Working class girls and the culture of feminity. In *Women Take Issue.* Edited by Center for Contemporary Cultural Studies. London: Hutchinson and Co.

Mead, G.H. 1967. *Mind, Self, and Society: From the standpoint of a social behaviorist.* Edited by Charles Morris. Chicago and London: University of Chicago Press.

Merleau-Ponty, M. 1962. *Phenomenology of Perception.* London: Routledge.

Offe, C. 1984. *Contradictions of the Welfare State.* Edited by J. Keane. London: Hutchinson and Co.

Palmer, R. 1969. *Hermeneutics: Interpretation Theory in Schliermacher, Dilthey, Heidegger, and Gadamer.* Evanston, Ill: Northwestern University Press.

Peshkin, A. 1990. A postnote: Tales from the rear. In *The Paradigm Dialog.* Edited by E. Guba: pp. 347-59. Newbury Park, CA: Sage Publications.

Quantz, R. 1992. On critical ethnography with some postmodern considerations. In *The Handbook of Qualitative Research in Education.* Edited by M. Lecompte, W. Millroy and J. Preissle. San Diego: Academic Press.

Sartre, J-P. 1956. *Being and Nothingness.* New York, Philosophical Library.

Saunders, P. 1981. *Social Theory and the Urban Question*. London: Hutchinson and Co.

———. 1983. *Urban Politics, A Sociological Interpretation*. London: Hutchinson and Co.

Seung, T.K. 1982. *Structuralism and Hermeneutics*. New York: Columbia University Press.

Shacklock, G. and J. Symth, eds. 1998. *Being Reflexive in Critical Educational and Social Research*. London: Falmer Press.

Sinari, R. 1974. The experience of nothingness in buddhism and existentialism. In *Contemporary Indian Philosophy*. Series Two. Edited by M. Chatterjee. pp. 273-93. London: Allen and Unwin.

Spivak, G. C. 1974. Translator's preface. *Of Grammatology*. By J. Derrida. Baltimore: Johns Hopkins University Press.

Staten, H. 1984. *Wittgenstein and Derrida*. Lincoln, NE and London: University of Nebraska Press.

Taylor, C. 1979. *Hegel and Modern Society*. Cambridge: Cambridge University Press.

Thompson, E.P. 1963. *The Making of the English Working Class*. London: Victor Gollancz Ltd.

———. 1978. *The Poverty of Theory and Other Essays*. London: Merlin Press.

Tugendhat, E. 1986. *Self Consciousness and Self Determination*. Cambridge, MA: MIT Press.

Vahiduddin, S. 1974. Aesthetic experience and beyond. In *Contemporary Indian Philosophy*. Series Two. Edited by M. Chatterjee. pp. 294-312. London: Allen and Unwin.

Willis, P. 1975. "How working class kids get working class jobs. University of Birmingham Occasional Papers.

———. 1976. The main reality. University of Birmingham Occasional Papers.

———. 1977. *Learning to Labor: How Working Class Kids Get Working Class Jobs*. London: Gower.

INDEX

A
absence, concept of, 53, 54
access
  privileged, 98, 106, 107-108, 233, 234, 235-236
  shared, 233, 234, 235-236
accuracy, 103-104
action
  forestructure, 137-138
  horizons of, 142-144, 254-255
  impetus prior to, 144-145
  impetus to, 135-137, 148-150, 201-202, 215, 217, 218, 219
  interactive syntax of, 142
  monitoring of, 139-141
  multiple meanings of, 130-131
  relationship with power, 80-82, 85-85
  role of meaning in, 128
action consequences, expectations, x, 60-61
alienation, 37-39, 42-43
Althusser, Louis, 35, 36, 37
American pragmatism, 13-14, 23
anonymous power, 48-50
Apple, Michael, 44, 110
arche-trace, 164
"archeology of knowledge," 46-47
assumptions, tacit, 70-71
audience-dependent recollection, x

B
Being and Nothingness, 240
Blumer, Herbert, 7, 25-26
body, awareness of, 169-171
capacity, concept of, 81, 82

C
Caputo, John, 154, 166
certainty
  desire for, 55-56
  and truth, 58
Chicago school, 7, 25
claims, concept of, 57, 233
claims, tacit, 71
communication, 24, 82-84
communicative actions, x-xi, 69, 71-72, 77, 79, 227
  and power, 109-110
communicative action theory, 33, 116
communicative anticipations, 90
communicative expectation, 64
communicative goals, 83-84, 86, 87-88
components, action, 130-131, 131n.1, 132-133
compression, concept of, 204-205, 208-209, 230
"conditions of action," 44
consciousness
  active, 239-240, 242
  desire's role in, 245-246
  ideologically distorted, 271-273

internal time, 156-160
multiple drafts model, 201
passive, 237-239
consequence goals, 84
construct, concept of, 19
constructivist paradigm,
social research, 8, 19-21, 23, 26, 104
contingent claims, 262, 264
Counter-Enlightenment thought, 27
Crisis of European Sciences and Transcendental Phenomenology, The, 168
critical ethnography, xii, 5, 33
emergence of, 33-34
critical paradigm, social research, 8
critical social research, portrait of, 14-17
critical theory, 10, 27-28
Croxteth Comprehensive school, 271-276
cultural production, 40-41n, 41, 43
cultural typification, 75-76, 142
culturalists, Marxist, 35, 36-37

D

Das Kapital, 37
"death of the subject," 32, 46, 48
"Death by Text," 30
deconstruction, strategy of, 50, 56, 58, 161-164
deference, 52-53, 67
deference structure, concept of, 55-56, 57
deferment, 52-53, 67
Dennett, Daniel, 201
Derrida, Jacques, x, 25, 27, 28, 44, 45, 50-58, 68-69, 99, 107, 108, 114-115, 116, 155-156, 157-161, 165, 166, 182, 248, 249
desire
body awareness, 171-175
Hegel's view of, 239, 241, 245-246, 250
postmodern view of, 55, 58
as symbol, 150
Dewey, John, 23, 24, 25, 28
direct experience, concept of, 53
"discourse-practices," 47-48
"doubles," theory of, 46, 47
Dunayevskaya, Raya, 37

E

Eastern philosophy
impact on west, 180, 181-183
nothingness in, 240
self in, 229, 231, 248
Economic and Philosophical Manuscripts, The, 37
educational ethnology, ix
embodied meaning, 123, 256
empirical double, 46
empiricism, 58
empowerment, 84, 85, 94, 96-97

Index 291

Croxteth Comprehensive, 271, 272
epistemology, concept of, 21
existentialists, views of, 56
expectations
    action consequences, x, 60-61
    concept of, 187
    explicit intersubjective, x, 65-66
    layered categories of, x
    mediated action consequences, x, 61-62
    role of, x
    tacit intersubjective, x, 63-65
experience, knowledge-imparting, 24-25, 64, 66-67
explicit intersubjective expectation, x, 65-66
expressive action, 91
expressivism, 39, 230
"expressivist," 28
external validity, 7

F
facts, concept of, 20
fallibility, 116
fear
    Hegel's view of, 243, 246
    postmodern view of, 58
feeling body, originary scene two, 123, 153, 167-184, 248
feeling-configuration, action, 145-148
feminist theory, 8
first negation, 237
first person position, 191-192, 193, 195-197, 210, 217, 232, 234, 235-236, 253, 258-259
"Five Third Person Positions and Their Relevance, to Reflection, Validity, and Systems Analysis," 5-6, 255
flattenings, 178-179, 234
flux, 22, 25, 26, 181
force, concept of, 237, 238
forestructures
    accumulation of, 175-177
    concept of, 133-134, 154
    perception and, 154-155
form and flux, originary scene one, 122-123, 152-154
form, concept of, 152-154
Foucault, Michel, x, 44, 45-50, 81, 114-115
"Four Scenes for Posing the Question of Meaning," 5, 12-13, 28, 119

G
Geist, 38, 178-179
genealogy of knowledge, 46-47
generalized others, in Mead, 193-194
German romanticism, 27
gesture chains, 216-217, 218
gesture, significant, 220-222, 225-226
gestures, 190-192, 212, 214, 215-216, 220-222
Giddens, Anthony, 9, 40-41n, 44, 81, 82, 100, 229

Guba, Egon, 7-8, 10, 12, 14-23

H
Habermas, Jürgen, x, 8, 9, 25, 28, 33, 49, 69-82, 101, 104, 107, 115, 185, 224-226, 229, 232, 233, 254-255
Hammersley, Martyn, 22-23, 26
Hegel, G. W. F., x, 39, 40, 43, 56, 87, 125, 179, 185, 186, 188, 228, 231, 236-248, 250-251
Heidegger, Martin, 118, 155, 182
Herder, Johann Gottfried, 28, 39, 40, 43, 253
hermeneutic method, normative/evaluative claims, 103, 105
hermeneutic theory, 110
"hermeneutics of facticity," 154, 155
horizon, 154, 254-255, 256-257. See also spatial horizon, temporal horizon
Husserl, Edmund, x, 28, 50-51, 52, 53, 54, 57, 58, 59, 123, 154-159, 161, 166, 168, 236-237
Hyppolite, Jean, 239

I-J
idea unit, 129
ideal speech situation, conditions of, 79, 80, 95, 102, 104
idealism, 58
identity claims, xi, 76, 87, 94-96, 99, 110, 184, 234-235, 256
  relationship to power, 96-97
  as truth claims, 97
ideology
  concept of, 15
  in critical social research, 14-15
  role of, xii, 106
image clusters, 119
impetus clusters, 214-215, 218, 219
index, 59-60
indicators, 73
"indirect teaching," 165
induction, concept of, 58
inference procedure, 101, 107
"Institute for Critical Cultural Studies," 30
intention, concept of, 136
interests, concept of, 106
internal validity, 7
intersubjectivity, 66, 108, 236
  origins of, 123-125, 153, 185-187, 239
James, William, 24, 28

K
Kierkegaard, Søren, 56, 166, 181
knowledge
  concept of, 57
  interactive nature of, 20-21
  relationship to truth, 81

Index 293

Knowledge and Human Interests, 79
Kuhn, Thomas S., 10-11, 12

L
language, role of, 63
Lather, Patty, 14
"layered categories," x
Learning to Labor, 37, 40, 41, 85
LeCompte, Marki, 9
Lincoln, Y., 7-8
logical positivism, 18

M
MacGillivray, Laurie, 258, 269
mahatatva, 181
Main Reality, The, 40
Marx, Karl, 27, 37-40, 43
Marxism
  power debate in, 35-37
  theoretical debates in, 33-34
McLaren, Peter, 123, 256
McNeill, David, 129
McRobbie, Angela, 44
Mead, George Herbert, x, 24-25, 99, 125, 185, 186-203, 206-209, 213-214, 228-229, 230-231, 235, 246, 247, 248
meaning
  model of, 126
  subjectivity and, 57-58
meaning horizon, 254-255
meaningful action
  articulation, 130, 130n

impeti, 136, 138-139
model of, xii, 125-126, 252-257
meaningful acts, analysis of, 118-122, 127-152, 229-230, 232, 252-253, 254, 256
mediated action
  consequences, expectation, x, 61-62
member checks, 264, 273, 275
"mental movement," 168
Merleau-Ponty, Maurice, 123, 155, 156, 157
metaparadigm, 11-12, 28-29
metaphor, text as, 255-256
method, concept of, 33
modern period, conception of, 45
modernity, Habermas's view of, 69
moments, action, 130-131, 131n.1, 132-133
monitoring, xii, 90-91, 93-94, 253
monological epistemology, 69
monologue, internal, 68
"multilogues," 69
multiple access principle, 101, 102, 104

N
Naturalistic Inquiry, 7-8
naturalistic method, 25-26
negation, 237-238
neo-Kantianism, 10, 22, 26-27
normative/evaluative-

referenced claims, xi, 73-74, 77, 103, 105, 261-262
normative-evaluative validity claims, 258, 265-266
normative realm, 232-233
norms, 225
nothingness, concept of, 240-241

O

objectification, 37-38
objective realism, 27, 232
objective validity claims, 258
objective-referenced claims, 72, 74-75, 77, 85
objective-referenced truth claims, 101-102
objectivity, meaning prior to, 127-128
Of Grammatology, 160-161, 179
offers, tacit, 71
ontological needs, 100
ontology, concept of, 21
oppositional acts, praxis of, xi
Order of Things, The, 45
origin of intersubjectivity, originary scene three, 123-125, 153, 185-187, 239
originary, concept of, 13, 121
originary scene, 12-14, 120-121
    Mead's, 24-25

P

paradigm, concept of, 10-11, 12
"paradigm dialogue," 8-10, 28-29
Paradigm Dialog, The, 9, 10
"Paradigmatics of the Paradigm Dialogue," 5
paradigms, social research, 8-10
passive perception, 17, 19, 21, 22, 26-27, 27-28, 29, 58, 67-69
peer debriefing, 264
perception
    concept of, 237
    constructed nature of, 167-169
    deconstruction of, 155-156
    knowledge-imparting, 26, 28
perceptual acts, 128-129
phenomenology, 28, 50-51, 58, 236-237
    analysis, 121, 124-125
Phenomenology of Meaningful Action, The, 5, 119
Phenomenology of Spirit, 87, 236-237, 238, 239, 245-248, 250
Philosophical Manuscripts of 1848, The, 37
physical science, social research, 8
Pierce, Charles, 24
point, 129-130
positivism, 58
positivist paradigm, social

Index 295

research, 8, 10, 17-18
postmodernism, 8, 32, 33
postpositivist paradigm,
   social research, 8, 18-19, 25
power
   and communicative action,
      109-110
   concept of, x, 33
   forms of, 80
   Foucault's view of, 46-47,
      48, 81
   functionalist analysis of,
      35-36
   human creation of, 43
   postmodern views of, 44,
      48-50, 56-58, 77-81, 101
   relationship to truth, 77-79,
      117
   role of, 26
   structural side of, 44
"Power, Truth, and Method;
   Outline for a Critical
   Methodology," 5, 28
pragmatism, 23, 115, 116. See
   also American pragmatism
praxis
   concept of, ix-x, 33, 37-38,
      39-40, 110
   importance of, 110-114
   reformulation of, 40-43
praxis philosophy, Marx's, 27
praxis theory, 39, 85, 101, 113
pre-pain sensation, 205-208
premonitored action, 92-94,
   124
   impeti, 124, 142, 163
presence
   knowledge-imparting, 53
   metaphysics of, 50, 51, 53-
      54, 57, 99
presentations, 235
primal scene, 70
protention, concept of, 54,
   156-159, 160

Q
qualitative research
   argument for, 7-8
   pragmatism, impact of, 25
quantitative research, role of,
   7

R
"realist ontology," 17-18
recognition, 92, 94, 95, 97, 98,
   99, 101, 105, 110, 242-243,
   246, 247
recollection, concept of, 166,
   183-184, 231-232, 234-235,
   247-248
reconstructive analysis,
   Croxteth Comprehensive,
   273-275
reflection, 258, 259-260, 263,
   265
   Croxteth Comprehensive,
   274-276
reliability, 7
   concept of, 58
repetition, concept of, 166
representation, 68
researcher, third person
   position of, 101
resistance, praxis of, xi

"responding to one's own acts," 187
response, 192
retention, concept of, 54, 156-159, 160, 161
rhetoric, concept of, 31-32
rules, regulating, 25

S
Sartre, Jean-Paul, 56, 240
scene, xii, 119
    concept of, 12-14, 121
Schooling as a Ritual Performance, 256
"scientific paradigm," 12
second negation, 237-238
second person position, 189-191, 203, 209, 211, 217, 232, 234, 235-236, 253, 258, 259
selection process, 219-220
self, sense of, 227-228, 230-231
self-consciousness, 244-245, 247
self-knowledge, desire for, 98-99
self-production, 37-40
Seung, T. K., 68-69
shared interests, concept of, 74
"sign structure," 52-53, 56, 66
signification, theory of, 68-69
signs
    concept of, 53, 234
    theory of, 155, 158, 159
snarl, gesture of, 190-192, 212, 214, 226

social existence, 35
social mobility, Croxteth Comprehensive, 271, 272
social ontology, 34
social research, contemporary practice, 10-11
social researcher
    normative/evaluative claims, 103, 104
    and power relations, 102, 103-104, 105-106
social typifications, 198-199, 217-219, 225-226, 229
somatic compression, 205-209, 210, 212, 213-214, 219-220
sous rature, strategy of, 182
spatial horizon, action, 143-144
speech acts, 131
Spivak, Gayatri, 99, 179, 248
Staten, Henry, 12-13, 119, 154
stimulus, 192, 212-213
stretching, concept of, 164-165
structural power, 44
structuralists, Marxist, 35, 36, 37
"structuration," 40-41n
"structure versus agency" debate, 34, 35
subject-object distinction, 23-24
subjective realm, 232, 233-234
subjective-referenced claims, 72-73, 77, 105, 106-109, 265

subjective validity claims, 258
subjectivity
  communicative expectations, 67, 227
  in modern philosophy, 45-46, 57-58
  as product of discourse-practices, 48-49
  of social researcher, 107-108
  uncertainty and, 135
symbol
  concept of, 24, 25
  significant, 193-194, 219-224, 225-226, 229-230
symbol theory
  flaws of, 194-197, 226
  of Mead, 187-194, 227-229
  remedies for, 197-199
symbolic action, 24
symbolic communication, phylogenesis of, 125
systems analysis, Croxteth Comprehensive, 273-276

T
tacit intersubjective expectation, x, 63-65
Taylor, Charles, 39, 253
teacher-student relationships, Croxteth Comprehensive, 272
temporal horizon, action, 142-143
theory
  concept of, 20
  social activists and, 31-32
  "theory window," 25, 26
Theory of Communicative Action, The, 9, 79
Theses on Feuerbach, 37
third person position, 101, 232, 234, 236, 253, 258, 259, 260-261, 263-265
  external-absent position, 268, 274
  internal-excluded position, 268
  internal-included position, 267
  internal-universal position, 269-270
  performative position, 266-267
Thompson, E. P., 35, 36-37
time, concept of, 4
trace, 51, 54-55, 162, 163, 233-234, 249
  subjective experience, 108-109, 160-161, 164, 235
traditionalists, Marxist, 35-36
transcendental double, 46
transsubjectivity, 124
"true paradigm," 12
truth
  concept of, x, xi, 8, 33, 58
  Hegel's view of, 241, 246
  postmodern view of, 56, 115, 117
  pragmatists view of, 115
  as product of discourse-practices, 47-48
truth claims, 65, 76-77, 84, 97,

99-100, 116-117
types of, 72-74
Tugendhat, Ernst, 185

U

uncertainty, in meaning, 134-135
understanding, 128, 163
universal claims 261, 262-263, 264-265

V

valid inference, 101
validity claims, xi, 72, 75, 77, 111, 113-114, 258-259, 261-262, 264-265
validity, concept of, 58, 72
value claims, 73-74
"value window," 17, 25, 26
values, in critical social research, 15-16
vanishing point, 151-152, 163, 181, 184, 234
visual perception
   in critical social research, 16
   western philosophy, 182

W-Y

will to power, 84, 95, 117
Williams, Raymond, 35
Willis, Paul, 33, 37, 40-44, 85, 110
Wittgenstein, Ludwig, 13
yoga meditation, 180-181

Studies in the Postmodern Theory of Education

General Editors
Joe L. Kincheloe & Shirley R. Steinberg

Counterpoints publishes the most compelling and imaginative books being written in education today. Grounded on the theoretical advances in criticalism, feminism and postmodernism in the last two decades of the twentieth century, Counterpoints engages the meaning of these innovations in various forms of educational expression. Committed to the proposition that theoretical literature should be accessible to a variety of audiences, the series insists that its authors avoid esoteric and jargonistic languages that transform educational scholarship into an elite discourse for the initiated. Scholarly work matters only to the degree it affects consciousness and practice at multiple sites. Counterpoints' editorial policy is based on these principles and the ability of scholars to break new ground, to open new conversations, to go where educators have never gone before.

For additional information about this series or for the submission of manuscripts, please contact:

> Joe L. Kincheloe & Shirley R. Steinberg
> 637 West Foster Avenue
> State College, PA 16801

To order other books in this series, please contact our Customer Service Department at:

> (800) 770-LANG (within the U.S.)
> (212) 647-7706 (outside the U.S.)
> (212) 647-7707 FAX

or browse online by series at:

> www.peterlang.com